D1255590

Stefan Zweig

Stefan Zweig

A Critical Biography

ELIZABETH ALLDAY

J. PHILIP O'HARA, INC.
CHICAGO
A Howard Greenfeld Book

J. Philip O'Hara, Inc. 20 East Huron, Chicago 60611.
Published simultaneously in Canada by Van Nostrand
Reinhold Ltd., Scarborough, Ontario.

First Printing G

Library of Congress Cataloging in Publication Data
Allday, Elizabeth. Stefan Zweig. Bibliography. p. 1.
Zweig, Stefan, 1881–1942. PT 2653. W42Z58 1972
838'.9'1209   74-190753   ISBN 0-87955-301-4

I dedicate this book to my mother,
who first introduced me to the work
of Stefan Zweig

Acknowledgements

I should like to thank Dr Richard Friedenthal, Mrs Friedenthal, Mrs Eva Alberman, Mr and Mrs Graham Hole, Mr Leonard Sansbury, CBE, Miss Ivy Miller, and Dr R Kahane for their help and information.

My thanks also go to my family, whose patience during my preoccupation has not gone unnoticed.

And finally, I wish to record my sincere gratitude to Shelagh M Cartwright, without whose practical assistance and continual encouragement this book would not have been completed.

EA

Acknowledgements to Publishers

I should like to make acknowledgement to the following publishers; Cassell and Company Ltd, for extensive extracts from *The World of Yesterday* and other works; Constable Publishers, for an extract from the *Plays* by Emile Verhaeren; the Hogarth Press Ltd, and the Translators' Literary Estate for the extracts from Gorki's *Reminiscences of Tolstoy, Chekhov and Andreev*; St John's College, Oxford and the Hogarth Press Ltd for the extracts from J B Leishman's translation of *The Selected Poems of Rilke*; the Navajivan Trust, India, for an extract from *My Experiment With Truth* by Mahatma Gandhi; Oxford University Press, for a passage from *The Kreutzer Sonata* by Tolstoy, translated by Maude; Penguin Books Ltd, for two excerpts from Fyodor Dostoyevsky's *Crime and Punishment*, translation © David Magarshack 1951; the Viking Press for passages from *Jeremiah* and *Romain Rolland—a critical Biography*. EA

Contents

Chronological Table

1881	Z born Vienna
1886	Z enters elementary school
1891	Z enters Gymnasium
1899	Z graduates from Gymnasium
1899	Z's trip to Brittany
1899	Z enrols at University of Vienna
1900	Z's first collected edition of verse published by Schuster & Löffler
1901	Enrols Berlin University (remains only one term)
1901	First contribution accepted by Neue Freie Presse
1902	First visit to Belgium, and first meeting with Emile Verhaeren
1902	Publication of Verlaine biography
1903/4	Obtains degree in Philosophy at University of Vienna
1904	Paris, first prolonged stay
1904	Meeting with Romain Rolland, Bazalgette and Rilke in Paris
1905	First meeting with Auguste Rodin in Paris
1906/8	Visits to England, Italy, Belgium, Spain and Holland
1908	First meeting with Friderike
1910	Visit to India
1912	First visit to USA, Panama and Caribbean
1912	Second meeting with Friderike
1913/14	Z and Friderike establish residence in Kalksburg
1914	Friderike's first book published in Berlin (Call of the Homeland)
1914	Outbreak of first world war
1915	Z's visit to war zone at Tarnow
1916	Death of Verhaeren
1916	Death of Emperor Franz Josef of Austria

1917	*Publication and production in Zurich of the play* Jeremiah
1917	*Russian Revolution begins*
1918	*First world war ends*
1918/19	*Z and Friderike establish residence at Salzburg*
1919	*Austrian Republic formed*
1919/20	*Z offered diplomatic post, which he refuses*
1920	*Hitler becomes Leader of National Socialist German Workers' Party*
1920	*Establishment of USSR*
1922	*Walter Rathenau assassinated*
1922/3	*Inflation of the German mark*
1925	*Hindenburg elected German President*
1926	*Death of Rainer Maria Rilke*
1928	*Z's trip to Russia (Tolstoy centenary)*
1929	*Death of Hugo von Hofmannsthal*
1933	*Hitler becomes Chancellor of Germany*
1933	*Appointment of Charlotte Elizabet Altman (Lotte) as Z's secretary*
1934	*Z's house in Salzburg searched by Nazis*
1934	*Chancellor of Austria (Engelbert Dolfuss) assassinated*
1935	*Z travels to London*
1938	*Z divorces Friderike*
1939	*Z marries Lotte at Bath*
1939	*Sigmund Freud dies in London*
1940	*Z and Lotte leave England for USA*
1941	*Z and Lotte sail for Brazil*
1942	*Z and Lotte die in Petropolis, Brazil*

Preface

In considering my reasons for writing this biography, Hans Arens's tribute to Zweig, which refers to the 'heroes of your youth', comes to mind.

I realize that I, too, found in this man and his writing all that seemed admirable; and three decades after his death there seems no reason to change that view.

While attempting to record the difficult passage of his life, with its restless inquiry into God's purpose for creating the human psyche, I feel that my task has been made easier by the hope that I have perhaps earned Stefan Zweig's own approval.

EA

Introduction

Almost three decades have passed since Stefan Zweig, playwright, historian, biographer and poet, died by his own hand in Petropolis, Brazil.

The passing of one man from the scene, and in a comparatively remote geographical spot, when so many were delivering up their lives in the amphitheatres of war, could not be regarded, except by those near to him, as remarkable, or even, at that time, a cause for deep national mourning. Even so, the news of his death was a violent shock to his reading public in many nations, though they were already anaesthetized against the vileness of concentration camps and mass murder.

That his death, remote from the scene of genocide, nevertheless resulted from it, added even more sorrow to this deed.

Perhaps it is only now that we are able to stand back and view, with nostalgia and regret, the untimely and apparently unfathomable act of self-destruction.

Those of us young at the time, yet old enough to realize we had suffered a great loss, read the tributes published later by his friends and literary contemporaries. Their names—Carl Zuckmayer, Bruno Walter, Romain Rolland, Richard Friedenthal and many others—brought to mind an epoch between two world wars, and although vastly different in their approach to and indeed in their pursuit of art, they were bound by a universal sense of loss.

If it is presumptuous in this era of the seventies, separated by a gulf not yet long enough to be labelled history nor short enough to have provided personal contact with the subject of a biography, it falls to the writer to use one of Stefan Zweig's own explanations when faced with a similar task: '. . . that which is confused craves for clarity . . . that which is in darkness strains towards the light'.

In this attempt to 'strain towards the light', it is hoped not only that events surrounding his life and death may be drawn into illumination, but that the light of discovery and rediscovery may be turned on the work to which he dedicated his whole existence.

A critical analysis should be of help and use to the newcomer, and perhaps it is long overdue for the student and disciple. The 'humanitarian' approach in Zweig's writing, often deplored by the classicists, makes him unashamedly a man for all eras; and the fact that the numbers of his works on the library shelves has shrunk is a matter for mourning and some concern. What was our physical loss in 1942 becomes, unaccountably, a literary loss only thirty years later. 'The homeless man becomes free in a new sense, and only he who has lost all ties need no *arrière pensée* . . .' So wrote Zweig, Austrian Jew, author-psychologist extraordinary, just before he took his own life in February 1942. Not young—at sixty-two not yet old.

This man, product of predestined racial wandering, yet cushioned against the harsh reality of it by virtue of his own birth and the relative security of his time, nevertheless held fast, whether by instinct or desire, to the bitter germ of insecurity that was his heritage.

And yet success, or what the public thinks of as success, came to him early and unsought. While still at school he emerged as a contributor of some talent to the selective and erudite periodicals then published in Vienna.

In twenty-eight years his monumental output has been translated into most languages. The peak of public acclaim was perhaps reached in the late thirties, when his plays appeared on the New York stage and his first full-length novel, *Beware of Pity*, claimed universal attention.

From 1902, when *Verlaine* was completed, to his passionate exposition of Mary Stuart and her political and emotional existence, Zweig wrote only biographies. The subjects he chose were a continual source of speculation and criticism. *Erasmus*, a product of full maturity and a subject few biographers have succeeded in tackling with such perception and at the same time so readably, achieved great success and plaudits for its author. He worked always at fever pitch, frequently in a climate of tremendous marital and domestic tension. That he himself possessed some of the ingredients necessary to counter such conditions, he rarely conceded.

With the advent of the 1939 war and its inevitable brutality, Zweig's works, among those of many other of his countrymen, were consigned to the flames by the Nazis; and this public holocaust, although effectively and nationally destroying the creative work of a man, served only to preserve his creation in the minds of his reading public beyond the German frontiers. Fortunately we in England were still able to obtain and read the works of this remarkably versatile author, until he demolished his mortal frame and there was nothing to follow *The World of Yesterday*.

In the gap yawning between that publication and the world of today, the name 'Zweig' has become a sort of half-remembered sound, and the memory is probably one of a film adaptation of his work, a stage production or a television play.

And yet who but Zweig, psychologist and literary surgeon, had the courage and insight to probe so deeply and surely into the mind of a deserted woman? In *Letters from an Unknown Woman*, would not filmgoers and readers witness this literary operation with the same astonished reaction now as they did then?

The contradiction which is Zweig, makes him alternately soul-searcher and domestic tyrant, peace-lover and neurotic. In the light of ensuing events and in the spotlight of retrospect it is tempting to adjust the facts and come up with what could be too obvious a judgement, both on him as a man and on his work. External pressures, working on these apparent internal contradictions, in fact continued to produce in him a state of equilibrium.

Legal, political and marital entanglements persistently surrounded his slight form, yet Zweig weathered them with the strength of an athlete. This physical strength probably owed its lasting quality to the fact that it was rarely tapped. The neuroses and 'artificiality' about which he frequently complained produced a certain irritability and impatience in middle life, but that later mellowed into a withdrawal and a melancholy introspection.

His relationships with women give a prime example of his apparent contrariness. Though they were varied and often referred to as 'necessary' rather than enjoyable, he nevertheless won the fanatical devotion of two wives, one of whom he rejected after almost twenty years, the other a girl twenty-seven years his junior who accompanied him willingly on his last mortal voyage of discovery.

On a retrospective journey to the world of so-called security, an era so beloved of, yet frequently and bitterly maligned by Zweig himself, and for whose loss he claimed he gave up his life, we are caught up in two world wars, witness to a mass movement of population, and observers of the destruction of all that was once held sacred.

Dictators toppled empires, the waltz was drowned beneath the roar of cannon and the birth screams of the charleston. The beer cellars of Germany and the attics of Paris were emptied of the young men so piously dedicated to art reform, and in the uneasy peace between the ending of one war and the beginning of another, the 'world of security' went a step further down the perilous incline of human miscalculation.

It was then that Zweig, 'the Jew', as he was labelled by the Nazis, began his wandering in earnest. His burden was that carried by members of all minorities at all times. His compassion and guilt were indivisible, springing as they did from the same ancient source.

With the dull repetitiveness of history, we are again living through an era balanced on the edge of insecurity, where the cry is always for something new, some panacea for all our political and social ills. But there is nothing new. Zweig, who longed for 'freedom' and 'security' with a passion amounting to obsession, never discovered the path, and emptied his soul in the search.

As we read his works, he takes us with him, in turn casting us down, then lifting us to the heights, enabling us to share his own incredibly sensitive handling of the follies, corruption, heroism and strength that is the sum total of being human.

Chapter One

By the mid-nineteenth century the Zweig family, industrialists, bankers, professional men and, almost without exception, successful in whatever they undertook, were firmly entrenched in Vienna.

From Bohemia and Moravia and from Italy they had come, bringing with them their hard-earned wealth, their intelligence and their ambitions. Others of the family had spread further afield across Europe, providing a well-established family-cum-business network.

They were weavers of textiles and finance, past masters in the subtle twists of law, and respected and successful in the world of medicine. They worked hard and diligently and respectfully gathered up the harvest of such work.

Out of this diligence and moral excellence there grew a self-styled family 'nobility', cherished by many of the older members of the family, faintly ridiculed by the last surviving children of the tree, and entirely without official support from any of the social registers. If the Zweigs saw themselves as part of a Jewish nobility, their claim would seem to have much to commend it.

Scrupulously honest in all its undertakings, the Viennese branch of the family was respected and revered by all who came into contact with it. Security, it seemed, was theirs, and only those whose destiny it has been to wander the earth in search of a resting-place can know what magic lies in that one word.

Atavistic memories of injustice and flight die hard, and the pursuit of security takes on a deeper and more intense meaning. If wealth will help achieve it then it is essential to work to this end. The Zweigs, without exception, applied themselves to this enterprise.

Thus, as the old century was drawing to a close, these members of the most ancient minority group found themselves dispersed but blessedly becalmed in the pseudo well-being of pre-war Austria.

The country of their adoption had so successfully licked her old war wounds that she had come to believe that the loss of her possessions in Italy, originally regarded as tragically irreparable, were not so important after all; and her defeat in 1866 at the hands of Prussia's 'Blood and Iron' Bismarck, although a shocking disaster at the time, was now almost mercifully forgotten.

Even the humiliation, at first so keenly felt and bitterly resented, of Austria's diminishing part in all German affairs, once the key rôle in her political and economic structure, was now easing out of the public conscience and in its place there was the steady growth of a national *élan*, a wholesale dedication to the pursuance of the arts. The muses, it seemed, had temporarily ousted the military from Austria, and the firmament was bright with ever newly discovered and creative stars.

Franz Josef, the ageing and unfortunate Emperor, clung like a withering fruit to the remaining branch of what had once been the mighty Hapsburg tree. Statesmen and politicians went about their affairs with suave and confident mien and not too much obvious concern for the already ailing 'Dual Monarchy' of Austria and Hungary, and the Austrian people, their national characteristic a delightful admixture of despair and gaiety, accepted what seemed on the surface to be a satisfactory situation.

They knew of old the art of political dissimulation, and the Austria–Hungary Empire had teetered too often on the brink of collapse for them to take the various crises too seriously. Rather like their old Emperor, the Empire survived by virtue of an in-built stubbornness. Resting on its laurels of autocracy, it simply had to be indestructible, and while fully aware of the geographical, historical and political vulnerability of their country, Austrians persistently immunized themselves against the fever of intrigue and disenchantment raging through Central Europe at the time. Their penchant for side-stepping the disagreeable amounted almost to foolhardiness, and even when the tragic and unsolved death of Emperor Franz's only son and heir, Prince Rudolf, was followed later by the assassination of the Empress, the national conscience stirred but sluggishly, and failed even then to ring the warning bell.

As the pressures built up to explosive point beyond the Austrian frontiers, to culminate in the assassination in Sarajevo of Franz Josef's nephew and heir, a near suicidal degree of political myopia was present in the court antechambers, confusing the conclusions of political conclave, and suppressing national apprehension if it was incautious enough to show its head.

Vienna, ancient garrison city of the Romans, and centre of the dynamic Hapsburg power through the latter part of the Holy Roman Empire, stopped its eyes and ears to the rumblings of war and deliberately turned its attention to the more serious business of culture.

With an admirable if perhaps lopsided view, the nineteenth-century Austrian devoted himself to art as diligently as his Prussian counterpart regarded his army boots. Coffee-houses were the high altars housing the adored literati and their worshipful following of student acolytes. Philosophical pronouncements and debate were as necessary to life as the endless coffee, torte and chess games.

If, during a lull between the production of a new play, the publication of an erudite or controversial book, a declamation by a poet or a new opera by Strauss, the public became a little restive, there was always the astonishing reassurance that it was nevertheless only too glad to hear from those in high office, that '. . . the situation was desperate—but not serious . . .' This quaint twisted axiom trotted out by the Emperor's advisers always seemed to work, and the public returned to its daily round with a sigh of relief, determined to ignore as far as possible the occasional disturbing foreign press reports which so annoyingly distracted the reader from the delight of consuming the gossip and art columns of the daily press.

A peculiarly Austrian inclination to self-delusion or misplaced optimism was vindicated by the national rejoicing of the country in its abundance of artistically creative talent. It is an obvious and facile exercise to condemn this attitude in the light of ensuing historical events. At the time these ostrich-like tactics succeeded in great measure in insulating the populace against the horrors of impending war, and enabled full and uninterrupted enjoyment of a steady diet of art in all its forms. It is perhaps incidental that such an attitude has provided a great artistic heritage, which has also benefited those countries more inclined to devote their attention to matters of military might than to music.

The theatre, the beer garden, the coffee-houses, spawning grounds of the Central European intellectual, became the pivot upon which Vienna, indeed all of Austria, balanced. Meanwhile less 'civilized' Europeans looked on with disapproval tinged with envy. 'How is it possible to be so gay . . . There is disaster in the air . . .' But the Viennese, reflecting the mood of the whole country, were contemptuous of this Grundy-like attitude, and pursued even more assiduously their flower-strewn path.

It was into this magnificent and ersatz security that Stefan Zweig was born, the second son of wealthy Jewish parents. The nineteenth century had just under two decades to go. The year itself was dying—November 1881. But as another star emerged in the intellectual firmament of pre-war Austria, the shadows of military conflict were receding even further.

Zweig, destined to take his place amongst the great names of European culture, the last-born in a clutch of international geniuses, who included Freud, Verlaine and Rilke, made his entrance into the world on the crest of a violent wave of artistic reaction.

The war against formality in art was well under way throughout Europe. Emile Verhaeren, the Belgian poet, and later to become

Zweig's own adored master, had already launched and headed an attack against *parnesse*, the rigid and restrictive measures by which poetry and writing had for too long been governed. Arthur Rimbaud, tortured, capricious and brilliant, was his able lieutenant, and Paul Verlaine, Rainer Maria Rilke and later Paul Valéry all added their youth and fanaticism to the verbal bomb-throwing. All were determined to destroy an unpalatable and enfeebled art form. A new image was to be forged in the world of sound, words and music, and they saw themselves as the angry young men deputed to carry out the task. In place of metrical coldness there was to be warmth and passion. The old hypocrisy which clothed reality was to be torn aside and a new approach born.

Bohemianism was the fashion. Tragedy, impoverishment and even spells of imprisonment were accepted by the disciples of the new order with a certain philosophical optimism. No price was too great to pay for freedom in art and expression, and what had begun as a cry in the wilderness now developed into a clamour as the ranks of the art-anarchists continued to swell. Mysticism and sensuality were given full reign, and the young men marching under their banner of symbolism had all the fervour, righteous anger and determination to flout authority of the young.

Even so, the old tenets, scorned by the *avant-garde*, and doomed anyway by impending world catastrophe, were an unconscionable time a-dying, because of the undeniable romanticism so deeply embedded in the hearts of leaders and rank and file alike. They were genetically incapable of forsaking romanticism, so this noble style was unrepentantly preserved while other, lesser, deeply scorned postures were tossed overboard. So, in bliss or wilful ignorance Austria, at the heart of Europe, sang, danced and applauded as her sons poured out more and yet more artistic delights with, it seemed, the ease of water flowing from a fountain. And if there was sometimes a certain feverishness in the hunger for emotional and artistic expression, it went unmarked by those caught in the colourful and heady pageantry of the nineties.

To those around him, the infant Stefan Zweig was indeed a

fortunate child, born with the proverbial silver spoon in his mouth. He should want for nothing, and his advent into the wealthy and secure circle that made up his family was a matter for great rejoicing.

His mother, a God-fearing, elegant and ambitious woman, and an exile from her native Italy, no doubt gave pious thanks that her son should see the light of day in so benign a country. Her own formal upbringing and devotion to tradition was heavily ingrained, and when, later in her life, she was expected to adjust to the new order, she was totally unable to cope or even accept. Sadly, it was to be her lot to witness destruction and terror and the final disintegration of everything she held sacred.

Stefan was the antithesis of his mother, and it is significant to mark that early on he subconsciously rejected those traditions she held dear; yet later, though he considered the rarefied and often neurotic atmosphere which had surrounded him in his youth 'claustrophobic' and unpleasant, he still clung to the 'old' world he knew, and its final passing left him an exile, the eternal wanderer, face to face with emptiness and utter despair.

It was this fissure in Zweig's personality, already evident in his youth and more strongly defined as he reached maturity, that enabled him to place his fingers delicately but accurately on the pulse of all human problems. That it also produced his own conflict and oppressed his spirit was tragically inevitable. Ironically, this division served to increase the clarity and power of his observations, as surely and clinically he exploited through his writing the shortcomings and triumphs, the grandeur and the triviality, the strength and the frailty of man. Every facet of the human character was dragged out, explored and analysed with unremitting persistence. Every ingredient, that is, bar one. The student, disciple or even the casual reader will search Zweig in vain for what the Greeks in their ancient philosophic wisdom declared precious, even vital, to complete the human personality: *humour*.

In his continual searchings Zweig either never discovered this magnificent human attribute, or, if he did, he failed to recognize it by virtue of his own melancholy introversion. Although a sense of the ridiculous occasionally invaded his thinking he refrained from using this in his writing; even the driest of humour was markedly absent from his work, and it is only in retrospect that the reason for the omission is understood. That life was a serious business for Zweig there was no doubt. It was essentially a pilgrimage where work and application to work marked the milestones. He rarely gave voice to what he considered the ultimate indeed he ever envisaged one. Sufficient to accept one's ethnic goal, if heritage of toil, if only to justify an existence in the world.

The dependence and gaiety of childhood was not high on young Stefan's list of priorities. Although his was the third generation to enjoy real security, he discovered very early on the nagging discomfort of some as-yet unrecognized and intangible unrest, and although his sensation was smothered and at times nearly forgotten beneath the beneficent influence of his family circle, its existence could never be denied.

By turns spoiled and severely disciplined by a succession of relatives and servants, the boy's behaviour vacillated between a precocious aggression and a natural introversion.

It has become almost trite to cast the psychological problems of a man at the feet of his mother, yet Zweig, on his own admission, deliberately set about severing the umbilical cord quite early on in life. Whether his determination to do this arose from fear or respect or from an inverted desire for the affection never too abundantly showered on either of the Zweig sons, can only be judged by close examination of his early declaration and from his later conduct.

Stefan made no bones about 'freeing' himself from the parental apron strings, but the knot existed, it seems, only in his own imagination. His mother was undoubtedly a self-indulgent woman, and having once discharged the material function of producing two sons, she pursued her own life as nearly as she could under the social conditions of the era. Far from being over-possessive, she was infuriatingly casual in her attitude to her family. She saw

Stefan, together with his brother and her always kindly and amiable husband, as part of the economic and domestic equation. Husband, children, possessions, all played the same role in her arithmetic. All must occupy their predestined niche and behave accordingly.

But having fulfilled her traditional role as a wife and mother of the Jewish upper middle class, her inherited and national vivacity took over, creating a ruthless determination to exist in her own right, unfettered by the bonds of a family which nevertheless was a necessary adjunct to her security.

That the pursuit of her pleasures was condemned as something less than intellectual and still less pleasant by her younger son, left her blissfully unmoved. This ultra-feminine dedication to self seems to have been a persistent irritation in Stefan's life, and even more so his inability to do anything about it. With what seemed to him incredible selfishness, his mother diligently pursued her own comfortable way of life, unrepentant or unaware that her son saw her as a fairly poor copy of the model mother he considered should be his by birthright. Her continual chatter and its (he considered) trivial content, the fetish she made of fashion and her perpetual travelling about, affected him like the wearing of a hair shirt. He had inherited little of his father's calm tolerance and was impatient of his brother's. Mother and son frequently crossed swords on many issues, but it was left to Stefan to reap the negative effects. The skirmishes, as he commented, seemed to leave her unaffected and indeed eager for the next round.

If there was always a measure of discontent in the young Stefan's breast, it seems in no way evident in any of the immediate members of his family. The ebullience of his mother was regarded indulgently by his father, an industrious and tranquil descendant of the Jewish communities living in and around the country villages of what was then Moravia. Like so many minority communities, the solid and working members of the earlier Zweig clan sought their fortune through trade and with the advent of the industrial revolution, moved into manufacturing. With the accumulated know-how and wisdom of his forebears, Stefan's father had already established a weaving mill of considerable size in northern Bohemia by the time he was thirty, and this single and solid achievement was the beginning of the Zweig family fortune.

Seen through his younger son's eyes, Zweig the father emerges as the most kindly of men. All the great human attributes are heaped upon his memory. Industrious, compassionate and amiable, he provided the necessary antidote to his wife's ebullience, and his extreme honesty both in human relationships and in the world of commerce and industry were regarded by the youthful Stefan as nothing short of miraculous.

In his last book and autobiography, *The World of Yesterday*, Zweig describes him in glowing terms. Unlike many other personalities moving within the orbit of Stefan's early life, his father escapes the retrospective and sometimes sceptically critical analysis of the professional observer. The affection which he felt his mother had rejected was directed to his father.

Along with many of the artificial and stylized characters peopling his immediate circle, Zweig also damns with faint praise the educational system of the time; and in this condemnation the rift in his own mental process is again revealed. While accepting, even appreciating, the inestimable value of a *gymnasium* (higher) education, its students invariably destined for entry into the University, Zweig disliked the idea of attending it so much that he went to quite ridiculous lengths to disguise the fact. He loathed the respectability and dedication to maturity, twin gods of the Viennese bourgeoisie, but possessed neither the strength nor the absolute desire to dispense with either.

While secretly relieved that he was not expected to go into his father's weaving business, he still experienced some guilty discomfort that he was to have many advantages denied his elder brother, who had reluctantly given up the idea of becoming a doctor to assuage parental concern regarding the future of the family business. It was tacitly assumed that Stefan was to enjoy the benefits of an academic career.

As a *gymnasium* student and later at the University in Vienna, Zweig was also uncomfortably aware that he was not suffering the honourable pangs of impoverishment. Hunger and the delight of being publicly misunderstood, the two basic requirements for automatic entrée into the cellar-world of Bohemianism were, for a while, denied him, and he fretted under the injustice imposed by his too wealthy parents. The privations that Verhaeren and the others were enduring in France for art's sake, he could only imagine. Even his first literary effort, which had been no effort at all, met with instant success, and at eighteen, while still at school, he was writing for some of the best periodicals in Vienna. Poetry, the accepted medium and safety valve for all young Viennese intellectuals, flowed from his pen with ease and style. Everything submitted to the publishers was automatically accepted, and while he rejoiced as the first cheques arrived, the youthful author felt a nagging discontent. With a Doctor's Degree of Philosophy almost a certainty, and a string of poems and articles already accepted by the most respected publishers in Vienna, Stefan rode the crest of the success wave with a mixture of excitement and shame. What the others, his idols in art were suffering to achieve, he had accomplished more or less effortlessly, and he admitted, if only to himself, that the hollow feeling beneath his belt was not the honourable result of hunger, but of intellectual discomfort. Increasingly he became aware that if he were to develop his art and claim entry into the sacred atmosphere of 'anti-ism', he must relinquish the plushy, insulated environment into which he had been cast; and so, at twenty, he took himself off to Berlin in order to 'study' at the University there—already exercising what was to become an established Zweig compromise. Determined to immerse himself in the lives and impecunious antics of the *avant-garde*, he nevertheless made quite certain that the bridges he left behind were intact and substantial, just in case it was necessary to beat a hasty retreat.

Stefan's parents watched the emergence of their second-born with tolerance and a complete lack of understanding for the great issues at stake. As far as they were concerned, family honour was vindicated and its future ensured in their two sons. One of them was 'in the business', the other about to claim his University degree. Bourgeois ambitions were thus appeased, and they returned complacently to their own literary pursuits, which, as Stefan frequently complained, were confined to consumption of the pronouncements on page one of the ultra-respectable *Neue Freie Presse*.

Once free of restrictive parental observation, Stefan flung himself into the smoke and cellar-life of Berlin with a gusto and marked lack of inhibition he was later never to recapture. With an ecstasy that surprised even himself he embraced the life of the cafés and the minds and bodies of their habitués. In a sincere attempt to identify with the cultured and not so cultured drop-outs of the early nineteen-hundreds, he wore the shabbiest of clothes, grew his hair and tried his hand at 'protest' poetry.

Excerpts from *The Brothers Karamazov* were read aloud by bearded and 'genuine' Russian emigrés, and Stefan's soul seemed to melt as he listened to the impassioned words of the great writer. Dostoyevsky's genius, his involvement, almost obsession, with the planes of human development from the mentally retarded to the ecstatic metaphysical, enraptured the young listeners, not least the newcomer from Vienna, who had already endowed the former Siberian political prisoner with immediate literary canonization. In Dostoyevsky's tragic life, his literary achievements, his frequent incarceration for political beliefs and, last but by no means least, his horrific escape by a mere five minutes from the firing squad, Zweig saw the epitome of human joy and sorrow.

It was during these formative and exhilarating sessions underground that Zweig first experienced the impact and influence of a prophetic and fiercely refined intellect. The Russian's appraisal of guilt and expiation, his brilliant dissertations and exposition of man's true nature, and the sheer complicated genius of his writing, installed him for ever in the mind of the young writer who was in many ways his successor.

If the deeper realization of all he was witness to came later, colouring and influencing his writing in maturity, the immediate impact on Stefan of this 'other' world was terrific. This, his young heart sang out, was living and suffering. The fact that his own suffering was limited to the observation of others in their various predicaments was unimportant. How had he ever endured those

29

cramped years at the *gymnasium* and even later at the University?
Berlin, with its excitement and newly formed, carefully nurtured
band of anarchistic intellectuals, made Vienna seem by comparison
staid and over-hygienically philosophical.

Stefan swore to himself that this was but the beginning. His
mind was seething with ideas, but first he must travel, see the
world, meet the great ones—that is, if they would deign to meet
him. As ever, at this point, humility seized him. Who was he, after
all, that he should presume to write? How could he ever compare
with his adored Verhaeren, the monumental Dostoyevsky, the
exquisite Verlaine . . .? He had not even got his degree yet—not
that he attached any importance whatever to such 'success', but
he knew that it was imperative to perform the last act of homage
to his parents. Waves of indecision swept through him as he
attempted to place matters of importance and urgency in some
sort of chronological order.

His father's kindly face came strongly before him, and suddenly
Stefan's mind was made up. He would return to Vienna, cram
frantically night and day in order to make up for all the lost time,
then launch an all-out assault in an effort to get his degree.

With family demands satisfied he would then be free at last.
Free to explore the world to the west, to venture into the mysterious countries of the East. To meet, he hardly dare dwell on the
prospect, Rabrindranath Tagore, Indian poet and mystic, long
endeared to Stefan's heart. And, if fortune still smiled upon him,
why should he not seek a meeting with the angry young pacifist
from India, whose declamations and writings were already per-
meating the thinking of his country's millions.

The mere prospect of such an interview made Zweig's senses
reel; and in imagination he vividly saw the slight but dominating
figure of Karmachand Gandhi. Now would be a time spent in
apprenticeship at the feet of the masters; a time for learning and
storing up what he had learned. He would, perhaps, if he were
allowed, make translations of the Verhaeren poetry in German,
thus bringing the joy of his own discoveries to thousands more in
his homeland. He would watch and worship in the shrines of

literary and artistic perfection throughout Europe—throughout the world, if possible. Stefan's heart thudded ecstatically at the prospect and his enthusiasm almost suffocated him. Yes, this is what he would do—watch and wait and learn—and then . . . and then, he would write.

Although perhaps ignorant at the time of the underlying significance of these youthful but weighty decisions, Stefan Zweig's obsession for travel and his fascination for the word 'freedom'—it occurs with marked repetitiveness throughout his writing—reveal the start of what was to develop into a tragic mental and spiritual dependence on flight. Freedom was a state to which he aspired, if only subconsciously, from his earliest intelligence, and its pursuit took him on endless wanderings and through a variety of intimate aesthetic and sometimes erotic relationships. Yet in his dedication to this elusive, maybe unattainable state, he succeeded only in binding himself ever more securely within the fetters of humanity.

But at twenty years of age his enthusiasm and belief in the shaping of destiny to one's own desire was vibrant and strong, and only occasionally disturbed by the still, small voice somewhere deep within him.

There was so much to do, and this was the beginning of a new century. Youth was on the march and would make itself heard. With a mixture of sadness and joy Zweig went the round of the meeting places in Berlin, bidding his new-found friends farewell. He had learned much from this cross-section of young people, coming as they did from all walks of life, their existence and background entirely opposite both physically and culturally to his own, now despised, middle class. Vows of eternal friendship were made, and bitter-sweet, rarely too-satisfactory affairs with lion-hearted but fragile female leftists, terminated. (Stefan, on his own admission, regarded any relationship formed at that time more in the realm of male vindication than an exercise of pure joy.) And so, with the fearsome portents and prophesies of Fyodor Dostoyevsky still ringing in his ears and a secret promise made only to himself that one day he would write a book on the mighty Russian, he packed his bags, carefully disposing of the romantically shabby garments he had flaunted in Berlin, and boarded the train for home.

Clean and spruced up he presented himself to his family, to his professor and to the University. A period of dedication to duty was about to begin. His deliverance into a state of freedom would have to wait for a while.

Chapter Two

As an adolescent Stefan Zweig had been fascinated by the works of the Belgian poet Emile Verhaeren, and by the personality of the man himself.

His own early excursions into the world of poetry were influenced and coloured by the Master, and the desire to meet him personally now outweighed all other considerations. After returning from Germany he began to feel more than irritated that he had still to fulfil what he had always subconsciously regarded as a semi-sacred and filial responsibility, the obtaining of his doctorate; yet to return to his onerous studies and the confines of home and University dragged his soul down; he knew it had to be done, but the desire to seek out Verhaeren temporarily won the day, and he put off yet again the prospect of another term at University.

As events turned out, the procrastination was a mixed blessing, producing an avalanche of artistic achievement, an out-of-this-world relationship and the almost inevitable emotionally disastrous climax.

Zweig's own words as he recalls his first contact (at the house of the sculptor Van der Stappen, in 1902) with Verhaeren give some indication of the passion and humility consuming him at that time. There is in the uninhibited description and specific choice of words a rapture which could have been purely aesthetic or unconsciously homosexual.

'Now he stood facing me', he wrote in *The World of Yesterday*.

33

'For the first time I felt the strong clasp of his vigorous hand, and for the first time I saw his clear, kindly glance.' Forty years after his first encounter with Verhaeren, Zweig was able to record with undiminished admiration, 'In those three hours I learned to love the man as I have loved him throughout my entire lifetime', adding rapturously, in an explanation of his presence during a sitting given by Verhaeren to the sculptor van der Stappen: 'So for two hours I gazed deep into this face, this unforgettable lofty brown face, already ploughed by the furrows of evil years, and over this a wealth of rust-brown locks . . . When I look at that bust today—nothing of van der Stappen's ever turned out better than the work of that hour—I know how genuine it is and how completely it embraces his nature. It is a document of his poetic greatness, the monument of an immortal power'.

This eruption in Zweig's artistic and emotional consciousness produced a tidal wave of Verhaeren translations, and in prostrating himself before the Belgian and his work, he subjugated his own creative ability in order to carry out what had become for him a holy task. He became virtually a member of the Verhaeren household for almost two years.

At forty-five the Belgian poet exuded such physical and mental attraction that few could resist him, and Stefan, his memories of Berlin, the smoke-laden atmosphere of the beer cellars and the haggard face of their habitués still fresh in his mind, found it but a short step to transfer his devotion from them to this lonely, Tolstoyish figure whose works he had admired even as a schoolboy. He found it incredible that Verhaeren deigned to acknowledge him, the unknown, but attributed this splendid trait to the fact that early poverty frequently moulded man into an intellectual giant.

Of Verhaeren's wife, Marthe, a painter, and referred to by Friderike, Zweig's first wife, as 'exemplary', Stefan characteristically says nothing. Verhaeren the man, the artist, filled his entire visual orbit; for Stefan his wife did not exist.

Whether Verhaeren was aware of it or not, Zweig had already decided to cast himself in the rôle of disciple-cum-apprentice, and for the next two years he toiled unceasingly at translations of the poet's work. Occasionally they would journey together around Europe, Verhaeren lecturing and writing and, consciously or not, inspiring his companion with so much love and admiration that Stefan's emotional burden moved him to a written declaration of his attachment. 'I credit this encounter [Zweig's first discovery of Verhaeren's work] to one of those accidents representing the true and perhaps innate necessities in all human decisions . . .'

Zweig's early life was dominated by Verhaeren's influence. At the same time his apprenticeship, offered gratis eventually produced professional and artistic results in the form of a crop of translations which rapidly spread throughout France and Germany.

Verhaeren's earthiness, his shirtsleeved garb and unpredictable temperament, his choice of the always controversial subjects of Church versus State, the People versus the State and the perfidy of Monarchs, all intrigued Zweig. If, without causing domestic uproar in Vienna, he could have disowned all and everything responsible for his social, educational and domestic background at that time, he would have done so. (Yet who but a son generously indulged by his family could have supported the type of existence he enjoyed during the two years spent in the company of the Belgian writer?) Detached from the necessity of earning a living, freed temporarily from the restrictions of home and the ever-increasing irritations produced in him by his mother, Zweig tried to shut out unpleasant memories, and dedicated himself afresh to the work in hand. Verhaeren was then at the peak of his literary strength, and was utilizing all that he had learned from the earlier symbolists. The tragic caperings and stark brilliance of his erstwhile friends Rimbaud and Verlaine had provided the foundation on which much of his work depended; and to the cossetted son of the Viennese Zweigs these torch bearers of the new era hardened his determination to shed once and for all the despised bourgeois outlook and heritage.

Zweig's depression, present even from childhood although as yet only intermittent, deepened as he pondered the circumstances under which Arthur Rimbaud had met his early death a decade before. Rimbaud's agony poem *Hunger*, produced while the poet was near to starvation on the streets of Paris, was a perpetual reminder of the brutal indifference of the public: He wrote of his own hunger pangs:

> 'Nigh the only taste I feel
> Is for earth and stone. So peal
> Dinn-din! Dinn-din! Make your meal
> Air and rock and coal and steel . . .'

The words of the Rimbaud sagas of hunger and poverty caused Stefan considerable discomfort, although amidst the frenzy of artistic creation that marked the whole of his stay in Belgium he enjoyed periods of gaiety that alternated with his bouts of melancholy, and, mercifully for his sanity at the time, romanticism was *not* finally laid to rest.

The same streets of Paris which had reduced Rimbaud to skin and bone and poetic sublimity, still called the groups of ardent poets from their stuffy rooms to meet at the boulevard cafés where, in an effort to be fashionable, Stefan attempted to consume quantities of absinthe, which he hated. The passing girls, with their rounded figures, trailing their wafts of violet perfume, drew the young poets' glances and temporarily eased them out of the introspection with which they tortured themselves; but Stefan, his incurably romantic nature reacting automatically to a burst of sunshine, a rustle of silk or an elusive perfume, was often hard pushed to imagine what the bitterness of poverty was really about.

Above and beyond all the human qualities with which Zweig endowed Verhaeren was the admiration he felt for the Belgian poet's dedication to a cause for promoting a universal love and truth. Verhaeren's insistence that love between man and nations could and must exist if man was to survive through the perpetuity of his soul, was highly idealistic, if, as he himself ironically proved later, totally unworkable. Social and political ills, he claimed, would only be counterbalanced and understood if the true nature and expression of man's spiritual content was realized.

This admixture of idealism and realism dominated their endless discussions on art, literature and philosophy, and Stefan's mind, thirsting for just such knowledge, moved to meet the more mature, if extreme and sometimes contradictory thinking of the older man.

But the work of translation, prolonged and dedicated, kept his nose to the grindstone; and the task he had set out to do was begun in earnest and meticulously completed over those two years. During that period all of Verhaeren's poems and a selection of his dramas were superbly translated by Zweig, and ultimately published in Germany up to 1910.

Despite his determination to break free from the bonds of established metrical rhythms and rhyme, the Belgian's use of the new lyricism was still partly subjugated to the old diehard and diametrically opposed method; and in a reply to Arthur Symons, the intrepid English translator of his work *The Dawn*, Verhaeren wrote: 'If the French verse without rhyme existed, I would have employed it myself; only the blank French verse tells me nothing. In English this must be my wish. I approve your sentiments. I agree with you entirely'.

The Cloister, which eventually (1910) appeared on the Berlin stage, was the dramatic result of Verhaeren's earlier stay in a monastery, in order to 'absorb the atmosphere', and presented the avant garde audiences of Brussels, Paris and Berlin with intellectual entertainment of the highest order, plus a certain amount of puzzled head-scratching. The collection of monks in the all-male cast and their verbal battles had a distinct flavour of anti-ism spiced with the eroticism of flagellation.

As Zweig continued with his self-imposed toil, Max Reinhardt's productions of Verhaeren's plays continued to attract select audiences in Germany, and the name of the translator, Stefan Zweig, appeared more frequently before the public.

At about the same time, several young Englishmen tried their hand at translating the somewhat revolutionary Belgian, and audiences in London and the provinces were given their first taste of a new and exclusive literary diet. Pre-nineteen-fourteen-war theatregoers felt very daring as they heard Dom Balthasar query, for instance, the absolute sanctity of Confession; and in the exchange between this character and his superior, there was much ecclesiastical dissension for the devout layman to ponder.

Esmé Percy, with the actor-manager's usual caution, was not so concerned, however, with things spiritual as with calculating audience reaction to '. . . a play without a woman . . .'. Sex, the unrivalled route to healthy box office returns, was markedly absent, and it immediately labelled Verhaeren 'abnormal'. Even so, the play was presented and met with unexpected if short-lived success.

Verhaeren's influence on Zweig cannot be overestimated. The younger man saw in the Belgian poet the sublime nature of man as he was before sin had stained him; and if this adoration of one man for another smacks of exaggeration of fringe eroticism it should be remembered that because of his extraordinarily affluent background he was able to indulge this obsession and remain physically and mentally in contact with his master, and over a considerable and highly impressionable period of time. Zweig, already an habitué of all Europe, passportless, wealthy and intellectually fully endowed, roamed the literary and artistic paths without let or hindrance. As a member of the ever-widening circle of artists whose work and culture at the turn of the century was to have lasting and powerful impact upon the pre- and post-war world, he became part of that Europe, peopled not with the ghosts and memories of the great, but of a Europe actually resounding to their physical vibrations: Rainer Maria Rilke, the withdrawn and tender poet, the lusty Frans Masereel, almost indistinguishable from the great wood blocks from which he carved; Rodin, of the peasant hands, whom Stefan was later to meet, and the ageing Renoir, whose studio and presence confirmed Zweig's breathless devotion.

This early and relatively calm period of Zweig's life, marred only by a brief return to Vienna in 1904 in order to obtain his doctorate—a happening he brushes aside with impatience, even contempt—contributed towards the emotional and spiritual awareness which afterwards developed in depth to the mature yet contradictory attitudes we see through the eyes of the characters he uses.

When he was twenty-three, Stefan's life, notably free from any feminine complication, reached what he felt was the peak of ecstasy in his wanderings through Paris with Verhaeren's moustachioed and rangy figure beside him. 'Oh, how easily, how well, one lived in Paris, particularly if one was young', he wrote in *The World of Yesterday*. 'Merely walking about was a pleasure and a lesson at the same time, for everything was within reach'.

His own work and the form it would take was gradually becoming clearer to him, yet still he hesitated to take up where he had left off. Still he clung to the familiar and affectionate ambience of Paris, and particularly to Verhaeren's Saint Cloud dwelling.

Zweig's mental and emotional development, though often threatened by doubt, was on the whole subordinate to the joy of just being alive in Europe at that time and in the company of such men. The gloomy prophesies, an unsought-after facility, and too often tragically proven, had not yet thrust themselves to the forefront of his consciousness.

He loved, adored and worshipped at the high altar of art, and with all the strength and vitality of youth he dedicated himself to this sacrament. Always restrained in social matters, Zweig became the extrovert only when expatiating on the greatness of art in human form. He baulked at no word, however extravagant, if he felt it described truthfully the genius in others. He chose to cultivate his position at that time as an observer, and to a certain degree he retained this habit as he moved through each of the different patterns of his existence.

Before this particular existence crumbled under the violence of the 1914–1918 war, and with it the friendship of Verhaeren, Zweig pursued the difficult task he had set himself as translator, bewailing the fact that there were never sufficient hours in the day, nor adequate supplies of mental agility to fulfil the exacting demands of his work.

With the war as yet a decade away, and the muses, as far as he was concerned, still the dominating factor in Europe, Zweig's love for the Continent and its abundance of literati became a passion.

Even in his darkest moods he could not contemplate a world without Verhaeren, much less his friendship; but he was reckoning without the violence that exists at the kernal of human love. This naïveté persisted in Zweig to the end.

He had come to accept as a fact that the Belgian's attachment to him was indestructible, and while translating Haineau's speech from Verhaeren's *The Dawn*, he attributed little of the violence of the characters to the author. Yet many times Verhaeren spoke clearly through the mass of his poetic trappings:

'I conclude then, as I concluded yesterday; in a revolution it is essential to strike at the ideas in the person of those who represent them. It is essential to go slowly, not to be carried away, and to make for immediate ends. Coldly each of us will choose his man, his victim. No one shall lie down to rest until the three Regents and the two Consuls of Oppidomagne are dead. It is the work of terror that brings the work of safety.'

Thus spoke Haineau, the coldly calculating warlord, determined to overthrow his opponents, if not by physical then by psychological methods. But when, in 1914, the whole of Europe was involved in war, Zweig was utterly bewildered that Verhaeren should regard him as an 'enemy' simply by reason of his birth. Where, he asked in vain, had all the protestations and declamations of Universal Brotherhood gone . . .? Why should this act of insanity extinguish a relationship which he believed surpassed all human frailties, and in addition produced volumes of artistic achievement . . .

Verhaeren, on the other hand, was clear on the subject. It was a question of black and white, and he seemed not to care that he had wounded his young devotee so deeply. As far as he was concerned, one world had come to an end, another, a more violent, crude and unsympathetic one, was to take its place. Belgium, his homeland, was to feel the vile suppression of the German jackboot. Therefore he was on one side of the warring nations, Stefan Zweig on the other.

Only once, and in the briefest and coldest of terms, did he again communicate with Zweig, and at the age of sixty-one, in 1916, he died. The realization of his loss brought on Zweig's first truly overwhelming depression, but the act of death was not so grievous to him as the loss of their communication. He simply could not believe that such a thing had happened; and many of the shadows that were later to gather in his mind were already present when he wrote of Verhaeren in 1917: 'Together with memories of my great, lost friend, I tell the story of my youth'. He was then thirty-six years old and deeply involved with Friderike von Winternitz, who was later to become his first wife: 'This gratitude goes out to the master of life', he went on, 'giving my youth the first imprint of truly human values, teaching me in every hour of his existence that only a perfect man can be a great poet, giving back to me, together with enthusiasm for art, an indelible faith in the poet's human purity'.

Many more complicated relationships were to follow before the instrument of war finally separated Zweig forever from the past to which he had clung, partly adoring, partly despizing it.

His own creative urge was now so insistent he could no longer ignore it, and with what he felt was enormous courage he began to write—not a continuation from where he had left off before the Belgian episode, indeed he felt some contempt for the earlier prose and poetry he had so easily and successfully published; but using his own developing craftsmanship.

Chapter Three

Paris, past mistress in the art of seducing her unsuspecting visitors into a state of bemused indecision, found a more than willing subject in Stefan Zweig. Even when the self-imposed task of the Verhaeren translations was more or less complete, he found it easy to talk himself into prolonging his stay. There was still so much to do, to see, people he longed to meet.

The city itself beckoned him. He felt the magnetism of the past and the pulse of the exciting present emanate from the very stones of the buildings; and this welcome imprisonment of his senses served to sharpen his perceptions.

The geographical land mass of Europe was, for Zweig, 'home'. Equally at ease in its capitals and languages, he tried even then to stop his ears to the rumblings of insurrection which would inevitably produce its rash of shifting frontiers, and political and human miseries, and terminate once and for all what he considered the priceless gift of freedom in cultural commuting.

While part of him accepted and even welcomed the struggle for political and social equality, he realized that its advent meant the demolition of certain structures he had always considered necessary for the continuance of man's higher mental survival. Any appraisal of his work and the approach he continually uses in the handling of his subjects must, therefore, be based upon an understanding of the inherent and compassionate reverence he had for all human bewilderment caught in the toils of higher, often corrupt power.

In many of his books he deals with the *effect* rather than the cause; with the residue of great historical and political manoeuvres. In the human flotsam from momentous happenings he saw the only abiding truth. The creature left on the beach after the tidal wave of political upheaval or of racial discrimination has subsided, was at the centre of his most profound and sombre meditations. In his mature years, and influenced by personal experience in this bitter field, his compassion for the human pawn carried him to the borders of literary evangelism. Consider, he calls out through his writing, the plight of this creature who, because of physical or mental fragility, or from political persecution, is cast out by the others of the tribe. Look hard at him, he commands. Whose indifference and what twisted social system is responsible for such a plight?

Not a few of Zweig's short stories deal deliberately with the outcast, and *Leporella* in particular, illustrates the appalling calamity arising from the sheer careless disregard of a woman's loyalty. If, like Leporella, she happens to be merely a servant and a fairly incoherent member of a minority group at that, the guilt of her master, Baron von Ledersheim, is shown to be even greater. In the last of only a few sentences Zweig allows the girl throughout the story, the sum total of selfishness is discovered: '"Thank you, Sir", [Leporella] said, in a broken voice: "I'll leave at once. I don't want to be a trouble to you." Slowly turning, she shuffled from the room'. An item in a newspaper reporting the drowning of a woman in the Danube the following day completes this cycle of discovery, surrender, love and abandonment.

Zweig traces the story of the servant girl and her fanatical love for her master in relatively straight forward style. In what must now be regarded as an outmoded setting, master and servant are used to illustrate the result of social injustice, and with his usual 'mode d'emploi' Zweig manoeuvres his victim of circumstance into a state where self-destruction appears to be the only solution to an insoluble situation.

Leporella, with almost every mark in the book against her, illegitimate, ugly, incoherent, nevertheless develops an unexpected refinement of fidelity in her passion for her master who, as Zweig explains, has the good nature of most 'libertines'.

The coming together of this unlikely couple is made credible by her presence in the Baron's erratic household as a maid of all work. A product of the orphanage system, the girl slaves away willingly, unaware of even the meanest privilege to which she may have been entitled: and when, during the neurotic storms that broke out frequently between the Baron and his wife, other servants abandoned the battlefield, Leporella remained to hold the fort—unmoving, immovable.

With the suicide of the Baroness after discovering her husband's infidelity, and his own cowardly rejection of Leporella, after she had sought only to please him by serving him during his extra-marital exercise, unable and unwilling to face the dumb and adoring peasant girl, von Ledersheim loads his own guilt upon her, while she, with her dumb animal-like devotion and limited intelligence, fails to grasp the reason for her master's loathing.

Zweig's handling of von Ledersheim's cowardice is simple to the point of brutality. In order to rid himself once and for all of the servant girl's presence, and thus a constant reminder of his disastrous marriage, he instructs his valet to give her notice to leave. When, after an agony of doubt on her part, she challenges him to his face, he confirms the order, adding 'and the sooner the better!' her reason for existing ceases.

Of Leporella's suicide following upon her final rejection, Zweig makes no comment, merely recording the fact that it was: 'Not until next day, when they read a news item in the paper to the effect that a woman about forty years of age had drowned herself in the Danube, did master and man know what had become of Leporella.'

No fierce moral indignation here, only the sadness of plain statement of fact. Zweig reserves the more ruthless indictment of selfishness, corruption, and folly for some of his later historical biographies. Leporella, within her orbit, nevertheless points the

44

way to what he saw as the common denominator of all human frailty.

In these years immediately preceding the outbreak of the war, he was already embarking upon his long voyage of emotional and spiritual conflict. During the search he revealed through his characters his absolute belief in the unquenchable purity of the human spirit and its endeavour. Parallel with such commendable ideology, however, is the bleak sadness of enforced acceptance— that somewhere along the line, that which is Divine in man appears to be extinguished by his ignorance, and he turns away from the 'light of knowing'.

This emptiness, which on later occasions was to claim Zweig as its victim, is nowhere better illustrated than in one of his disturbing yet tender 'Legends', *Rachel Arraigns God*. Here he points out that the silence which is God is not understood or accepted by Rachel; and the futility of her earthly existence and of the sacrifice she made drains her soul, driving her to a near-pagan harangue. Both aspects of humanity's eternal dilemma, faith and denial, are clinically yet humanely investigated by Zweig in this story, one of a collection based on the Old Testament.

As yet, however, these mature, often crystal clear reasonings and analyses were dormant. For the present, he was willing to exist from day to day, pursuing his deliberate plan of watching, listening and learning, only occasionally hearkening to the movement of a higher and restless consciousness.

Today, the sun was glistening on the wet pavements of Paris and sparkling in droplets on the leaves of the plane trees; and the still, small voice deep within him was temporarily silenced by the outward and visible signs of wellbeing all around. It was not even necessary to affect the standard Bohemian garb any more. With some relief Stefan now sported his good quality, conservatively tailored suits. At least Paris had the common sense to accept an artist's work if it was good, whether he wore a smock and beret or trousers and a homburg.

Stefan's ecstatic reaction on his first visit to Renoir's studio typifies his worship of art in any field. Breathing deeply of the

45

atmosphere, still heavy with the thought and visual forms of the Master, he felt rather like a grimed and unworthy mortal on an unexpected confrontation with God. It is worthy of comment that when recalling this visit almost forty years after, Zweig, who loathed, almost obsessively even the mention of the word 'money', particularly in connection with art, refers with some awe to '. . . the *hundreds* of pounds Renoir's pictures are fetching today . . .'

Renoir, Rodin, Valéry, Rilke—whichever way he turned he was surrounded by these men of creation, these giants of self-expression. At times his entrée into such an elite circle completely mystified him. He felt so unworthy, so untried, that he doubted whether he would ever regain the early confidence which had produced with such comparative ease the poems, short essays and articles already published in Austria. However *Silberne Saiten—Silver Strings*—one of his first poems to be published, and doomed by its critical young author never again to see the light of day after its first edition, was even then having such a tremendous effect upon a young woman living in his native Austria, that she swore instant and lasting devotion to its author. After a series of 'fateful' happenings, as she romantically described them, or as emerges on closer examination, a few carefully manipulated feminine devices, the first, extremely involved, relationship between Zweig and a member of the opposite sex was established in 1901.

This rather tenuous beginning to what was destined to become a most dynamic association rarely troubled Stefan during his commuting between countries. He was vaguely aware that there must have been good reason for the adoring letters that occasionally reached him, and that casual meeting amongst friends which Friderike referred to so nostalgically must have taken place. But the image was blurred. What was the name of the Garden Inn she mentioned . . . the Stelzer in Rodaun . . .? He had been there, of course, but he could not possibly offend her by stating flatly that he was unable to recall meeting her.

For Friderike, however, *Silberne Saiten*, and the serious-faced young man sitting with a group of other artists at a table in the beer garden, were synonymous with the turning point in her previously uneventful life.

Her heart beat faster in her maternal, youthful, bosom whenever she thought of the author of those melting words; and Stefan, blissfully pursuing his predestined role amidst the higher echelons of French art, would have been astonished, even dismayed, to learn of such devotion and from such a source.

At that time Friderike was to all intent and purposes safely married to Dr Felix von Winternitz, with a small daughter and many in-law connections in high diplomatic places to prove it. She was, therefore, undeniably bound tight within the confines of her domestic and social circle, but no bondage, however stringent, could imprison her heart; and this had already been given, if not directly to the author, then without any reservation to his work.

Later on, inflamed by the passion and melancholy of Zweig's early drama *Tersites*, she ascribed every human and most of the heavenly attributes to this weaver of words. During the weeks and months of their inevitable separation she recited the gentler poems, already condemned by Zweig as 'adolescent', but balm to Friderike's tortured soul. The young poet's work was the bridge she never allowed fall into disrepair; and her avowal to bring the 'Zweig cause' to some sort of fruition, despite what were seemingly insuperable difficulties, was no less determined than Zweig's own dedication to his poet's progress.

Paris, in the meantime, laid prior claim to him; and although his sorties beyond the French capital were on the increase, including later on a stay in London rather 'different' from the intellectual teach-ins with which he was familiar, he yet lingered amongst those friends through whom he was beginning to discover himself.

All, as may be imagined, was not continual poetic peace and harmony in this star-studded gathering. Clash of opinion was frequent, and as sharp and wounding as any sword-play; but the wounds were only superficial and nearly always inspired by a genuine desire to purge beneficially rather than to destroy.

Of his friends and critics, Zweig refers often and affectionately

47

to Leon Bazalgette who, with forthright honesty, rejected Stefan's early work (apart from the Verhaeren translations) because of its 'escotericism'. It took Bazalgette, who had devoted many years to translating Walt Whitman into French, nearly a decade before he gave his seal of approval to Zweig's work. Approbation so hard won was doubly cherished by Stefan and he regarded it as the turning point in his early literary career from the esoteric to the more realistic and incisive approach.

The outbreak of hostilities and his violent emotional reaction to the brutality they unleashed eventually found tongue in his dramatic play *Jeremiah*, and this, more than any other vehicle, laid the foundation for the writer Zweig was to become. (The timing of its first production, in Easter 1917, when suffering was at its height, probably lent weight to what was in any case a message and prophecy of universal peace that much of the world's wearied populace *wanted* to hear.)

Approval of his work in the earlier style, however, his poems and essays, was early forthcoming from a poet of very different calibre: Rainer Maria Rilke. This gentle and delicate exile from Germany, already at the remarkably youthful age of twenty-three an established poet with a huge following, rates high in Stefan's list of friends. In the withdrawn, introvert personality of the man he found many echoes of himself. But whereas Rilke, by the time they met, had already crystallized into what his present work showed him to be—mystic *and* human in the highest sense of the word, Zweig was more concerned with earthly problems than he with his symbolic 'spirit mothers and angels'. However Rilke quickly recognized and encouraged Zweig's budding talent, even though his own had probably surpassed the levels with which the slightly younger man was involved.

Zweig singles him out from amongst the more temperamental and fractious members of the Paris circle as unique. On Rilke's vulnerable nerve endings a harsh voice or a sudden sound would vibrate unpleasantly; and intermittent withdrawal from the crash of humanity seemed the only way of escape. For Zweig, and those in the majority, forced to remain within this vortex of sound,

Rilke's words and thought-forms pour like cool water. In certain of his Elegies his choice of words is never less than sublime:

> Hark, how the night fluted and hollowed, you
> stars,
> is it not from you that the lover's delight
> > in the loved
> one's
> face arises? Does not his intimate insight
> into her purest face come from the purest star'*

Rilke's loving and lovers rarely descend from the astral planes and remotely passionate regions of the spirit. His personal attachments were so finely wrought as to be almost non-existent; and yet he was greatly loved by many of his contemporaries, who probably saw in his special brand of luminosity the image of what they themselves wished to be. Zweig admits that even his name was 'precious', and many years after the death of this gentle poet he asks:

'Is it not a lost tribe that I am bemoaning—Rilke, Verlaine, Verhaeren . . . a tribe without visible successors in this day of exposure to every storm of fate.' His own tempestuous and involved emotional and sex life no doubt prompting the self-questioning, he continues: 'These were the poets who made no demands on society—neither the regard of the masses nor decorations, honours or profit—who sought only to bind verse to verse in silent yet passionate effort, every line saturated with music, flaming with colour, glowing with images. They constituted a guild, an almost monastic order in the midst of our clattering time.'

Yet even Rilke at times hankered after the more robust qualities of man, denied him from early childhood by a perverse Nature. In *The Boy* he calls out forcefully:

> I'd like above all to be one of those
> who drive with wild black horses through the night

* Stephen Spender and J. R. Leishman toiled long and devotedly to produce their superb translations of the Elegies, of which this is a part.

49

torches like hair uplifted in affright
When the great wind of their wild hurling blows
I'd like to stand in front as in a boat,
tall, like a long floating flag unrolled,
And dark, but with a helmet made of gold,
restlessly flashing. And behind to ride
ten other looming figures side by side.

Allegorical or realistic, Rilke's choice of heavier-weight words than usual in this poem put him into an easier perspective. Despite Zweig's high regard for the 'precious' Rilke, he is not everyone's choice, and many critics have possibly extracted not a little pleasure in their condemnation of this remote, provocative poet.

By his relatively early death, at the age of fifty-one, however, he rescued himself and his work to some extent in the eyes of his realistic detractors. Posthumously, our faults rarely seem so damaging.

Rilke's early and disastrous marriage with one of Rodin's pupils, Clara Westhof, provided him with an idyllic period of love and fulfilment, but very little financial support; and from the peace of the country, where the two artists had planned to sojourn, alternately loving and working, he was forced to make his way to Paris, the city of 'railways and noise'. Here he hoped to reap, not financial gain, but at least a measure of financial support. He hated the harshness of 'the big town', yet was realist enough to appreciate the density of talent and its enormous public gathered in and around France's capital. However, the stones and the smells, the chattering crowds on the boulevards and the eternal discussions supplemented with coffee and absinthe, wearied him beyond measure. All the accumulated sound, creation and ostentation that so attracted Zweig, even though at that time he was still on the sidelines in his capacity as observer, had the opposite effect on Rilke. The noisier and more inflamed the scene, the further away he drew, yet, like all the other exiles quartered there, he seemed unable to break the shackles of Paris.

In the vast collection of letters which Rilke wrote to known and unknown correspondents in many countries, he challenges the priestly confessor on his own ground. Thoughtfully, lyrically and always humanely, he answers his correspondents' queries, soothes their emotional agonies and delivers a considerable quantity of profound common sense. Reginald Snell, his champion and translator, bravely puts him in line with the great European letter-writers, Goethe and Shelley, and adds, defensively, 'almost with Keats'.

Zweig's assessment, then, of Rainer Maria Rilke, is not perhaps so biased as it would at first seem when viewed through the rosy glow of friendship.

Even now, after the second world war, which Zweig himself saw as the death-knell to all that is spiritual and creative in man, the poet posing the eternal question:

> Did I fall from the cart, or was it
> the lightning that
> struck me?
> Was it pierced by a poison or hurled by a horn
> that I
> fell?
> Was it I struck earth, or was it the earth that had
> struck me?
> Take all of me up to your image, perhaps you can
> tell!

strikes our ears with much the same clarity, wonderment and persistent childishness as when it was first published. Rilke is here, wandering the gusty, teeming streets of Paris, sheltering from the city's onslaught in hard-to-find quiet corners, exposing his vulnerability only in the torrents of words that poured from his pen; and in the few intimate discussions he had with Zweig, recalling the pallid, precious child we try in vain to protect from his atavistic night terrors.

Measured against this particular artistic alchemy, the 'others' appear violent, even coarse-grained. But Rilke's somewhat ethereal presence within the vivid spectrum of art, poised over the Paris scene, is necessary, even vital, if the whole range of shade and colour is to be preserved and understood.

Was Zweig, particularly in his youth, biased or uncritical in his judgement on artists and art? At first glance it would seem so. Superlatives flow easily from him as he recalls the activities and personalities of his friends and colleagues. Yet much later, when friendships and fashions in art had changed, when violence and exile had forced him into the stateless area of exile, still he held fast to his earlier convictions, rooted as they were in the people to whom he had given his unstinting affection. The doubt one finds in his bewailing of 'the lost tribe of artists' was not self-pity, but rather an expression of fear that the post-war world would forget that work which he knew to be of the highest artistic merit. If, in retrospect, some of Zweig's critical or benevolent assessments of his contemporaries are not today fully vindicated, it is with some difficulty that the names come to mind—for they are few indeed.

In the case of Auguste Rodin, for instance, whom Stefan first met in 1905, when the great sculptor was hard upon his three score years and ten, any prediction, whether it comes from Zweig or from the uninitiated, sixty years after, would seem superfluous. Rodin's work stands before us, alone in its magnificence. Comment is unnecessary—as Zweig discovered when he found himself in Rodin's massive studio at Meudon:

'. . . I stood among his statues like one of them'. He remembers with reverence the moment, and the one stupidly inadequately word—'admirable!'—that escaped from him upon seeing for the first time an unfinished Rodin in the process of completion by the master.

We tend to use the materials with which a man expresses himself as a yardstick to measure his personality; and this empirical assumption is reasonably near the mark when we consider the masses of unyielding stone which Auguste Rodin reduced to the genius of living form.

Reaching for words that convey the ultimate to the reader was not difficult for Zweig. By his choice of expression he touches that emotional and mental nerve which had seemed non-existent in us, or at least slightly underdeveloped; and we discover with amazement that his burning enthusiasm is transmitted, and then shared. 'Finally, the master led me to a pedestal on which, covered with wet cloths, his latest work, a portrait of a woman, was hidden. With his heavy, furrowed, peasant's hand he removed the cloths and stepped back.' Zweig recalls how his admiration for Rodin turned into adoration as the sculptor donned a smock, grabbed at a spatula and proceeded to pay him, the unknown, the greatest compliment, by ignoring his presence while he made the superb and sure strokes that would reveal to succeeding generations the genius behind a curve, a fold, a line of exquisite symmetry. 'He no longer spoke', Zweig writes, with the homage of a pilgrim at the shrine, 'with a masterly stroke on the shoulder he smoothed the soft material so that it seemed the skin of a living, breathing woman . . . Then he no longer spoke . . . His eyes, which at table had been amiably inattentive, now flashed with strange lights and he seemed to have grown larger and younger. He worked and worked, worked with the entire passion and force of his heavy body; whenever he stepped forward or back the floor creaked. But he heard nothing. He did not notice that behind him stood a young man, silent, with his heart in his throat, overjoyed that he was being permitted to watch this unique master at work. He had forgotten me entirely. I did not exist for him. Only the figure, the work, concerned him, and behind it, invisible, the vision of absolute perfection . . .'

The various assaults on his senses to which Stefan was frequently exposed during those days in Paris had a lasting impact upon him. They were the basic structure upon which he built his own art form. Work, above all, and the act of grace which enables the human being to apply himself to it, was Zweig's lodestar, and in witnessing those engaged upon it, whether in mighty or in humble form, he renewed his vow of dedication to this singular blessing.

In describing the final, exquisite moments spent in Rodin's company, he brings the master back to vigorous life: 'So engrossed in his work was Rodin that not even a thunderstroke would have roused him. His movements became harder, almost angry. A sort of wildness or drunkenness had come over him; he worked faster and faster. Then his hands became hesitant. They seemed to have realized that there was nothing more for them to do . . . Then he replaced the cloths gently above the figure as one places a shawl round the shoulders of a beloved woman . . . His figure seemed to grow heavier again. The fire had died out . . .'

With Rodin's passion spent, the fire in Stefan's breast threatened to consume him. With what he refers to as a 'strangled lover's sob' he forced himself back to earth, grasped the peasant hand Rodin proffered, and only just managed to stifle an overwhelming desire to kiss it: 'Great moments are always outside of time', he cries. And this, for him, was undoubtedly one of them.

Continually refreshed at this fountain of self-expression, living and working in the very midst of Europe's artists, Zweig laid his plans for future work. There was still much to do, many countries to visit. So far only Europe had claimed him. Rilke, with his tales of Russia and the 'solitary emptiness and spiritual purity', had intrigued Stefan, bringing back to him the excitement of the 'Dostoyevsky Days' in Berlin.

The brooding lands of the Czar were contrasted starkly with the intimate sophistication of Paris; but the country that had bred Chekhov, Tolstoy and Gorki was automatically elevated to the summit of desirability in Stefan's estimation.

There was also a vague thought about establishing some sort of pied à terre. He felt, rather guiltily, that perhaps this may have been dictated by social rather than physical need, but as he had collected many precious bits and pieces during his travels, it seemed that, even if he was not too interested in a permanent resting place, these items, which he liked to think of as his collection, probably deserved a more fitting setting than the cupboards and suitcases in which they now rested.

The enchantment which he felt as he watched others work must, he knew, be replaced by his own efforts. The Insel-Verlag, a publishing house of great quality and reputation in Austria, and the Neue Freie Presse, the great left-over but still respected newspaper of the Hapsburg Monarchy, had already published some of his articles and essays, yet still he would not commit himself.

Zweig's hesitancy was probably subconsciously related to the earlier part of his life which, with its domestic restrictions, and not least, the thorny relationship between himself and his mother, he was trying to forget.

Eventually a decision was reached, although in the light of many future 'decisions', it was a typical compromise. He settled in Vienna and eventually found a reasonably attractive apartment; but even this substantial evidence of his citizenship failed to satisfy him. He saw himself as a 'European', and as such he would continue to travel abroad and wander wherever his desire or his work would take him.

Chapter Four

When Zweig finally moved to his pied à terre on the outskirts of Vienna, he promptly filled it with books, a valet-cum-general factotum and his zealously collected assortment of first editions, autographs and sketches. Collector's fever had caught him while still a boy at school, and many of the scrawled signatures he had waited patiently outside stage doors to collect, were now carefully stowed away in his 'haven'.

He refused to consider the apartment as anything but a haven or a port, for use between trips. Subconsciously he always cast himself in the rôle of wanderer or exile although at that period of his life, indeed from the day of his birth, there was not the slightest reason to suggest that his social or financial security was in jeopardy and about to crash around his ears. Political security was something else entirely, however, and Zweig, with his ultra-sensitive Jewish heritage and its memories, at present dormant but always alert to the smell of persecution, was even then intermittently on the watch. His increasing determination, running counter to common sense, to regard himself as a European and not as a Jew is an indication of his fear—a condition not implanted by events or circumstances, but as biologically inherited as his pigmentation or perspicacity.

If during those early years of the twentieth century he had been questioned bluntly regarding his views on Judaism, he would have made short shrift of the issue by substituting immediately the word 'Europeanism'. He did not want to see the dividing line, wanted to ignore its implications.

The label 'intellectual' also had great attractions, and gave a sense of security to those whose artistic work qualified them to use it. The cultural life of Europe was at that time to a large extent in the hands of Jews, especially in Austria and Germany, and Zweig eagerly subscribed to this elite and its euphemistic subtitle, and became one of its most active members.

It was only later that he cast aside this self-deception, and later still that he managed to call a spade a spade, actively taking up the moral and literary cudgels of his race, defending it against marauders, and finding at long last a latent moral strength in its history of tribulation.

Ironically, his future mistress Friderike, Jewish by birth, had added to the shackles of matrimony and society that of religion, by converting to her husband's faith. In addition the Catholic Church, to whose camp she had defected, would certainly censure without sympathy its converted daughter's anticipated act of treachery. Friderike certainly had plenty to think about during this period, and what made the whole thing more difficult was the fact that she was not even sure of Stefan's reaction to all the legal and illegal manoeuvring which the dissolution of her marriage required. She knew him sufficiently, however, to have observed his instinctive withdrawal from everything that hinted at legal intricacy, and as she recalled this, her unease increased daily, along with her determination to overcome the difficulties. Stefan, for his part, rationed his domestic sojourns in the capital with admirable caution. He was caught up in a steady stream of literary work, and his play *Tersites*, written in 1906 and so beloved by Friderike, had already been promised its première at the Prussian State Theatre.

Zweig never quite recovered from his astonishment that so august a theatrical body could be interested in this play, continually criticized by its author as containing the youthful excesses that he was labouring so devoutly to forget. In his eyes the play was already stilted and outmoded and he now disliked the idea of presenting it, as he had at first agreed, in Greek costume. However if the directors of the State Theatre liked it enough to put it on, he felt that he should not refuse. And when with a mixture of delight and apprehension he heard that Adelbert Matkowsky, one of the heroes of the German stage, was to take the rôle of Achilles, the play seemed set for success. Then the first of many theatrical blows fell. Shortly after the commencement of rehearsals they were abruptly ended by the sudden death of the famous actor, and in due course the play was abandoned.

Zweig recounts at some length the extraordinary series of mishaps and tragedies that followed on nearly all his ventures into the world of the theatre. One by one, artists who accepted roles in his dramatic plays seemed to become victims of some unidentified 'bone pointing'. Only *Volpone*, *Jeremiah* and *The Lamb of The Poor* escaped the jinx, although even this last, when produced for the Athens stage, resulted in uproar and public demonstration. A mature if troubled association with the great Richard Strauss began when the composer musician asked Zweig to act as librettist for his latest opera, *The Silent Woman*; but this was also doomed to fall on the theatrical rocks, this time through political strife.

It is easy to see, then, why Zweig falls back on the word 'superstition' to describe his attitude of mind when recounting the always uneasy relationship between himself and the theatre.

Although his not wholly enthusiastic farewell to Paris a year or so before meant leaving many of his artist friends, Zweig was to discover others in Austria and Germany, many of them destined to reap even greater laurels than their French counterparts.

It was perhaps a singular privilege for one so young to be permitted to hobnob with these representatives of the muses. No one was more surprised or deeply sensible of the honour than Zweig himself; although it later became fashionable for his various critics to attribute his early success to these privileges, rather than to his talent.

Zweig welcomed all criticism, however. For him it proved two things: that he had established a sufficient European following to merit such professional reaction, and secondly, that he must never relax in his striving towards what he saw as perfection. Because of his youthful success with his poetry and articles on art and artists, he had distrusted anything achieved with too much ease; and if anything, the adverse criticism that some of his work had attracted merely provided the spur later on to fine down and prune away all that which he later saw as expendable.

How far he succeeded in doing this should be judged against the demand of the public for a 'good story, well told', and for accounts of the great personalities in history. Did Zweig satisfy these requirements? His detractors find refuge in their distrust of the 'emotional' or 'romantic' treatment, but even they rarely denounce his humanity. The dividing line between emotion, romance and humanity is extremely thin, and Zweig's personality would not permit him to stand too far off from a subjective approach. His concern, as I have said, lay with effects rather than causes—and the more tragic those effects, the more interested he became.

This human approach was no compromise for him. And even his very early work, which he himself criticized, has withstood the test of time, and still occasionally invokes a literary blessing.

Zweig was about to reach a turning point. He was shortly to declare himself as the man, the writer he knew he was, and what he had always striven to be, a humanitarian. His compassionate enquiries into the human psyche were now increasingly tempered by careful analysis. The embryonic and still suspect system of psychoanalysis had always attracted him and later, through his long association with Sigmund Freud, was to give a studied balance to what might have deteriorated into an emotional seesaw style of historical presentation.

In his Mary Stuart biography (written, admittedly, in maturity), this approach facilitated an uncanny and accurate penetration into the minds of Mary and Elizabeth, two women diametrically opposite in every way. There is also a striking objectivity in his treatment of a subject notorious for its ability to trap the unwary author

59

in emotional pitfalls. Shortly after his return to Vienna, Zweig's early attachment to Austria's 'princely' poet, Hugo von Hofmannsthal, was renewed. In Hofmannsthal he saw the sum total of everything he himself had worshipped in his youth.

If here the name Goethe dare be mentioned, the risk must still be taken in an effort to place Hofmannsthal in his correct perspective. Although nowadays it is difficult to come across any translations of this poet's work on the library shelves, he was then accorded only slightly less homage than his great nineteenth-century predecessor. And so sacred was Zweig's homage to the leonine Goethe, it seemed blasphemous for the uninitiated even to breathe his name, let alone hammer it out on the unsympathetic keys of a typewriter.

'I discovered by chance', Zweig recalls, 'that the most unusual and most valuable literary museum piece was treasured not in my closet, but in the same house'. The carefully guarded original text —the so-called jewel of his collection, Goethe's *May Song*—now seemed almost pallid since his discovery that in the same house, in an apartment above his own, lived an old, half-blind lady who had actually shared the physical presence of Johann Wolfgang Goethe.

'I nearly fainted', Zweig says; 'there was still one person on earth in the year 1910 on whom Goethe's sacred glance had rested.' The lady upon whom he in turn worshipfully gazed was in fact the daughter of Goethe's physician, Dr Vogel, the great poet himself having actually been present when the old lady, then a babe in arms, was baptized. Throughout his life, these vicarious encounters with creatures he regarded as god-like, brought Zweig the greatest possible joy.

Better than any biographer Zweig was perhaps able to sum up one important facet of his own personality. 'I agree with Goethe perfectly', he observes, 'when he says that to understand completely great creations one must have seen them not only in their perfection but have pursued the process of their creation. The sight of one of Beethoven's first sketches with its wild impatient strokes, its chaotic mixture of motifs begun and discarded, and with the creative fury, the superabundance of his genius, compressed into a few pencil strokes, is physically exciting to me because it is mentally exciting.'

Here lies a key unlocking one of the many doors to Zweig's mind. Physical excitement, even passion, stemmed more often from the aesthetic than from the corporeal stimulus; and it is fairly obvious that his eventual attachment to Friderike was based on her literary enthusiasm. In her devotion to art lay, for him, the attraction. No rounded breast or elegant thigh was more appealing to him than a woman's lips framing the precious and sacred names of Goethe, Hofmannsthal or Rolland.

In between the complicated meetings with Friderike, he discovered that Vienna was still synonymous with the words 'art' and 'music', and once again he found his literary path leading him towards the theatre. Arthur Schnitzler, physician turned dramatist, Luigi Pirandello, Sholem Asch and many others marching the dramatic and literary routes through Austria and Germany, were numbered amongst his intimate friends.

Having now reached his thirtieth birthday, Zweig could already see a substantial array of published work to his own credit. He was much sought after as contributor to all the finest newspapers and periodicals; but his latest play, *Das Hause am Meer—The House by the Sea*—brought down yet again the curse which the author was beginning to dread. Due to be produced at the Burgtheater under the direction of Alfred Baron Berger, it was the Director himself who this time succumbed to the unseen forces apparently at work in the arena of Zweig's dramas.

Berger's sudden death, within a fortnight of the first rehearsal, renewed Zweig's morbid belief in the presence of some dark angel hovering above his work, descending only to strike at or before the first performance. Throughout his life he never got rid of this superstition.

Europe had never been so appealing to him as in these years of 1910–14. Even Vienna, which he had tried to 'outgrow', claimed now his deepest affection; and perhaps would do so even more after his self-imposed trips to India and America.

His mental vision of Europe was frontierless, one country blending almost unnoticeably with another; and the whole gathered together in an amalgamation of brotherhood based on an ever-increasing devotion to culture. For a while he determinedly shut his eyes to the undercurrents of discontent which had disturbed him only recently, and succeeded in deluding himself that Austria and Germany, indeed the whole of Europe, represented a social paradise even for the armies of the workless and underprivileged.

He confessed himself relieved to see stuffiness and hypocrisy give way before the new, fresher outlook on life; although this 'new look' appealed to him more because it was the final break with an age which for him epitomized the outlook and approach of his mother and her generation. He recalls with an unreasonable contempt, for instance, the rather comical habit of draping chairs with protective covering and hurriedly dashing round to remove them each time a visitor arrived. His mother, however, was quite satisfied with the way family matters were turning out. Stefan had eventually obtained his doctorate, as she knew he would, and she could now mention the fact—casually, of course—in her rounds of social chatter.

The family business, too, was in good if somewhat unwilling hands. The elder son, now resigned to his rôle as 'head of the family', with father Zweig feeling the strain of advancing years, had taken complete charge. The two brothers, however, according to Friderike, when eventually she was drawn into family squabbles, refused absolutely to see eye to eye on any single issue. Stefan wanted nothing to do with the weaving and textile mill which, the others were constantly at pains to remind him, provided their incomes and consequently their comfortable upper-middle-class surroundings. Stefan continually refused to provide such necessary trivialities as signatures or verbal approval, and he seemed to find a perverted and childish delight in causing such annoyance.

What was responsible for the unshifting resentment that Zweig felt for his mother? The restrictions and regime of childhood about which he complains are the almost inevitable lot of any child whose parents are not entirely delinquent, and the Zweig parents certainly did not fall into this category. From his own words and examination of the progress of his life, it seems that his early precocious development prevented him intellectually from 'communicating' on a natural and uninhibited level with those around him. Too immature to recognize the true content of his feelings towards people who, for him, were on a lower level of consciousness, Stefan deliberately isolated himself, then wondered fretfully why no one in his immediate family circle understood him.

The enraptured outbursts on all his meetings with the great men of art and letters outline this attitude, this worship of mental and spiritual activity. Only with the advent of war was this sincere but singular attitude modified.

It will be seen that his destined entanglement with Friderike and afterwards with Lotte, coinciding with his strongly-established intellectual life resulted in a whole new set of traumatic changes and crises.

His work and his personal experience are inextricable; this can particularly be seen in *Beware of Pity*—an almost frightening autopsy on the emotion of compassion—and in many views expressed in the second Balzac biography. But as yet the major exercise in analysis, both of himself and of humanity, lay in the future. For the present he was content to play out his time working on the Verhaeren translations. Occasionally he would indulge in an essay or somewhat erudite article, which always found an easy market among the Viennese periodicals and daily press, but he attached little importance to this. Already his thoughts were drawing him from the confining intellectual climate of Austria to where his developing enthusiasm for pacifism might find further stimulus.

And here began a new treadmill of vacillation. He had long admired the writing of Tolstoy, and adored that of Dostoyevsky: pacifists both, though the one turned in horror from the thought of bloodletting—indeed, of all things physical—while the other was realist enough to acknowledge the existence of such violence, and to accept all the consequences if the cause justified them.

Already he was longing to venture forth into India, where he felt he might find some of the answers to what he now recognized as unquestionably pacifist views.

Beyond the frontiers of Europe, and even beyond Russia, lay yet another intriguing personality in the forty-one-year-old Indian mystic Mohandas Karmachand Gandhi.

But Zweig's idealism, spurred on by the writings of Tolstoy and the declarations of Gandhi, suffered a severe setback when he reached India. His own fastidiousness was deeply offended by the poverty and sickness endemic.

Gandhi's protest against caste segregation, as epitomized by third class travel on the railways, was like a magnet for Zweig. With much the same negative but dramatically effective gesture Leo Tolstoy used when deliberately drinking from a cup used by one of his own syphilitic serfs, so Gandhi identified himself with the misery and illiteracy of his people by travelling with them.

Third class in the India of that time automatically meant the social stigma of low caste or no caste, the great army of untouchables. 'Third class passengers are treated like sheep', Gandhi records, 'and their comforts are sheep's comforts. Entire carriage sections were converted into spittoons, the floors covered with betel-nut saliva and the air thick with foul language and uncontrolled yelling. I can think of only one remedy for this awful state of things—that educated men should make a point of travelling third class, and also never to let the railway authorities rest in peace until an improvement comes about.'

The literary reformers, through their art, were everywhere becoming active, and bent upon making the more affluent parts of the world sit up and take notice. The actions of these men and many others constantly needled Zweig's conscience. He knew that he must make a move. Must see for himself and suffer as they were in Tolstoy's Russia, and as in Gandhi's India, they were doubled beneath the yoke of serfdom.

He began to lay his plans for the Indian visit. It would be the first time he had set foot beyond the cultural hot-house of Europe.

But in the records he left concerning his Indian safari, there is little to indicate that he found it necessary to travel third class in order to identify with the national misery. Even Darjeeling, that sacred refuge of the British Raj, was scarcely bearable; and after several somewhat hurried investigations into acknowledged areas of disease and squalor, he withdrew, sick at stomach and heart.

India was to leave him scarred, frustrated and even more concerned with humanity's eternal problem.

Chapter Five

At this period of his life nothing short of artistic perfection seemed of importance, and he found it easy at times to denigrate that system from which he sprang and which until then had provided undeniably important financial succour.

The Vienna of Franz Josef's last years alternately charmed and irritated Zweig. But if, as once happened in a small cinema in Tours, he saw the dear old gentleman with the white whiskers and doddery gait ridiculed by the French audience viewing the newsreel, he felt an over-protective concern for him, for the Austria that was personified in the little, frail old man, and for the whole social and political framework that was, after all, his own country. Forgotten temporarily were his youthful, acid comments about the 'hypocritical' social set-up, the incomprehensible attitude of his mother and her chattering relatives, and the steady application, the almost ox-like plodding which was the driving force of the family's hard-won industrial success.

The idea of ridicule and humiliation mortified him, and this characteristic, so early and powerfully developed in his personality, was one of the principal sources of later agony when, for instance, under the Hitler regime:

'University professors were obliged to scrub the streets with their naked hands . . . pious white-bearded Jews were dragged into the synagogue by hooting youths and forced to do knee exercises and to shout 'Heil Hitler' . . . Innocent people in the streets were trapped like rabbits and herded off to clean the latrines of the S.A. barracks'.

Zweig had a foreboding of persecution right from the days of his adolescence. It would seem a strange companion to his censure of a liberal system he reviled as 'bourgeois', but it sprang from the unusual depth and quality of an inordinately compassionate process of thought. In its turn it led, later on, to an increased identification with the Jewish people.

Only youthful indecision prevented the crystallization of such thinking. But the blackness of depression born of his accursed 'second sight' was to lay a shadow across him that even the brightest and warmest of friendships could not dispel. 'All the sickly, unclean fantasies of hate that had been conceived in many orgiastic nights found raging expression in bright daylight. . . .' So Zweig in retrospect damns the beginning of a war which, more perhaps than any previous conflict, used the vile and unhealthy weapon of racial persecution to stimulate the seed of hatred.

But in the frothy music of the waltz and in the comfortable plushy atmosphere of the restaurants, resplendent with palms and heavy with the perfume of the much-criticized bourgeois culture, there was little to presage the nightmare of Hitler's reign. Yet Stefan, with his ear to the ground, and with memories of the privations of Verlaine and Rimbaud fresh in his mind, knew that behind the prosperous façade, millions waited restlessly for what they hoped would be release; and millions more, those in the minority groups, trembled as they anticipated the form that their 'release' would take.

The first world war was to generate the more mature and artistic impulse in him, giving tongue eventually to the drama *Jeremiah*. It was left to the second of the world wars to extinguish forever the flame of his literary creation. An understanding of Stefan Zweig and the literary harvest that he left comes into perspective as he reaches his thirtieth year.

Unfettered by the usual domestic bonds of marriage and family, free to wander amidst countries and people, his bondage was of the severest kind: the Jewish inheritance that he could never disown. More frequently he refers to the 'freedom' he enjoyed, the 'security', scorned but necessary; and parallel with such statements the cautioning phrase of the impermanence of both these priceless gifts.

Throughout his life he was unable to correlate the acts of humans with those of humans in government or power. His literary practice was to hold off for as long as possible before producing a work of major importance. This watching and waiting period provided him with what he considered incontrovertible proof that humanity manifest in a single mortal frame was, or could be, the epitome of grace, strength and mental and spiritual freedom. It was, he frequently said, only when the human being was made part of the whole structure, caught up in the whirlpool of government policies and social edicts that he lost his identity and became what his masters dictated, a coward, a hero, a bully or merely a cog in the wheel.

It was in alternately bemoaning acts of inhumanity and glorifying individual moments of spiritual triumph, that Zweig found the material for his work.

The development of his thought, his communication with an ever-widening circle of European intellectuals and increasing selectivity in the choice of his subjects, formed the major part of his existence in the years up to 1914. Zweig knew for sure that if he was to enter the literary arena and, what was more important, make his own mark there, he must emerge from the melée of collective thought, and show himself under his own colours with a formed and mature approach. His primary preoccupation was with universal brotherhood and pan-Europeanism, and he pursued it diligently even though he knew it to be unworkable. The presence of two conflicting major ideals is not always disastrous except when, as in Zweig's case, they happen to be those of idealism and fatalism, each dispensed in equal and formidable quantities.

By comparison the woman who was to be his companion for so long, and who was to prove a major influence in his literary career, appears forthright and almost crystal clear in her objectives. Friderike von Winternitz was as much a product of Austria's pre-1914 era as Stefan himself; but while his critical faculties had appeared as early as his schooldays, and were probably fanned by the prickly attitude he adopted towards his immediate family, her acceptance of the 'good' life in Vienna remained unquestioned, until, that is, her eyes alighted on the slim, boyish figure of Stefan on that night in Rodaun in 1908.

For a variety of reasons he always found it difficult, even impossible, to refer directly in any way through his writing to the women most vitally concerned with his life and his work; no mention of Friderike, or, later, of Lotte, is found in Zweig's autobiography.

The dramatic play *Tersites*, and his poem *Silver Strings*, both of which Stefan had already rejected, are the literary links to which Friderike clung so tenaciously. In a romantic and rather pathetic third-person account of their first encounter, she writes: '. . . the young woman threw a fleeting glance at the young man honoured by this retrospective praise. Had not such maturity necessarily been preceded by a great loneliness? Had not great solitude devoted to ceaseless meditation finally led to such precocious spiritual development? And had not she herself, although so carefully sheltered during her maiden days, lived through similar experiences?' Every incident of that evening, each nuance, is recorded by Friderike, almost thirty years after; and if the cynic should feel that this remembrance was kept alive only by the enchantment of distance or in the light of Zweig's then recent and tragic death, the fact remains that the impact Zweig had on this young woman was almost unbelievably instantaneous and enduring. She refers to his recurring state of melancholy, and records her dismay when he drew attention to the fact that many intellectuals had ended their days in mental institutions.

Yet still she saw in him everything she desired, and although weighed down by family problems, she saw nothing strange in the fact that she proposed to add to them by including in her plans the young poet seen over the distant tables in the romantic atmosphere of a beer garden.

Just how all this was to be brought about, she could not imagine; but whatever faculties Friderike had so far displayed, determination was high on the list.

She refers to Stefan's constant travelling abroad with an admirable restraint; but at the time her patience must have been sorely tried. Here was a young woman, bursting with an emotional and physical appetite that her somewhat profligate spouse was apparently unable or unwilling to satisfy; and there, at times so near that she could almost touch him, yet legally so far away that her blood became ice in her veins when she thought of the gruesome legal machinery necessary to unlock the nuptial fetters, stood Stefan Zweig, unattached, brilliant young poet and author. Already acclaimed by the press for his contributions to the Insel Verlag, that exclusive and élite publishing house which, to the literary minded, represented the authors' paradise, Zweig's unavailability made him seem even more desirable.

Friderike's own ventures into the literary world, although rendered necessarily spasmodic by the demands of motherhood, were nevertheless a useful link between them when Stefan's continual travelling interrupted their correspondence. She had two small books published—*Call of the Homeland* (Berlin 1914) and *Birdie*.

Zweig's physical appearance was somewhat pale and unvigorous and he had almost everything on his mind except women and their usual complications, yet her passion was to harass and enthrall him. Stoically she accepted his raves about countries, artists and authors, and dutifully echoed his reactions to any new experience. At times, she later confessed, she felt this remote attachment would never reach physical fulfilment, but it was all she had at the time, and with commendable vigour and what must have been many a heartache, she forced herself to accept with good grace the occasional gifts with which Zweig reciprocated her lyrical outpourings.

Meantime, she pursued her usual domestic round, wrote an occasional article, taught French and German History, and finally produced a second daughter in the respectable von Winternitz tradition.

Her life was, on the surface, that of any young matron in upper-middle-class circumstances. A doting father-in-law with connections at court and in the Foreign Service kept alive for her the presence of the aged Emperor and the picture of an affluent Austria. She accepted unquestioningly that this was the home of civilized thought, with its capital concerned with art and politics (in that order), both wide open to the professional and dilettante.

She was never less than staunchly approving of her home and background, even after five decades. The coffee-houses, with their learned habitués and newspaper racks, deferential, well-informed waiters, and sickly mounds of confectionery topped with whipped coffee cream, were all part of her background, as were the evenings of music, beer and wine, and the folk singers' unrepentent senti-mentality, bringing forth the nostalgia and tears with which Austrian bosoms and eyes were always ready to be filled.

Her family's connection with the various Ministries meant an abundance of framed and signed photographs around the house, each allocated a specific spot on the overmantel or the artistically draped piano, according to the position of the subject on the social, ministerial or court ladder. Surrounded by aunts, cousins and, on occasion, an uncle decked out in military uniform from some far distant and sentimentally remembered Empire outpost, she fondly recalls a childhood memory: a nearly demented aunt who burst into the room with the news—'Rudolph is dead!'—drawing the entire family together in common despair and mourning over the loss, not, as one would imagine, of a dearly beloved cousin or son, but of the Crown Prince of Austria.

From this protected and protective environment Fridereke had made few excursions. Her knowledge of the world was governed by the Austrian attitude of 'art for art's sake', and the newspapers' dedicated line of letting politics take care of themselves. Her in-stant attachment to the remote figure of Zweig can perhaps be better understood if one remembers the role of the romance of poetry in her upbringing. Poets were allocated an automatic shrine in the hearts and on the bedroom walls of nearly all gently brought up girls in the Austria of that time. The murmurings of fountains and glittering moonlight, belaboured in the sighings of this army of young men, found an immediate response in heaving feminine bosoms, and relieved the monotony of trudging through the interminable three R's as dictated by school authority. No dashing officer of Hussars, resplendent in the black 'do or die' uniform could have matched the slight, rather pallid and later bearded face of the poet who spoke to her personally, she was certain of it, in the words of his own poem:

'And yet remembrance often makes me pensive
Ah, what sweet tremor at the dawn of day!
Ah, were I home midst childhood's pure, cool rivers!'

even though the sonnet, she was later forced to admit, referred originally to Ellen Key, the Swedish educational reformer, whom Stefan had met in Paris and later again in Italy.

While Friderike wrestled to escape her shackles, at the same time keeping Zweig firmly within her sights, Stefan filled in the waiting period before his Indian trip with mental and literary exercises which invariably found their mark both in the publishers' and the public eye.

With the extremely controversial question of 'caste' both the Indian and the Austrian varieties—very much in his mental foreground, Zweig mulled long and arduously over this particularly loathsome invention.

He had no idea where the answer lay, but he was sincerely and fearfully caught up with the problems it caused. Bloody revolution, so soon to be launched in the Russia of the Czars, he was convinced, merely replaced one evil with another. The pacifism of Tolstoy, or the newly thought-up 'civil disobedience' in India, were obviously some sort of antidote, but with utter frustration he had to admit that what history placed as an unchallengeable truth before us, one man could not remedy in his relatively minute life span. He considered, however, that there may well be an opportunity for the individual to bring to the forefront of public conscience the plight of the underdog, the consequences of dictatorship, the loneliness of the mentally ill. All these and many more turbulent thoughts took Zweig's mind over as he grappled with his self-imposed task.

A deepening concern for all forms of social injustice occupied much of his thinking, and in his indictment of the old educational system, he wrote with bitterness: 'I cannot recall ever having been joyous or blissful during that monotonous, heartless and lifeless schooling which thoroughly spoiled the best and freest period of our existence.'

He loathed, too, the system which forced young men to seek their sexual pleasure down the sleazy back streets of the cities, and maintain a holier-than-thou attitude upon returning home; and in castigating the propogation of such a hypocritical set-up, he uses words that reflect his contempt for much of the social structure of the day. 'No young man must deflower the daughter of an upright and socially correct family, but at the same time he was expected to sojourn whenever his fancy seized him with these poor creatures, badly dressed, tired and often unkempt.' Zweig strips off the outer layers of bourgeois respectability in this autobiographical revelation, but can offer no alternative other than the then much-maligned emancipation of women: 'Generally speaking, prostitution was still the foundation of the erotic life outside of marriage; in a certain sense it constituted a dark underground vault over which rose the gorgeous structure of middle class society with its faultless, radiant façade.'

There is no evidence to show that Zweig followed those intellectual and social reformers whose repugnance for their youthful erotic adventures eventually led them to total abstinence. Leo Tolstoy claimed that his greatest spiritual burden was of his thoughtless and inexcusable abuse of women. That it was condoned by the society in which he lived only made the act more vile in his eyes. Gandhi was assailed by a similar guilt, but even as they

73

condemned a social evil, neither man saw anything suspect in subjecting their respective and legitimate wives to the severest form of mental distress by withholding their physical and frequently their mental communication.

The whole complicated and less than perfect social structure which so horrified him—whether as onlooker or participant we are never sure, as he persistently withholds any personal involvement here—is summed up expertly and with typical Zweig eloquence: '. . . then the sidewalks were so sprinkled with women for sale that it was more difficult to avoid them than to find them. To this was added the countless number of "closed houses", the night clubs, the cabarets, the dance parlours with their dancers and singers, and the bars with their "come-on" girls. At that time female wares were offered for sale at every hour and at every price, and it cost a man as little time and trouble to purchase a woman for a quarter of an hour, an hour or a night, as it did to buy a packet of cigarettes or a newspaper . . .'

He did not march against the tide, however, or even organize a spirited protest. He was as much a part of that scene as 'the poor creatures' he describes. But while yet part of it, he stood, as always, on the observing lines, his mind deeply occupied with the whole procession of humanity, engaged in every exercise from kneeling in prayer to scrambling into bed.

Chapter Six

In just over forty years Stefan Zweig travelled the earth, not once but many times. It would be interesting to log his mileage; but after the first excursions covering almost the whole of Europe and trips to the United States, Indo-China, Russia, India, and South America had been completed and repeated, the fantastic sum total would seem to illustrate some inner compulsion for flight rather than the merely pleasurable indulgence of a world traveller.

Unlike, for instance, Somerset Maugham, who appeared to dredge from his junketings in banana boats and coal barges an endless supply of human material for the books he wrote, Zweig used his travels, particularly in his youth, at first simply to escape a constricting background, but later to seek out those personalities in whom he had always placed a sort of reverent trust.

Romain Rolland, the already eminent French novelist and playwright who, while Stefan traipsed the streets and the studios of Paris during 1900 and again in 1904, was engaged on writing his novel *Jean Christophe*, 'the first great novel of the twentieth century', was later sought out by the younger man. Zweig had no inhibitions when it came to winkling out those artists he admired. With naïve enthusiasm he would cast his bread upon the waters and invariably it returned tenfold. Here I am, he would say, Stefan Zweig—a nonentity. I crave the honour to sit at your feet, and to listen and to learn. Just as he had done with Verhaeren and Rilke, so, in

1904, he did with Rolland, and sure enough Rolland responded. This time physical contact proved somewhat more difficult, as Rolland spent long periods shut up in his apartment during the production of his monumental work, Stefan hit on the idea of sending the French author one of his own small publications. It did the trick, as Rolland later communicated with him, inviting Zweig to visit him in person. Thus, as Zweig comments, '. . . a friendship began which, together with that of Freud and Verhaeren, was the most fruitful, and at certain times, the most decisive for the future course of my life . . .'

Zweig's regard for Rolland communicated itself to Friderike when later Zweig introduced them. If some of her husband's friends afforded her only a somewhat enforced and dutiful pleasure, there is no doubt that Rolland was not one of those. Her affection for the frail author was obviously sincere and deep. 'Nobody', she recalls, 'could look into those heavenly blue eyes, merging infinite goodness and keenest understanding in an incomparable way, without feeling secure.'

When later, in 1915, at the age of forty-nine, the owner of the heavenly blue eyes was awarded the Nobel Peace Prize, his massive novel *Jean Christophe* playing a large part in the award, Stefan's youthful and uncanny artistic nose was fully vindicated by this world literary acclaim.

The Rolland-Zweig friendship appears, above all other connections forged by Stefan, to have come nearer fulfilment than would seem possible in any human relationship, apart from the association with Verhaeren.

'And so a friendship began which, together with that of Freud and Verhaeren, was the most fruitful and, at certain times the most decisive for the future course of my life . . . No virtuoso—and I have listened to Max Reger, Busoni, and Bruno Walter in the most intimate setting—ever gave me such a feeling of direct communication with the beloved masters . . . I sensed with the joy that such recognition always gives me, a human, moral superiority, an inner freedom without pride, the taken—for—granted freedom of an independent soul. At first glance I recognized him—and time has

76

proved me right—the man who was to be Europe's conscience in a crucial hour.'

It was certainly the most enduring friendship. Already mentally removed from the narrow confines of limited materialism, Rolland acknowledged no frontiers, no enemies and harboured no bitterness; incessantly travelling the length and breadth of Europe in pursuit of his great mission, he spared himself nothing. Frail and stooping, and frequently the victim of ill health, this one man's colossal literary output was geared to exposing the uselessness of war.

Zweig's homage to Rolland in his biography of him, published in 1921, was repeated forty years later by a variety of English critics on rediscovering *Jean Christophe*: 'Here's something you mustn't miss . . . a great novel', raves the Daily Express, and in the same vein, 'To anyone who wants a change from the fragility of contemporary fiction, let me recommend *Jean Christophe*', echoes the Yorkshire Post. Un-Zweig like and racy in their approbation of this worldly yet spiritual author, they were nevertheless moved to deep appreciation of Rolland's apparently dateless literary approach.

Although it was inevitable that to some extent the people he met, their countries and the political climate in which they existed, influenced his thinking, Zweig's journeys were in the main undertaken as pilgrimages. His early zest for casting himself in the role of 'subject to liege' or pupil to guru never deserted him. Even in the last wearied days of his life, he displayed rare pleasure whenever he came into contact with those minds concerned with the humanities. He was always a dedicated listener, and this facility encouraged the most profound if diffident personality to blossom and eventually reveal itself.

Now, with preparations for his trip to India well under way, and with Friderike still on his conscience, he thought back to the brief spell he had spent in England, with which India was linked in his mind. London had appeared on his itinerary with about as much enthusiasm as he had accepted aperients in childhood, and for precisely the same reason—it would be good for him. But the aperient, though perhaps more unappetising, certainly produced a positive effect, whereas England, Shakespeare's land of such dear souls left him absolutely numb.

Zweig, with an almost comical fairness, realized that it was probably his own fault that no immediate rapport was established between him and the land of dear, dear souls, cloistered as he was in the British Museum day after day, almost too terrified to emerge. Whenever he did venture forth in Joseph Chamberlain's London, or sometimes further afield into the country, he felt like a man from Mars. He found the English character paradoxical, indeed enigmatic. The easy-going friendliness of the cab drivers, and the over-pompous declamations from celebrated patrons of the arts at the one or two parties he forced himself to attend, drove him back to the safety and silence of the B.M. like a badger scuttling back to his stuffy but familiar hole.

And yet the sceptr'd isle often seemed to him to be a series of sealed-off compartments, with the ants all busily engaged on carrying out their appointed tasks and not caring a damn for the ants in the next cell. They were kind enough, of course, once one had penetrated their territory—if one had the courage—but the open-handed comradely welcome, the universal badge of all artists, was noticeably lacking. He had come to accept the watered-down variety of invitation which seemed to be the accepted standard; but as England had appeared on his list of 'musts', he took his medicine like a man and lived out the allotted time, not with too much pleasure but now with an increasing curiosity.

A poetry reading by W. B. Yeats which Arthur Symons and Zweig attended, turned out to be a sort of mystical ceremony, over which W.B.Y. presided like a high priest. Here, surrounded by candles, in monastic garb and with a spellbound, select and dutifully sighing audience, the poet, enmeshed in his quasi-theatrical role, poured the words of his creation over their devout heads. Zweig's own description of this incident proves that nothing he saw or heard in England at that time seemed to add up. Devoted for long to Keats and the incomparable Shakespeare, he imagined that the country would be peopled by knights and angels with a background of idyllic birdsong and flaming sunsets. To his astonishment there was nothing very lyrical about the sound of cockney talk, nor particularly uplifting in the greyness of the city buildings. The language problem, too, isolated him to a certain extent. And while he knew that he was only making a surface judgement, he lacked the courage at that time to investigate further afield and find, in between the grandeur and the drabness, between robust, rather crude friendliness and the frigidity, that true art he thought must lie between the earthiness of London's locals and the ethereality of Matthew Arnold's appreciation of 'the tawny-throated nightingale'.

Zweig later realized that he had missed out somewhere on that first trip to England; and it was to be left to a much later period in his life, and that possibly the most tragic, that he discovered the peculiar metal from which the English race is fashioned.

The only truly magnificent memento, however, that he carried away with him from the ill-fated English visit, was the pencil drawing of King John by William Blake, long revered by him as a master of poetic spiritualism and mysticism. Of all England's bountiful supply of poets, artists and authors, it is perhaps significant that the work of this renegade, or at least off-beat, poet and artist had for him the greatest appeal. With due reverence, at a much later date, Friderike gazed upon Blake's mad King John, during the period it hung in her room at Salzburg as, she explained, 'a kind of wedding gift'. As for Zweig, he admits 'the genius of England, which I tried in vain to recognize in streets and cities, was suddenly revealed in Blake's truly astral figure and now I had added another to my many world loves'. From the country of his exile, just before his death, he recorded with resignation: 'Of all that is lost and distant from me, it is that drawing which I miss most in my wandering.'

One link was forged, however, and brought back for Zweig the early days he had spent with Verhaeren. He managed to contact and later meet, Arthur Symons, who had translated into English Verhaeren's drama *Les Aubes*—The Dawn. Zweig almost wept with nostalgia and homesickness as he recalled his first meeting with the Belgian author, and the relaxed and easy relationship they had maintained during the pleasurable agonies of the translations.

With consummate ease he had wandered the corridors of Europe, meeting with little effort on his part all those acknowledged personalities within the inner- and outer-fringe art circles. One meeting seemed automatically to lead to another; every house, apartment and studio opened its doors to him. Hospitality was received and reciprocated, and the Universal Brotherhood about which he dreamed seemed almost a reality.

If England had come as a cold shower, or at best a sort of dampening douche, India was to immerse Zweig in a bath of feverishly hot water. He was miserably conscious of the heat and all his youthful evangelism for identifying himself with the problems and miseries of the east was not strong enough to fortify him against the passive brutality that the westerner finds so hard to digest on his first visit to India.

Although a missionary, Zweig was not of the hardy variety. Physical discomfort was not easily borne by him, and the knowledge of its presence as endured by others, was as painful to him as if the sword was in his own side.

Meanwhile Friderike, sitting out yet a further session in the bosom of her family, records her disappointment that Zweig had now, it seemed deliberately, placed this distance between them. Even one of his earlier letters from Paris, in which he referred to a 'female involvement' with as much delicacy as would be used in plucking out a painful sting, had not given rise to quite so much concern as this latest separation. In the Parisian incident, after all, Stefan had merely confessed to meeting with 'a most enticing person', and later, in carefully worded though beautifully expressed warnings, he had felt impelled to remind her that 'Paris meant women', and later still that 'our love is fulfilled only in thought, not in deed'. Zweig was proving a reluctant lover indeed; but she had no choice, and now that he had decided to make the visit to India, she did the only thing left to her—she waited, anticipating the moment of reunion.

This was one trip, however, from which Zweig returned utterly sobered, his usual zest flattened, and the spiritual and emotional contents of his personality undergoing even then a tremendous change.

India was the springboard from which Zweig was forced to dive into the deep end of realism. Perhaps more than any other single influence, his visit there at last forced him to take the pen into his hand and with it compose, not a series of competent, technically correct translations or essays, but his own thoughts and reactions to what he was now compelled to admit existed beyond the hot-house climate of 'civilized' Europe.

It was all very well for Rilke to sing the song of angels or plunge into the demon world of fantasy, taking his readers to poetic heights and depths. But this was reality, the vicious and relentless march of humanity that had forced Rimbaud to compose his battle hymn of hunger, and Verlaine to record, not mystic pain, but the physical pain in mortal existence.

For Zweig the glory of the bejewelled temples, and the fabulously maintained palaces of the princes and the British Raj faded rapidly beneath the gloomy system of caste which so obsessed him. In the ancient and hidebound acceptance of such a social evil he saw the plight of all minority groups. Sick at heart and thoroughly uncomfortable in body, he trudged around the prescribed centres, temples and Holy Places, but the latter appalled him more than all the remainder of India put together. Holiness and hunger were not, in his opinion, synonymous, nor indicative of culture; and the overflowing beggar population, culminating in Benares, sent him at top speed for the nearest escape route. With memories of his English trip still fresh in his mind, Zweig's bafflement increased, as he imagined the almost impossible task of survival in this country of heat, ashes, jewels and hunger. Yet those stolid Englishmen and their families had been entrenched in this boiling and disease-ridden continent for nearly two hundred years.

On meeting Rabrindranath Tagore, the Indian poet, later on in Europe, Zweig was to find, however, an area of common ground, which enabled him to see, if not with clarity, at least with some understanding the other side of the Indian picture. Gandhi's later preaching, at that time only a thorn in the side of the British Government, was to show Zweig that his self-imposed and distressing Indian visit had not been entirely in vain. Hindu philosophy, on which Gandhi based his thinking, is itself based upon the belief in the psyche in God, and of its ultimate perfection through a mortal's conscious striving towards knowledge and truth. It was this that fascinated Zweig, and was later to permeate much of his thinking and writing. His later close association with Sigmund Freud did much to confirm his spiritual and psychological approach which he learned from India.

In a letter to the Editors of *20th Century Authors*, Haycraft and Kunitz, Zweig wrote: 'My main interest in writing has always been the psychological representation of personalities and their lives, and this was also the reason which prompted me to write various essays and biographical studies of well-known personalities.'

His technique of probing the thoughts of his subjects rather than dwelling on actions, still at that time regarded as exploratory, stands today as a means of drawing the reader immediately into the mind of the personality involved. The approach employed in this present biography of Zweig himself owes much, not altogether surprisingly, to his innovations.

Due no doubt to an inherent delicacy, Zweig always manages to avoid too much undiluted psychoanalysis. His central figures stand out sharply against darkling backgrounds of court intrigue, political strife and murder; and in deliberately concentrating, above all else, upon the entire, complex personality of his subject, he has helped many contemporary authors who, concerned with psychological reasoning, might otherwise have tended to irritate the reader by losing sight altogether of the focal point in a drama.

Zweig is never guilty of this omission. He holds fast to his subject, and if he sees in that subject's actions many and diverse reasons for seemingly inexplicable behaviour, he rations such findings, so that the diet remains palatable to the layman. Whether engaged in love, politics or mortal combat, Zweig's subjects remain firmly fixed before the eye. Classicists may bemoan his humanity; but its delicate, yet somehow larger-than-life appeal is undeniable.

When he returned from India Europe's bourgeoisie was still feasting its eyes and ears on the poetical, literary and artistic works of its sons and daughters, but Zweig's mind seemed able to grasp only half of all he now heard and saw. His thinking was coloured by the depression left over from the Indian visit. He was sure that this ersatz gaiety must end while millions, not only in India, but in Russia and Europe, still worked and lived below the bread-line.

In much of Zweig's later work, particularly his short stories, and most notably in the biographies *Marie Antoinette* and *Mary Stuart*, this concern shows how greatly his contact with Hinduism deepened his psychological insight. The principles by which the Hindu mystics interpreted the human psyche owed nothing to scientific method, yet by drawing upon them Zweig was able to achieve the most subtle interpretation.

What Emile Zola had only partly revealed in his scorching novels and essays twenty years before, still lay like a festering wound just below the smooth skin of the new era and the new century. Zola had shed a new light onto the evils of child labour, prostitution, unemployment and bigotry, but it was an uncomfortable light, and many people had chosen not to see what it had revealed.

Stefan was burning now to make his long-delayed start; he was filled with eagerness, this was to be his first cry to the world (apart from his earlier poetry, the ill-fated play *Tersites* and an essay on Verhaeren, which he had in his mind partially discarded anyway). This début was not to be, as he had often imagined, in the steps of Verhaeren, or even Rolland, but triggered off as violently as the act of war which inspired it.

Jeremiah was the prophet who preached peace in the very teeth of war; *Jeremiah*, the play, was Zweig's own lament and prophecy. The forebodings and nightmare visions he depicted were to become his own companions, growing in terrible and melancholy stature, but which he himself controlled—at a price—until at last events and the acts of humanity weakened his resistance.

It was 1914. Political events were hurtling towards Sarajevo, and Franz Ferdinand's tragic death; Hofmannsthal and his elite circle of poets still dominated the cultural heart of Europe; Zweig returned from yet another of his explorations; and Friderike, after a great deal of heart-searching, somehow or other severed herself from her husband and was entrenched, with her children, in a separate domicile.

Zweig's emotional involvement with Friderike is important, not because of its legal implications and emotional entanglements, or what must at the time have been almost unendurable amount of mental conflict and gossip, borne equally by both parties; but because in both resenting and submitting to it he exhibited fundamental traits of his personality that increasingly governed his life, and in the light of which we may better understand his work.

Chapter Seven

Restlessness had been Zweig's constant companion from early childhood, and although in his memoires he refers with some irritation to the habitual physical movement and travel of his mother, he apparently failed to recognize that he may to some extent have inherited this same trait from her. It was always the same—no sooner had he accomplished one mission, written one book, visited one country or confronted one eminent personality than he was laying plans for the next.

This pattern was to be the somewhat fragile foundation on which his entire existence balanced, the inner voice which dictated his physical and mental activity until, wearied by the long wait either for release or solution, he chose to terminate the struggle himself.

One advantage that accrued from his constant travelling was the astonishing array of illustrious friends and acquaintances that he had collected en route. Travel also enabled him to expand his collection of objets d'art, which he had started as a schoolboy and which now included some first editions and some quite valuable paintings and manuscripts; the possession of these treasures provided him with a substitute sense of security which, as his life continued, became more desirable and infinitely more difficult to obtain.

At this period of his life, the years between 1910 and 1913, it is a matter for some speculation about what would have happened had not the act of war intervened or the additional emotional responsibility in the guise of Friderike thrust him from the side line into literary action. It is very possible that Zweig would have remained what he then was, an informed, travelled and ultra-sensitive man with a string of brilliant translations to his credit, and much sought after as a contributor to the established periodicals. There was certainly a marked reluctance to take up his own literary cudgels; and this was possibly due to his overlong apprenticeship in the workshops and studios of the great. He had for so long cast himself in the role of student and admirer, he felt it somehow presumptuous to set foot on so illustrious a path himself. A desire to hold fast to the world of Rilke and Verhaeren contributed to his unwillingness to move forward.

It was not until he had severed himself completely from the hearth and home which he appeared to despise, and whose cloying security so frustrated him, that he had found a niche. The shifting art world of Paris, he believed, would give him lasting artistic security. Then the war shattered this hope, and the seed of despair within Zweig stirred towards partial germination.

It may well be argued that a young man living under such benevolent circumstances and with more than his share of intellect and talent, had little cause for melancholy; and indeed with a young man's instinctive desire for life and the good things it offered, Stefan presented a façade which appeared reasonably well ordered. But the deeper sensibilities, in him already acutely, even over-developed, never allowed him the respite which for the majority is as healing as dreamless sleep.

There is a little of de Maupassant, Balzac, even Tolstoy, in Zweig's handling of human problems and endeavours. Like de Maupassant in his short story *The Necklace*, Zweig points to the futility of materialism.

Mathilde Loisel, the French author's heroine, is obsessionally concerned with owning the jewels she cannot afford; and in order to create a good impression at a Ministerial Reception to which she has been invited, she borrows a magnificent diamond necklace from a woman friend.

De Maupassant relates her horror upon losing the necklace, and goes on to describe the misery she endures after her husband has purchased a substitute with money he has borrowed from various acquaintances. Mathilde and her husband pay the price of their snobbishness with years of toil and subsequent ill-health, only to discover, on redeeming the last promissory note, that the original necklace had been an imitation.

Madame Forestier's exclamation sums up the folly of attachment to possessions: 'But my dear Mathilde, how ill you look! If only I had known. You see, my necklace was an imitation. I think it was worth about four hundred francs.'

Critics find it easy today to denounce Zweig's pessimism, and yet at the time his literary quality was rarely in doubt and in constant demand in almost every country of the world. The name of Zweig only faded from the forefront of European literature when the shadow of Nazism was descending upon civilization and his books being publicly burned.

Whether he actually willed it or not, Zweig finally found himself caught up with Friderike in the year preceding the outbreak of war. Even then he knew that this union could only exacerbate his melancholy. On many occasions he had found it expedient to 'warn' her regarding his own darkling moods, the instability of his life and the as yet only half formed plans he had for his future; but when she confronted him with a ready-made domestic set-up, complete with fully-furnished villa, wife and children, his prudence and foresight seemed to desert him.

A woman needs only the merest suggestion of warning that she may not be able to handle a situation concerning a member of the opposite sex, and the whole affair, at least as far as she is concerned, is a fait accompli. Friderike was no exception to this golden rule, and apparently before Stefan realized it he found himself armed with the most indefatigable partner, lover, aide de camp and admirer.

In his almost complete preoccupation during his travels and work, he seems to have regarded her much as he would any member of any art circle to which he became attached. But this art student was no dewy-eyed teenager, nor was she yet that thing so beloved by all young male artists of that era, a sort of mother-figure, presiding over the gatherings, occasionally reading from her own excellent but rarely published poetry, or exhorting the un-informed on the finer points of art.

In fact entrée into most art circles usually depended upon ob-taining the blessing of these very matriarchs, a relatively simple task for a young man, a little more tricky for young women. But Friderike, as in most things concerning her attachment to Zweig, was successful in breaking down this barrier, and almost unnoticed became a 'one of the group'.

There was one snag to this arrangement, however, which even Friderike could not solve. Zweig, still clinging to his precious 'freedom', frequently left the 'group' in Vienna to return to his Paris haunts, leaving her to stay put and to draw what consolation she could from the wanderer's more intimate friends.

The tension in Europe was steadily building up, however, and a series of 'incidents' forced an unpleasant awareness upon the ostriches in Austrian diplomatic circles. The literary groups, mean-while, were united under their common militant pacifism, but rudderless and leaderless.

They published their warnings and prophecies, but the majority of Europe's masses saw the coming disaster as inevitable; one era would pass into another just as surely as season follows upon season.

Austria, where a way of life was embedded in the frail and age-ing Emperor, nevertheless accepted the wind of change. No one wanted it to happen, yet all subscribed to its advent. The once Holy Roman Empire, now under the uncertain and often irra-tional rule of Franz Josef, looked on now with growing alarm as sabres and gunshots rattled from the mountain fastness of the Balkans.

With feverish anxiety the habitués of the coffee houses and beer gardens now discussed the political and military manoeuvres to the east, their music and their chess games forgotten. What was happening to Serbia in 1913, after her involvement in the 'freeing' of Macedonia from Turkish domination, was a sobering lesson for the carefree Austrians. Already deprived of almost all her own possessions, she had attempted to exist as an independent entity, and now it seemed the time had come for her to take the long hard look at herself which is usually so painful. Drawing a diplomatic screen over her past losses and present miscalculations, finding that the eruption of art and artists had produced an imbalance she could now ill afford, Austria was becoming uncomfortably aware of her shortcomings.

Zweig was acutely conscious of the impending conflict: 'I cannot explain it otherwise than by this surplus of force,' he later wrote in his autobiography, 'a tragic consequence of the internal dynamism that had accumulated in those forty years of peace, and now sought violent release.'

Vienna, for too long played at politics, with a comic-opera cast of spies and counterspies dispersed throughout the hotels and rococo palaces and mansions of the capital, became only too well aware that every train now departing and arriving at the West Station had its quota of enemy aliens and espionage agents, all bent upon furthering the projection of war.

Even the Austrians had to admit that they were now in a highly vulnerable geographical position. While the summer of 1914 blazed its way through July, and the boulevards of Paris were so dry beneath Zweig's feet that the stones seemed to crack, the countries of Eastern Europe fell to examining the results of their confused, bitter conflict. Macedonia, recently liberated by Serbia, was now responsible for that country's isolation; and it took the intervention of Greece, Rumania and Turkey—ironically, the original aggesssor—to rescue Serbia from her present unenviable position. After a year of conflict, the countries of Eastern Europe were about to taste the first sharp agonies of a war which was destined to involve later the whole of Europe and ultimately all the territories of the Old World. Austria, quavering with uncertainty, stood on the sidelines, waiting, watching, and dreading what now seemed an inescapable fate.

Earlier, in 1908, Zweig had made a start on his Dostoyevsky biography, but had never come to actual grips with it, allowing his incessant travelling to interrupt the flow of concentration necessary for such a complex work. Now, however, in the summer of 1914, he was contemplating a trip to Russia in order to get the feel of Dostoyevsky's land, and to see for himself the 'tracts of silence' about which Rilke never tired of speaking. Rilke himself had earlier inspired Zweig with his stories of his own stay in Russia, and Stefan felt powerfully attracted to the land and its artists. But in the blazing summer months, when all the western world sweltered beneath the twin rays of the sun and power politics, long-term projects were temporarily shelved, and Zweig contented himself, as usual, with trips to Verhaeren in Belgium.

Friederike utilized this time apart for entrenchment; and while Stefan languished in the benign atmosphere of a beach resort near Ostend, she set about making final arrangements for moving Stefan's bits and pieces from his original apartment to the villa.

Zweig and Verhaeren, meanwhile, were debating long and fully on all that had happened since their last meeting. Verhaeren seemed overly concerned with the Balkan issue, and particularly with the affair of the assassination of the Archduke Franz Ferdinand and his wife in Sarajevo on June the 29th. Zweig too was now perpetually agitated with the national disaster; but typically became, through his anxiety, even more Austrian than the Austrians, and refused to subscribe to the theory that the double murder of the heir to the Austrian throne and his unpopular wife should necessarily plunge the whole of Europe into war.

Back in Vienna, the removal of the assassinated couple was hypocritically mourned in high places (they were not popular) for the requisite time, and almost as quickly forgotten by the populace at large. Franz Ferdinand and his wife were despatched with quiet and dignity to a remote and 'pre-designated' burial place, away from the scene of all previous Hapsburg state funerals; and Stefan Zweig, along with the majority of his countrymen, persuaded himself that the murder was just an isolated incident, having no bearing on the international scene of political unrest.

But it was happening; and all around him in Belgium, where panic was later barely contained, Zweig's was the only dissenting voice. He labelled as impossible the likelihood of Germany occupying Belgium in the event of France being attacked. He clung, like a drowning man to a reed, to the effectiveness of treaties which guaranteed immunity from such flagrant aggession; and he later recalls that in one of the many discussions that his group held only a week or so before war was actually declared, his was the only voice raised for peace: 'You can hang me to this lamp-post', he declared rather magnificently, if the Germans march into Belgium'.

It was all wishful thinking on his part; for many of the moods of melancholy to which he had fallen prey since early youth had their origin in his prophetic insight. But at the time, with all Europe boiling under the pressures of forty years of peace, and his personal life about to undergo what were obviously powerful and distressing emotional changes, he clung with child-like tenacity to those things he saw slipping from his grasp; and the fact that nothing he could do or say would halt this change, at times drew him to the edge of panic. The once-dreamed-of Universal Brotherhood was taking place before his eyes, born, not of knowledge and forbearance and compassion, but of universal necessity in the light of attack from the enemy. Men were united as they had not been for almost half a century; and in the crowded Orient Express, the last train to leave Belgium for 'enemy' territory, Zweig was forced to face the horrible truth that for those friends he was leaving behind he was now part of that common enemy.

With the wearied and worn-out clichés about peace scarcely expelled from their lips, the leaders of Europe's masses were now ready to commit their people's to a righteous and just war, the total cost to humanity, when the arithmetic was finally sorted out, a staggering eight and a half million deaths and nearly thirty-eight million casualties.

In Emperor Franz Josef's retaliatory military aggression against Serbia, Austrians felt he was doing the only thing left. After all, it was in Serbia that their beloved heir apparent and his wife had met their death, what else could Austria do but strike back? Forgotten already was the scarcely concealed relief with which the assassination of Franz Ferdinand had at first been received. The just and holy cause of war was thus deliberately fanned into a flame by misplaced patriotism, hypocrisy and persistent international news reports that brainwashed and bemused the European public into believing that the only way out of trouble was to lend its support to open warfare.

If Russia, for instance, dashed to protect Serbia, as she seemed inclined to do, what then more natural than that Kaiser Wilhelm's armies should align themselves to Austria? It was all as inevitable as the moves in a game of chess. France, as Russia's ally, could not possibly expect to stand aside, and to reach France it was but a short step to march through Belgium.

Earlier treaties, such as The Triple Entente of 1907, and an additional guarantee undertaken by Britain to safeguard the neutrality of Belgium (this was referred to contemptuously in Germany as '. . . the scrap of paper over which Britain went to war . . .') were the very instruments used to precipitate the conflict.

So Zweig watched the remorseless march of events, and tried to digest the horrible facts of and reasons for war. Nothing he saw or heard made sense. The political position was as complicated as the confused military movements now in train. Where did this conflict leave him with Verhaeren, with Rolland, Bazalgette and the others in France and Belgium? Were they hating his guts, as propaganda demanded they should; or could they see that this artificial drawing of frontiers, of making men 'enemies' or 'allies' was a loathsome invention, a weapon of war which had no place in his, Zweig's mind.

He was in a state of tension when he finally arrived back in Vienna, having already witnessed the movement of men and arms during the trip over the frontier. His desire to do something positive to halt such lunacy only resulted in more frustration.

He admits that he had no solution to this latest explosion of ideals.

But Friderike listened to his newly formed plans to 'join up' and bided her time. She had waited now for almost a decade, with only a few compensatory periods of reunion; and now this terrible war threatened to snatch from her grasp the man she loved and for whom she had undergone considerable humiliating emotional pressures, even to the extent of securing a 'secret' divorce from her husband in the teeth of well-nigh impregnable opposition. She was an Austrian, and she also loved her country, but the dear old Emperor, for all his sacred office, and the strutting and ridiculously moustachioed Kaiser, were not going to wrest one slight, if wiry, young man of thirty-three from her maternal grasp. Besides, what could Stefan do? He had not even completed his year of voluntary military service. There were others, far more ably equipped than he to serve in the field. If Stefan suffered from pangs of conscience then there were plenty of opportunities other than that of active service for him to serve his Emperor and his country.

Zweig listened to the arguments raised against his donning the honourable field-grey uniform, and with unease and a wretched sense of compromise, he finally agreed to offer his services to the War Press Bureau and War Archives Department, whose head-quarters were in Vienna.

Stationed for a while in a barracks, he tasted a modicum of military life while eking out the endless hours at a desk in an effort to list citations, produce translations when required and, in final desperation, to edit a war office magazine.

Friderike, like generations of camp followers before her, took up her belongings and found nearby lodgings. No doubt her physical presence brought Stefan some relief, but the hateful compromise he had made at her behest never left him, and his desire for action nagged away at him incessantly. One by one more and yet more countries were dragged into the war. Italy, his mother's birthplace, and regarded by him as a second home, had joined the Allies in their struggle against the Central Powers, and that decision to place herself alongside the allied cause meant that Zweig's own family, by virtue of its origin, would be in danger of becoming divided against itself.

Were all those people then, some his own blood relations, automatically his enemies? Would they regard him, Stefan Zweig, born and bred in Austria, as an enemy? Could an act of war, engineered by unknown, power-hungry personalities, dictate who should be one's enemy, who one's friend? Zweig knew now with the certainty of despair that this was indeed the case. His adored friend Verhaeren had made it quite clear through intermediate parties that as far as he was concerned, war had thrust its demarcation line between them. This single fact, perhaps caused Zweig more personal grief than any other of the war. It was not so much that he had lost the friend of his youth, but that he could not accept the failure of Verhaeren to reject those external forces which demanded their separation.

His work at the war bureau was intensely monotonous relieved occasionally by the appearance of Rilke, who had also found himself part of the army of 'desk soldiers'; but it gave him time to think, and plans for his play *Jeremiah* took root.

Always an acute observer, Zweig was becoming increasingly appalled at the war, and two aspects of it in particular: the massive and unremitting blood-letting, and the sight of those who stayed behind and cashed in on the remnants of existence—the get-rich-quick types, the black marketeers and the pilferers.

Somehow two years dragged by; then he accepted, with relief, an assignment which demanded that he visit the battle fronts of Tarnow following the Austro-German offensive there. He went not as a journalist, as he had earlier sworn that he would never write one word approving of or contributing to the act of war, but as an observer and collector of any relevant and precious documents that might have remained behind. This gave him the opportunity at last, to identify himself with the agonies of those involved; at least he could now stand beside them and know at first hand the suffering they endured.

As he moved into the areas of devastation around Galicia, the scene of suffering struck him so forcibly, he recalled later, that he must have passed quickly into a state of anaesthesia. His descriptions of the scene which met him, of the dead and the dying piled into cattle trucks on railway sidings, and into which he himself climbed in a vain attempt to comfort them, indicate the extent and depth of his own suffering and anger. In the masses of Russian soldiers, squatting apathetically behind their wire cages, he saw the greatest humiliation, and the shame he felt at witnessing such degradation eventually found tongue in the moving story of Buch Mendl the dejected survivor of international war.

Zweig's experience at Tarnow left a picture of suffering branded on his mind, and this, together with his disgust for those who applauded the act of war while remaining at a safe distance from the filth and degradation of it, produced an unfamiliar anger and desire to hit back. 'I had become almost reconciled to what at first had shocked me', he wrote. 'But unfortunately just then I came across a Viennese newspaper. I tried to read it; and only then was I filled with rage and disgust. Here were all the phrases about the inflexible will to conquer, about the petty losses of our own troops and the gigantic losses of the enemy. Here it jumped out at me, naked, towering and unashamed, the lie of war!'

And so the seeds of the play *Jeremiah* were brought to germination, and Zweig snatched at every free hour during the following year, in order to complete the cry of protest against 'the lie of war'.

Just as Erich Maria Remarque's *All Quiet on the Western Front* portrayed the emptiness that follows upon war, so Zweig's *Jeremiah* illustrates the senselessness of embarking upon a 'just and holy conflict'.

Both plays were, by virtue of their subject and timing, an unlooked for success; and later, in about 1929 or '30, when Zweig was approached by Remarque to translate *All Quiet*, it seemed as if the combined thought of the two authors of two different generations had completed full circle.

For the first time, Zweig freely acknowledged his Jewish heritage, and in the writing and completion of *Jeremiah*, which quickly found its way on to almost every stage in every country of the world, he also partially found himself. 'In choosing a Biblical theme', he recalls, 'I had unknowingly touched upon something that had remained unused in me up to that time; that community with the Jewish destiny, whether in my blood or darkly founded in tradition. Was it not my people that again and again had been conquered by all other people, again and again, and yet outlasted them because of some secret power? Had they not presaged, our prophets, this perpetual hunt and persecution that today scatters us upon the highways like chaff, and had they not affirmed this submission to power, and even blessed it as a way to God? I know today that, without all that I suffered in sympathy and in anticipation during the war, I would have remained the writer I had been before the war, I would have been "pleasantly agitated", as certain pieces of music are marked, but never fixed, composed and responsive to my very vitals . . . Now for the first time I had the feeling that when I spoke it came from myself and from my time.'

Jeremiah is dedicated to Friderike von Winternitz, and Stefan presented her with the first bound copy of the play, having composed an affectionate sonnet to her on the flyleaf. She was utterly overcome by this gesture, and the nostalgia for those early days with Stefan floods, understandably unstemmed, through her reminiscences: 'In his leisure hours, in his beautifully rounded script, he wrote *Jeremiah*, line by line. In the midst of war he composed a lofty song of peace . . .'

This lofty song was smuggled through the Censor and first produced in Zurich; and as soon as the war ended *Jeremiah* published in 1917, came upon its war-weary audiences as an elixir and a warning against future sabre-rattling. During the immediate post-war years, the play proclaimed its message throughout Austria and Germany, and after translations into many languages, it was soon playing to audiences in Palestine, England, France, and to thousands of spectators in open-air performances in Holland and America. *Jeremiah* became in turn a symphony and an opera, and tracts of it have been used for readings in churches and synagogues. Zweig's war lament kept the message inexorably before world audiences up until a production in New York by the Theatre Guild in 1938, barely nine months before the prophet's voice was drowned beneath the hysteria of the arch-racialist from Zweig's own country, Austria.

In the final act of his drama, Zweig speaking through his prophet, persistently entreats these same millions who listened in awe to Hitler to listen to the bitter futility of such claims. Might, he implores them to heed the message, is not Right. And then with resignation, yet still finding comfort in Divine Purpose, he adds that the advent of Adolph Hitler, or indeed any comparable evil, is still not sufficient to destroy the eternal spirit of God in man.

'Arise then, and cease repining,' Jeremiah fervently commands. 'Take up your faith as a staff, and you will march bravely through these trials as you have marched for thousands of years. Happy are we to be vanquished, and happy to be driven from home, by God's will . . . Kings who mastered us have vanished like smoke, nations which enslaved us have been scattered and their seed destroyed . . . but Israel still lives, ever young, for sorrow is our buttress and overthrow is our strength. . . . Praise the name of God who, through tribulation, has chosen us for all eternity . . .' And as if to make up for the many ill-fated starts Zweig had encountered in the theatre, the production of *Jeremiah* in all its various settings experienced none of the bad luck of his previous plays.

Jeremiah gave Zweig tangible evidence of his talent and dissolved his self-doubt for a while at least. It established him firmly in the eyes of the public as a pacifist, as a Jewish writer, as a man who was not afraid to come out strongly and forcefully with his own convictions and as a writer of acute literary perception.

In the eyes of Friderike, he achieved the stature of a giant, and there can be no doubt that her encouragement and enthusiasm contributed towards this, Zweig's first mature offering to the literary world.

Chapter Eight

The first two years of the war, enacted against a background of feverish patriotism, that involved even the humblest peasant, provided Zweig, ironically, with the anti-war protest material for his play.

At the same time it forced him to accept the fact that he could no longer regard the world he lived in, the Europe that had nurtured him, as his home if he associated himself with both sides of the picture. It was one thing to say, 'this is my home, it must remain the same at all costs', and quite another to expect that home to remain intact without being prepared to defend it against the marauder.

He often said that he could never envisage himself 'sticking a bayonet into the entrails of a Russian peasant'. But on the other hand he was not too anxious to be labelled a conscientious objector, with its attendant stigma of publicity. His role as pacifist, therefore, demanded that he take up his pen instead of the sword, while at the same time availing himself of every opportunity physically at least to stand by the side of those other innocents dragged into the 'lie of war'.

Even so, he still clung rigidly to an idealism which refused to accept that what was happening in Europe was a continuation of the human paradox. He still refused to discard the ideology of ultimate human perfection through development of the intellect; and he was, until his visit to the ravaged areas of Poland, in 1915, in much the same mental state, a sort of induced pseudo-euphoria, as his predecessor, Leo Tolstoy, when the author wrote his sentimental story *Family Happiness*.

Until that time, Tolstoy, an aristocrat of old Russia, whose early talent and affluent background had brought him unsought recognition, accepted his laurels with equanimity. Only after tremendous inner conflict was he able to reject, even publicly denounce, some of his own work, and start afresh, free from the shackles of the Church and other spiritual and secular restrictive influences.

Zweig, whose thinking almost unconsciously followed that of the majestic Russian, also wrestled long and solitarily with a similar problem and he, too, came gradually to the state where the sheer weight of the evidence around him forced him to admit the existence of ignoble human failure alongside the equally noble spirit of human endeavour.

Like Tolstoy before him, he conceded, and with perhaps even more reluctance, that without a preceding act of violence or episode of suffering there can be no compensating deed of compassion or heroism.

But there can be no question about his attitude to the universal pain of humanity. Humiliation and suffering in others affected Stefan Zweig to a far greater degree than that usually accepted as 'normal'; and until the advent of war he had always managed to turn away, deluding himself that he spared his own suffering and that of the victim by so doing. But now he knew that by a series of acts, violent, heroic or merely stoically patient, the home of Europe which he loved with such passion, could only endure by virtue of a colossal and dedicated mass effort of its citizens.

In the bloodbath of the Somme Zweig's idealism again took a severe beating. He saw in the battered and disfigured soldiers who were lucky enough to return from the front, the gruesome price extorted from the masses for the privilege of defending their homeland.

Despairingly he told himself that the life-or-death battle between nations seemed to have little to do with the natural longing of men for peace, nor even the slenderest connection with the political or territorial manoeuvres presumably originally responsible for it.

What Archduke Franz Ferdinand and his inglorious assassination had started, and the deathbed edicts from the old Emperor Franz Josef had given impetus, was now a world problem, demanding an equivalent universal sacrifice. The facts were obvious, but the reasons responsible for them were already obscure. In his imperial surroundings, Franz Josef lay dying, surrounded by luxury and the restrained apprehension of his courtiers; and in the trenches of the Somme were packed men of many nations, bewildered, terrified, courageous and also dying.

Zweig had no answer to this. The dreams of a Universal Brotherhood were already consigned to ashes; and his thoughts turned ever more frequently to his own Jewish heritage. '. . . sorrow is our buttress and overthrow is our strength', he had had the prophet Jeremiah proclaim in the final act of his play, and this philosophy of his ancestors, prophetically melancholy in its steadfastness, yet based upon reality, became in time his own.

His beloved Belgium, home of Emile Verhaeren, lay bleeding to death beneath some of the fiercest battles ever waged; and Brussels, the first foreign capital Zweig had visited in his trans-European commuting, was shortly to be occupied by Stefan's own countrymen under the hated banner of conquerors.

There was no balance left. These questions of why and how would have to remain unanswered until this outbreak of hate and violence between men of all nations was somehow brought to an end. And then, he knew—there would still be no answer.

But for one man at least, the answers to all questions were at last ceasing to matter one way or the other. Franz Josef, eighty-six years of age, and for long but a frail reflection of his strong Hapsburg predecessors, was preparing to relinquish his uncertain hold on the affairs of state, international politics and intrigue which for so long had occupied his thinking and energy. His sacred heritage, which time and again he had seemed unable to handle and often hopelessly bungled, now appeared meaningless.

Many had criticized his actions; many times he had paid dearly for his mistakes, but at least he had never given up. He had fought to preserve what he believed to be his holy office, and what he had seen as the wellbeing of his country and its people, to the very end. He waited now with resignation, almost relief, for the act of death to remove him from the arena where humanity was playing out its great tragedy.

In the year 1916 Austria, deeply involved in war, lost her old Emperor and turned to face a new era. The 'heart of Europe', the centre of an ancient seat of government and partner of the unsatisfactory Dual Monarchy, was preparing itself for the wind of change which was to sweep across its frontiers after the cessation of hostilities, transforming the once mighty empire into a rather dubious 'Republic'.

It was already written that the seat of the Hapsburgs, with their 'sacred' lineage, was about to succumb to the rather vulgar sounding but probably more workmanlike arrangement of a peoples' Republic; and God, as Franz Josef himself would have remarked, saw to it in His knowledge, that His faithful servant was removed from the scene with dignity before that humiliation became an historic fact.

Both Stefan and Friderike, he caught in the toils of introspection, military desk work and the frantic composition of *Jeremiah* and she, torn between Stefan and her daughters, one of whom was now grievously ill, heard the news of the Emperor's death with a mixture of relief and foreboding.

They knew that the system over which he had ruled was faulty, even dangerously inept; and yet what alternative was offered? The events of war, swamping all other considerations, reduced the impact of Franz Josef's earthly passing to just one more death in the midst of the holocaust.

For all those who had passed their youth under the mixed blessings of the Hapsburgs, where melancholy and joy, murder and romance, territorial gain and loss were all accepted as part of the monarchical system, the future, epitomized by the terrible and bloody present, seemed bleak indeed.

Stefan took up his stance with others lining the route along which the funeral cortège passed; and Friderike, accompanied by her father-in-law, the aged von Winternitz, a true adherent to the old school, and now reduced to tears at the sight of the small coffin on the gun carriage, also felt the emptiness of uncertainty. Her memories of the royal funeral are heavy with nostalgia, as she records the eerie half-sound of shuffling feet and the beat of muffled drums. The passing of an era synonymous with poetry, potted palms, hard-drinking Hussars and soulful damsels was hard to take; and the national and economic shambles of the present did little to compensate for such a loss.

Friderike's own domestic and emotional front was about as stable just then as the Russian lines in Tarnow, which had collapsed beneath the weight of the victorious Austro-German assault. The compromise she had brought about fell far short of the real thing, and she knew that its difficulties, dissimulations and necessary restrictions were repugnant to Stefan. But the need to persevere with such a compromise was as vital to her as breathing. She could imagine no future without him beside her, and if it meant that at times her patience and tolerance were pushed almost beyond even her elastic limit of mental endurance, she knew it would still be worth the effort, and the price she was willing to pay.

Zweig, with a ready-made family around him whenever he returned from his sessions at the Vienna barracks or from a visit further afield, found himself in the incredible role of pseudo-father-cum-husband without actually having lifted a finger.

Any doubt or suspicion that the arrangement might not work out was hastily lulled by Friderike's absolute concentration upon him and above all, upon his work. As this sacred task of work always headed Stefan's list of priorities, he was willing to allow the manoeuvring and counter-manoeuvring to go on around him, if it meant that he could make some sort of progress with his writing under what were at that time almost insuperably difficult conditions.

Work also meant an increasing ability to withdraw, and in the various tensions mounting around them, their domestic and Friderike's marital complications, Zweig appears to have ducked his head into his manuscripts and left her to deal with the various family factions which sprang up, denouncing at frequent intervals her union with him.

Nevertheless, he was now learning to utilize the presence of strife as a spur rather than a rein to his creativity.

It was under these circumstances that *Jeremiah* was completed, sometimes in 'a spirit of exasperation'. But whether this exasperation was entirely due to the events of the war or in some part to family tension, is not absolutely clear. But that it was completed and in record time, demonstrates his discipline and eagerness at last to embark upon his own literary path.

When later, in 1917, Zweig was invited to visit Zurich to discuss the production of *Jeremiah* with its producers at the Zurich Town Theatre, and attend rehearsals, he dispatched summarily and almost comically the difficulties and tribulations involved in attempting to leave a country in time of war, for any purpose other than official or military.

'I secured an appointment with the head of my department', he recalls, 'and made my request to him. To my great surprise he immediately promised to give the necessary orders . . . Four days later I had my leave and a passport to go abroad.'

Friderike, surrounded by her usual spate of domestic uproar and problems, not the least of which was her ailing small daughter, nevertheless determined to accompany Stefan, for he was again showing all the symptoms of wanting to pick up the thread of his earlier European wanderings, despite the fact that the whole continent was now in the grip of war.

Who could tell where his journeys might take him this time, or even when she might see him again? She decided to move heaven and earth rather than allow him to disappear from her life.

Her plans and interviews were somewhat more involved than Stefan's, but she found in their temporary union, away from the restrictive atmosphere of von Winternitz's Kalksburg home, at least an escape route from the mounting pressures from both sides of her family. A period of time alone with Stefan sounded like heaven, and Friderike was geared to remove all obstacles and the accompanying red tape in order to achieve her object.

After a series of false starts and further investigation by Friderike on the seemingly impossible problem, for an Austrian Catholic of getting a divorce, the two of them eventually arrived in the haven of Switzerland. The shocking comparison between the two countries only served to heighten their gloom about the ghastly present and the uncertain future of war-torn Austria.

Even the enthusiasm with which *Jeremiah* was received failed to obliterate completely the shadow that had fallen across their land, and to some extent over the entanglement of their own lives.

Chapter Nine

With the death of the Emperor Franz Josef, and the war about to enter its third year, the people of Austria seemed to draw even further from the distasteful German military aggressiveness. The precipitate action of their ageing ruler had pushed their nation into this hated conflict, and at the same time allied her to German military aims, and now they were beginning to examine the fruit reaped from such a disastrous harvest. Gone was the excitement of that initial nationalistic fervour, its true content never clearly understood, which bound Austria's destiny to that of the restless and aggressive German military machine.

Always historically independent of the mass of Germanic states which were ultimately welded into the German Empire under the rule of the Emperors of Prussia, Austria had somehow maintained a tightrope balance of political inviolability. Now, as her statesmen and politicians, under the untried leadership of Charles, the new Emperor, took stock of their battered and wearied country, they admitted sadly that the cost so far seemed grossly in excess of any advantages gained.

What were these advantages? Admittedly the Austro-German push through Galicia towards Russia had succeeded, but what did Austria want with Russia now? and how could she possibly justify her alliance with Germany on the Western Front, especially now that millions already lay slaughtered, and both Britain and America were flinging in masses of men and armaments to aid the desperate peoples of France and Belgium. Whatever territorial gains might accrue to Germany, Austria doubted that she would benefit.

But the bizarre drama of Ferdinand's assassination in Serbia, and Franz Josef's unbalanced assessment of the situation, wilfully forgotten by the majority of Austrians, were kept very much alive by the Germans as an excuse, if such were needed, to keep Austria bound to her side in a conflict which could well give the Prussians extended and powerful military gains throughout Europe, and even beyond.

However with over a million dead already and countless numbers of casualties yet unpublished, Austria longed to opt out of the war; and in her tradition of political plot and counter-plot, there was, at this juncture, a definite move afoot towards sounding the possibilities of pulling out while at least part of the country and a portion of her people remained intact. But Austria had got the tiger by the tail, and all her efforts in political and diplomatic conclave fell apart as month by month she was dragged deeper and deeper into the ever-widening areas of war.

Neutral Switzerland, with its bright and beautiful cleanliness, shocked Zweig, when after a four-day journey he managed to cross the border into that country. Gone was the greyness that in Austria had spread even into the faces of the civilians. The 'lie of war' became startlingly apparent in this division of fates. How was it possible to take a train journey from hell, lasting only a few hours, and at the end of it, find peace and well-being. As on so many other occasions during the war—Zweig could make no sense out of the contrast. In Austria people were queueing up for a loaf of bread, which would inevitably be mouldy; and in Switzerland chocolate and fruit were plentiful and available to all.

He saw the scene before him, not so much as a slap in the face for those deluded patriots beyond the Swiss frontiers, as a reminder that somewhere in the world sanity had somehow survived. With *Jeremiah* about to be produced in Zurich, a centre now for every group of intellectuals able to squeeze out of war-torn

Europe, Zweig again experienced the dragging discomfort of an ever-widening fissure within his own personality. 'Each tree', he recalls, 'looked greener, the sky more blue, and the houses sheltered no wailing women deprived of husbands and sons snatched from their grasp to attend the dance of war. . . .' But though misery and slaughter seemed far away, there was no escape from what the mind had seen and remembered.

An international audience of exiles flocked to his first night, and applauded the new play and above all, the Austrian playwright Stefan Zweig, who had seen fit to choose such a theme. Everyone hated war; and this particular conflict raging beyond the mountain stronghold of Switzerland seemed to have expanded beyond all reasonable expectations.

In a conglomeration of tongues the anti-war play *Jeremiah* was discussed and its theme approved. This man Zweig obviously knew what he was talking about, and was not afraid to say it. With some relief the refugees and evacuees associated themselves with this, the first positive and public movement towards peace. But while Zweig had pointed to the futility of war, carrying his audience along on the crest of 'militaristic pacifism' with the magnificent speeches of the prophet, many failed to interpret, or at least avoided the implication of the end message. Zweig, with the absolute certainty that the Jewish heritage is supremely more important than these temporary consequences, instructed his audience to fight for peace at any price, even though that peace will ultimately be wrested from the individual by powers that he himself as a member of society has unwittingly set in motion. Already he had no illusions about the vagaries of man's mental make-up; and although the period of time he spent in Switzerland in the company of those intellectuals who had earlier fled their countries, restored in some measure the literary camaraderie of his youth in Paris and Brussels, the ice of brotherhood was cracking under the weight of the war. His escape route was Switzerland, and he knew it. But he knew, too, that he must return to Austria, and face again the ravage of land and humans that lay beyond the mountains of this maddening neutrality.

Romain Rolland, who was staying in Geneva, welcomed Zweig when the younger man sought him out once more, this time in an attempt to bring some order to the chaos of his own conscience. 'I felt more entitled to live here [in Switzerland]' Zweig later recalled, 'whereas in a country at war, it had become embarrassing and almost an offence to be free of wounds'. His freedom from wounds caused him almost more discomfort than if he had in fact endured them physically. This limbo into which his thinking invariably placed him was becoming yearly more untenable. Possibly, in Rolland, there might be some sort of solution. Of recent months only his negative conclusions, as voiced in *Jeremiah*, were conclusive. He felt that he must find an alternative answer, a reasonable assurance for positive thought; and in Rolland he saw, as he later described him, 'the conscience of Europe—exhorting with gentle persistence, those in power and those who were ruled by them, to think, and think yet again, of the responsibilities of armed force'.

Rolland, with his saintly and inspired application, had devoted himself to his vocation, trusting implicitly in the power of God to enlighten those in darkness and to bring sanity to the field of human chaos. He felt himself to be the instrument of God, his articles and essays had always brought acclaim; but Rolland, his eyes on the Creator and his feet on earth, pursued his campaigns of peace with a rare dedication, while Zweig continued in his torturing vacillation. At times, carried away by what he called the essential goodness of Rolland, and at others experiencing the claustrophobia normally only found in dreams, Zweig attempted to reach through to God. The story which he later wrote about Rachel and her search for God reflected his own indecision and fear, which lent substance to the terrifying changes which Rachel undergoes in the course of her pleas for recognition.

These fluctuating thoughts on his spiritual existence produced little comfort and no respite; and while he was thus occupied with the contradiction between God's infinite compassion and His creatures' cruelty, Zweig passed the weeks and months in Switzerland, in a mood of increasing gloom, much occupied with discussions and lectures on international cooperation. Although he was not yet too deeply involved in his association with Friderike, he found in her presence a comforting realism which frequently tended to counterbalance his intermittent moods of melancholy.

With her usual tenacity, meanwhile, Friderike applied herself to the business of 'looking after' Stefan, welcoming his friends, applauding his sentiments and even writing a small book herself.

In between explorations into every legal avenue that might be a way out of her marital difficulties, she longed for the ending of hostilities; and if, as now seemed possible, there was to be a 'new Republic' in place of the old order in Austria, there might well also be a new legal machinery which would sort out her divorce.

Whatever added concern she may have had about her present and even more important, her future, she refrained from troubling Stefan too much with it. Her own and her children's return to Vienna long before Zweig, required that she again was filled with the dread that in her absence he might once more assume his role of wandering artist although at present, with the war still restricting all movement but that of the military, her fears were contained. But he alluded only rarely to their predicament. Friderike remembers him saying: 'we must do something about this'; but as, she adds rather sadly, she was presenting him with the first edition of her little book at the time and although she was convinced that he had every intention of making their union legal, she was not too sure on this occasion whether he was referring to her publication or their future marital and legal state.

It is indicative of Zweig's divisiveness of thought, particularly apparent during the war years, that his casual treatment of this woman who obviously adored him in fact fluctuated between affection and mere friendship. On many occasions, Friderike must have felt the cold fingers of Stefan's detachment, and his description of this period in his autobiography must have struck a familiar note. '. . . when war broke out,' Zweig wrote, 'I found myself alone in my Fatherland. In my inner resistance to the war and to the noisy frenzy that was so forgetful of consequences, I had, among all my friends and associates in Austria, no one to stand at my side.'

No one! In his subconscious awareness of utter loneliness, Zweig excludes, whether deliberately or unwittingly it is not clear, the woman who stood constantly at his side with such vigour and enthusiasm that her stance was often more like that of a defending warrior than of a lover.

The war was at last dragging to its close, and with the collapse of Germany now imminent, and the sum total of deaths and casualities still being totted up, the whole of Europe stood waiting for the final act.

While the exiles in Switzerland eked out their time, some anxious to return to their homeland, others dreading the day when this became necessary, from the theatre of war on land and on sea were reported the endless programmes of victories and losses. Each engagement, every confrontation, seemed more costly in lives and less decisive in outcome than the last.

Russia, with her eyes more on her internal problems than the world war into which her treaty with France had drawn her, now collapsed completely; and with what strength was left her people prepared for the coming Bolshevist revolution. Even before the world war had ended, Russia was to be plunged into yet another bloodletting; the civil war which Lenin and Leo Trotsky had planned for so long and with such meticulous care. In fact the same gentle Swiss ambience which had comforted the intellectuals gathered together in Zurich and Geneva also sheltered a very different community, the neo-Bolshevik conspirators. The pins, figuratively speaking, were already drawn from their stockpile of hand grenades. Plots and confused counterplots were the order of the day, and news was constantly being smuggled between Russia and Switzerland.

Bearded, overcoated and obviously conspiratorial, the Trotskyists moved furtively around their Swiss haunts. Everybody knew who they were and what was probably about to happen, but the exciting game of hunt-the-slipper—or the hand-grenade—went on childishly undaunted. Only those members of the inner circle were fully aware of the appalling outcome of the game.

In the homely atmosphere of various Swiss boarding houses, the final plans for the projected overthrow of Czar Nicholas's Holy Russia were being made. And in the massive arena beyond the serfdom and sanctity of Russia, the Central Powers, one by one, began to sue for mercy under the terms of an armistice. The armies of Germany, Austria, Turkey and Bulgaria were everywhere in rout, and the Allies started to mull over the Treaty to be signed at Versailles.

It was during this terrible time that Stefan Zweig, Austrian author, member of the already expiring pan-European cult, an 'enemy alien' to his friend Emile Verhaeren, and witness to the war that was to end all wars, reverted to the tribe of his forefathers. Now he was asking himself, 'where is "home"?'

In his early youth he had travelled throughout the continent with ease, deluding himself that 'home' meant Europe. But now that same Europe lay in shards. Treaties and frontiers shifted the problems of humanity from one area to another, until even those who manoeuvred the peace terms were themselves baffled.

The home of his birth, Austria, which he had been so anxious to leave as a youth, was now utterly vanquished. The greyness of war seemed forever to have extinguished the lights of the capital, and the spiritual light of its war-weary people. With a heavy heart Zweig knew that he must return, try to pick up the threads and continue to delude himself that somehow he still belonged there.

With the end of the war almost within sight, and the departure of thousands of her uninvited visitors, Switzerland settled back into the usual enviable state of national phlegm which, bolstered by Nature's mountainous barricades, has ensured her unique state of neutrality. Hotel rooms, attics, lodging houses and villas disgorged their multi-racial inmates. Zurich and Geneva, hosts to a veritable army of artists, espionage agents, revolutionaries and counter-revolutionaries, pacifists and died-in-the-wool bourgeoisie, now watched complacently as the train-loads of 'visitors' departed.

For Zweig, the road back to Austria was marked with misgiving, and a deepening apprehension for the future. His mind, already concerned with the problems of humanity in a post-war world, was now anxious to get to grips with them through his writing. He had already decided that he would choose as the subjects of his biographies those men who had ceaselessly championed the cause of the right to liberty: his old heroes Dickens, Balzac and Dostoyevsky. He had done much research in the first decade of the century and plentiful material was now in his hands; but it had taken four years of war before he actually got down to the task of sorting it out.

With what was now becoming the rule rather than the exception, Friderike had again gone about the tedious business of establishing some sort of acceptable domestic set-up which would enable them to graduate from a series of temporary homes to the real thing—which both she and Stefan had once spotted long ago during a visit to the Capuchin mountain in Salzburg.

Disenchantment on the part of its present owner and a series of discussions and bargainings with estate agents, resulted in the ancient and crumbling house atop a flight of crazy stone steps becoming their own.

Friderike was overjoyed to think that her interminable wait was now almost at an end, and as she dived into the whirlpool of domestic takeover, Stefan withdrew into his now familiar mood of detachment, and gave his delighted mate permission for their combined removal to the house on the hill.

While a vanquished and depressed Austria struggled back to something approaching normality, many of her neighbours were racked by revolution, anarchy and civil war. Faithful to her tradition of compromise, however, Austria still somehow scraped through the deadly aftermath of war with nothing worse than a coalition between the parties of the Social Democrats and the Christian Socialists. With wildly fluctuating monetary values, dilapidated property, insufficient food and little hope of ever returning to her glorious days of independence, the seat of the Hapsburgs and centre of the Holy Roman Empire philosophically tightened her belt and, sighing, promised herself that never again would she allow mistaken patriotism or ill-founded treaties to plunge her into a war that was really none of her business.

Politics, recriminations, and shortages. None of these mattered to Friderike as she prepared to move into her new home. There was still no definite news that the New Republic might ease Austria's narrow views on divorce and remarriage, but even this failed to dampen her enthusiasm.

'For the life of me', Zweig wrote later, 'I cannot recall how we kept house during that era, or in what manner the Austrians kept on raising the thousands and tens of thousands of kronen and the Germans, in their turn, the millions which were daily needed to keep body and soul together.'

If Stefan, as Friderike had intended, was insulated from the more sordid aspects of living in a house with a leaking roof, bulging walls, little or no fuel and the most meagre food ration, the effort on her part cannot have been less than heroic although even she could not perform miracles, and Zweig remembers how much of his writing at that time was done in bed in an effort to keep his fingers from freezing. But with the misery of decreasing rations, fuel and domestic labour, Zweig's creative ability steadily and stubbornly increased, and he began to assemble into some sort of order the material for a trilogy, to be called *Master-Builders*. The subjects were of course Balzac, Dickens and Dostoyevsky; he was more than ever determined to pay tribute to the latter, now that Russia was suffering under the revolution. However there was as usual a period of soul-searching to be got through before he actually got down to writing.

His reflections on the past four years of the war, and his own glimpse of the suffering involved, were to dictate much of his style and choice of subjects in the future. Although *Jeremiah* had been written in a mood of anger, he felt now that much of his idealistic prose was misplaced. Despite the words he had given the Chaldean conqueror to speak before the final curtain, he knew that he still could not entirely accept the lofty principle of the endurance of the spirit: 'Who can conquer the invisible? Men we can slay, but the God who lives in them we cannot slay. A nation can be controlled by force; its spirit, never . . .'

The tranquillity of absolute belief, that Zweig so desired was continually denied him by his doubts. Many years were to pass before he reached towards even a compromise. In the mean time he sought solace through the medium of his work.

Chapter Ten

In the immediate post-war period, with the new Austrian Republic floundering through a series of bungling attempts to restore something like law and order, and his newly found family now gathered around him in the battered but romantic old house at Salzburg, Zweig gingerly embarked upon what was then only a partially understood domesticity.

Friderike made valiant efforts to insulate him from the noise of the children and the squabbles of hangers-on who had taken over the house as squatters during the war, and who were still not eager to be dislodged by the new owners, and used all her physical strength and mental agility to maintain a tremulous peace.

It speaks volumes for her determination that, despite overwhelming domestic difficulties in these early weeks and months of their life together, Stefan enjoyed a period of relative solitude in which he began to sort out the material he had gathered over the years. He was now desperately anxious to make a start on the three biographies, the first of which, on Dostoyevsky, he saw as the pathfinder in that rather ponderous trilogy. As things turned out, the heavyweight plan misfired somewhat, and was eventually fined down, to be published as *Three Masters*; relatively short biographies on Dostoyevsky, Balzac and Dickens. Later, and at intervals, he added the works on Tolstoy, Stendhal and Casanova.

Of the first three subjects, Honoré Balzac presented Zweig with many extra problems, and he was happy about the inclusion of Balzac in this particular, very compact, series.

The great French author had occupied Zweig's thoughts since his schooldays in Vienna, and in Balzac's near-sacred dedication to work. Zweig felt he saw a symbol of man's earthly fulfilment. The man's physical vitality and mental prowess had fascinated him when, as a pupil at the gymnasium, he had listened as if hypnotized to Hugo von Hofmansthal while the poet roved restlessly around the class room, waving his hands and wagging his head as he extolled the glories and achievements of the almost legendary Frenchman.

Later on, when he himself lived in Paris in that first flush of freedom, Stefan gazed with wonder and awe at the stone steps up which Honoré had bounded two at a time, or touched with reverence a window whose glass had once reflected the author's heavy-jowls.

The immensity of Balzac's literary output and the astonishing circumstances under which it was produced never failed to enthrall Stefan. As he commented, 'even a Saint-Beuve employed help of sorts in a secretary . . . but Balzac wrote everything with his own hand.'

In many ways his involvement with the Balzac biography at that particular time of physical discomfort and difficulty mitigated Zweig's own somewhat complicated arrangements. If his literary hero could so insulate himself from the rigours of unheated rooms and the crash of creditors' fists on the front doors of his apartments, surely he, Zweig, could stop his ears to the distant sound of childish squeals, and female voices raised in anger or argument over imagined or legitimate rights in the disputed areas of the kitchen and laundry departments.

Although never presuming to measure himself against the lusty and genial personality of the Frenchman, the knowledge of Balzac's basic good humour, which rarely deserted him in times of extremity, frequently steadied Zweig himself when bouts of irritability threatened to throw him off course. Despite the serious, even melancholy make-up of Zweig's personality, close members of his family (Eva Alberman) recall a dry sense of humour which on occasion proved that he could appreciate a sense of the ridiculous.

The old house on the edge of the mountain was a delight to both Stefan and Friderike during the first years of their occupation. The accommodation, although hopelessly ill-equipped, provided him with the working solitude he needed, and she was happy that they were truly together at last. He was now working steadily, and while actually writing the drafts for the first subjects in the *Masters* series, his mind was occupied with others that he knew would follow. Sigmund Freud, whose personality had long fascinated Zweig, would, he hoped, take his place amongst them.

His earlier writings on Verhaeren, Verlaine and Rodin, mainly essays, now could be seen to have provided him with much valuable experience; although he had disowned much of his previous work, it was still finding its mark on the literary market. Whether he admitted the fact or not, the form he was at present working on emanated in some degree from his earlier experiments.

Divorced now from all those who had made up the circle in which he had lived and worked for so long, he was forced to rely entirely on his own judgement, and although he confessed to many misgivings, the quality of these earlier short biographical essays is very high.

Verhaeren had died in 1914, leaving no message of consolation or encouragement for his former acolyte—but Zweig's own belief in the Belgian poet and his work was never to be shaken. To the end of his life he never lost the emotion which the older man had awakened at their first meeting; and, looking back to his final parting with Verhaeren, Zweig deplored yet again the act of war which makes enemies out of friends: 'My friends were better friends than ever . . . the city was more carefree than ever before, and, being carefree ourselves, we loved the city for being carefree. During those last days I accompanied Verhaeren to Rouen where he was to lecture. At night we stood in front of the cathedral, its spire gleamed like magic in the moonlight. Did such gentle wonders belong to only one 'fatherland'. Did they not belong to all?'

That night Stefan and Emile Verhaeren embraced, caught up in that moment of wonder and their splendid good fortune in being part of it. Zweig records this, their last meeting, with heavy nostalgia. In retrospect it is clear that the outbreak of war and Verhaeren's death were the first links to give way in the protective mail with which he had surrounded himself.

An era, the earliest, and possibly therefore the most impressionable had ended for Zweig; another, which Friderike was to share as his wife, was about to begin.

With true feminine instinct, she did not presume at first to fill the gap left by the dispersal of his international circle of friends, being content for a while to assume the role of a sort of *eminence grise*—a counsellor, an advocate, on hand at all times and under all circumstances.

Her love for the man who was now legally her husband, under the somewhat delicate and ambiguous terms of a Government dispensation, sustained her when Zweig seemed to be torn from her grasp by his obsession with his work and not infrequently later on with his travels and the resumption of many literary friendships.

She had known from the beginning that the disadvantages of taking this man as a partner would often seem to out-weigh the practical and emotional benefits; but she gambled on her instinct. The almost careless, perhaps even unconscious tyranny that Zweig exerted over her was undeniable; but the man and his work were inseparable, and in accepting one she willingly embraced the temperament which powered both.

Stefan Zweig's work can best be evaluated in terms of his humanitarianism.

Ethnically a product of the ancient and wandering chosen tribe, he nevertheless felt remote from it, particularly in the cloistered atmosphere of his early youth. Later he deliberately detached himself from all that represented material security, but even then he still craved the comfort of its assurance and solidity.

In his passionate attachment to people and places, he always remained aware of the pitfalls of such earthly bondage, but was unable to discipline the emotion within him which demanded it.

Again, while illustrating vividly in much of his work the essential goodness in man, he is still driven to despair—somewhat illogically, one feels—by its rejection. With the progress of years, the dual paths of his thought grew until they threatened to divide his personality completely. By this time of his life he was able to recognize, though with some difficulty, this separation of thought, and utilize it as a literary device.

In his story *Impromptu Study of a Handicraft*, Zweig chooses as his subject a sleazy little pickpocket; he analyses him in a clear and almost humorous manner; then, after deciding that it was probably his duty to set the poor wretch on the path of righteousness, promptly and typically allows the man to slip through his fingers. In employing this high degree of observation Zweig seems purposely to avoid judging his characters, something he always viewed with the greatest caution; and in holding fast to the human element in whatever story he has to tell, he dismisses, many of the stylized literary notions of his predecessors, even of some of his contemporaries.

He obviously cares nothing for those upon whom fate or fortune bestow so-called strength of character, preferring instead the weaker or vacillating personalities whose misfortunes were his own. His growing interest in presenting the psyche rather than the mechanical problem places before the reader many of his own conclusions that our innermost qualms and hidden fantasies are often more real than so-called reality.

Thus, we see Erasmus, the scholar, the classicist, portrayed by countless biographers as an erudite but somewhat remote and dusty figure having little to do with us or our own restive existence, brought to life by Zweig, as a man beset by the eternal problem of humanity. Seen through Zweig's eyes, Erasmus becomes understandable, even to the twentieth-century mind.

His treatment of Marie Antoinette is also typical; her life was cloudy with romance and overloaded by bizarre circumstances, avoiding prejudice of any kind he clears away the fog of many devoted biographers to show her to us as a queen who was willing to commit treason if it would serve her end.

'Let us ask how, in strict conformity with the law', Zweig writes in his biography, 'the jury ought to have decided. In the above-quoted questions, the president had disregarded the political embroidery of the trial, and had reduced the accusations to one. The jury was not asked whether Marie Antoinette was an unnatural and adulterous, an incestuous and spendthrift woman, but merely whether the ex-Queen had been guilty of treasonable communications with the foreign enemies of the Republic . . .' Carefully and objectively Zweig places the legal machinery of Marie Antoinette's trial before us. Even the jurors' attitude is examined and analysed. No particle of human strength or frailty is ignored in this historic frieze of indulgence, lethargy, intrigue and murder.

And while the reader swings in sympathy, as Zweig intends he should, from one side to the other, always refraining from final judgement, he compels compassion by drawing a picture of her on the way to the scaffold: 'There was a stir in the crowd, and a sudden silence. This silence was broken by the savage shouts from the Rue Saint Honoré. A squadron of cavalry rode into the Place, followed by the tumbril in which was seated the bound woman who had once been queen of France; behind her stood Samson the excutioner . . . .'

Zweig's attitude to suffering is deeply dramatic; he concentrates all his attention on the sufferer, making no moralistic reference to anything outside, and it is in this sphere that the reader feels the greatest impact from his writing. In his Biblical Legend *The Buried Candelabrum*, the travail of old Benjamin, in his interminable wandering, becomes well nigh intolerable; even the ache in his bones comes through the printed word. Zweig is merciless in his determination that the plight of Benjamin's tribe be shared at least by those who choose to read his work.

The final paragraphs, written with near child-like simplicity, only serve to accentuate the tension and agony that has gone before.

'Next morning some traders on their way to market at Ramleh, caught sight of a human form lying in an open field close to the road which led from Joppa to Jerusalem. An old man, dead.

'The unknown lay on his back, with bared head. His arms widespread, seeming ready to grasp the infinite, he had his fingers likewise opened, as if the palms were prepared to receive a bounteous gift. His eyes, too, were wide open and undismayed, his whole expression being peaceful. When one of the traders stopped, with the pious intention of closing the dead man's eyes, he saw that they were full of light, and that in their round pupils the glory of the heavens were reflected. The lips, however, were firmly closed as if guarding a secret that was to endure after death.'

In the greying autumn mists and the inevitable beauty of the spring, the old house in Salzburg, with its crumbling walls and aura of an indefinable but romantic past, sheltered the members of the Zweig entourage. A somewhat unlikely collection of souls—family, servants—drawn together by Stefan and his work, they lived out the weeks and the months and the first two years after the end of the war in a mixture of moods, ranging from gay to melancholy. Occasionally the monotony and domesticity would be interrupted by a visit from one of Stefan's old friends from Paris or Berlin; and at these times he would emerge from the silence and solitude he imposed upon himself, and in some measure upon the others of his household, when he was working, to delve into nostalgia for his youth.

In this surreal atmosphere, oddly combining art and marital discipline, Zweig temporarily abandoned his plans for escape, although he still clung to the idea that a lonely and wandering existence was the only way to reach the state of freedom he secretly desired. He still thought about his plans for the larger and more satisfactory Balzac biography he would complete in the future, but at present contented himself with the production of the work on Romain Rolland, and a lesser portrait of Marceline Desbordes-Valmore, the French poetess, whose tragic life had earlier captured his imagination.

It was not long, however, before the old wanderlust took hold of him once more, starting him off on journeys which seemed to have no planning or reason. Whatever Friderike's private thoughts on these proposed trips, she took them in her stride and prepared to accompany him whenever she was invited.

One of the trips on which she did accompany him was to Italy, a country he had always regarded as romantic, but now to be a sad disillusionment.

Europe, as ever, was enchanting, but Zweig was not deceived. In almost a decade his idealism had worn thin: 'The war was over . . . the war was buried', he wrote. 'But it was not over . . . We merely did not know it. In Austria we knew no more about the Italian internal situation than that, together with the post-war disappointment, definite socialistic, even bolshevist tendencies had gained a foothold. Many walls bore crudely traced in charcoal or chalk, *Viva Lenin*. Furthermore, one had heard that a socialist leader, by name Mussolini, had separated from his party during the war, and had organized a counter-group.'

The early rantings of Benito Mussolini which so entranced the unemployed thousands in Italy and those 'comrades' still alive to endure further inquisitions by Holy Russia's dreaded secret police, were deliberately ignored by Zweig; instead he briefly enjoyed once more the delights of Venice. What was then embryo in Italy, and had already happened in Lenin's Russia, had an anaesthetic effect on Zweig. He still refused to come to grips with reality; and in his devotion to his social and political ideals, he refused to accept that such ideology cannot be put into practice without bloody civil war.

Chapter Eleven

In the relative peace of the house on the Capuchin mountain, Stefan Zweig moved at last from the role of onlooker and disciple to take up his predestined role in the centre of the literary stage.

His almost excessive devotion to the artists in whose circle he had orbited, and his translations of their work, had enabled him for a long time to postpone committing himself to the risks of a literary career of his own.

Jeremiah's success, however, and the popularity of his Rolland biography, not to mention the essay-cum-biography *Memories of Emile Verhaeren*, were still attracting such public interest—though with little enough encouragement from their author—that it became virtually impossible for him to rest on his laurels, however miserly he was with his critical self-esteem.

An added difficulty, again typically Zweigian, was his inability to reconcile himself to accepting due financial reward for the fruits of his labour.

This quirk, which dogged his thinking to an almost morbid degree, had its roots in the destiny which had seen fit to place him in so affluent a position; while many of those around him, particularly in his youth, had fought an unending battle with the bogey of near poverty. And yet Zweig is honest in his admission that, at least in his very early days of public recognition, he enjoyed a very natural and human reaction of pleasure in the knowledge that even notoriously hard-boiled publishers and critics commended his work and, in the case of the former, backed up their approval by willingly gambling their finances on him.

Yet even the substantial confirmation of his literary merit only added to the uncomfortable apprehension he felt on earning such a mark of respect. Nothing that he wrote satisfied him, and the more he was praised the more wretched he became. In addition to this lack of literary confidence, he was constantly doing battle with the enemy of uncertainty which blasted many of his ideologies sky-high.

His solitariness seemed to be increasing. He thought again of Romain Rolland, steadfast in his faith, and of Emil Verhaeren— although the Belgian poet had finally rejected his youthful champion, his singular and definitive thinking still drew Stefan's respect and admiration. So far, at least, Zweig discovered no clear answer to the eternal questions bombarding his mind. Was he the maverick in that clutch of artists because he found it almost impossible to attach himself with conviction to any single purpose? This treadmill of thought kept Zweig company during the solitary hours, and unconsciously provided him with yet more ammunition for the work which was about to be born.

He remembered the gentleness of Rainer Maria Rilke, now fighting a losing battle against continuing ill-health. Rilke seemed never to falter, always appeared spiritually supple within the bastion of his awareness; and in the remote and august figure of Hugo von Hofmannsthal, firmly entrenched as one of, if not the greatest living poet, Zweig thought he could identify the crystallization of lucid thought.

In Honoré de Balzac, with his agonizing childhood, brilliant literary output and near lunatic caperings around Paris and later across Europe, and in the self-confessed conflict of Leo Tolstoy, and the tragic but militant figure of Fyodor Dostoyevsky, he saw personalities subjected to the extremes of circumstances, yet emerging from the crucible tempered, not disintegrated. How could he, Stefan Zweig, compare with this nobility?

The rambling old house was now in some semblance of order, and with the satisfactory completion of his own working quarters

Zweig felt this division of thought even more keenly. Here there were no creditors banging on the doors night and day, no financial torment such as Balzac had experienced; but nor had he feminine distractions like Honoré's. Here was no violent social distinction, no serfdom, such as had driven Tolstoy and Gandhi to the production of works of literary reform; nor yet had he ever been reduced to the physically abject and spiritually purging extremes of Rimbaud or Dostoyevsky.

As external irritations were constantly smoothed out by the adoring Friderike, and with the public seeming now to acclaim each new publication with enthusiasm, Stefan Zweig nursed a mixture of cautious enjoyment and deepening dissatisfaction that so far, at least, he had not yet reached his desired goal: complete self awareness.

While almost irrationally discontent that his circumstances demanded none of the sacrifices required of his artistic heroes, Zweig on occasion wielded his domestic power despotically, reducing those around him to a state of tearful nervous tension. Near to despair, Friderike would rush from camp to camp in the family stronghold, attempting to soothe the frayed temper of her spouse and the legitimate protests of her rapidly developing daughters, who felt their isolation unnecessary and the worshipful attitude demanded of them by their stepfather somewhat unreasonable, particularly when it came to forbidding such basic necessities as the delivery of the daily newspaper or the presence of a radio in the house. But . . . as Friderike gallantly explained, 'the master needs isolation and absolute quiet when he is in the throes of creation'. For a while, at least, oil was poured on troubled waters, and Stefan explained somewhat apologetically that unless he remained divorced from the irritations and distractions of such extraneous matters he could not maintain the necessary flow of concentration.

Fouché, Zweig's first full-length biography after *Romain Rolland*, was written, he claimed, 'purely for my own pleasure.' That this 'pleasure' produced a first printing of ten thousand copies which sold like hot cakes, and the sale of fifty thousand copies in Germany alone in the first year, set even Zweig back on his heels, although the choice of his subject, the unscrupulous, anti-monarchist Duke of Otranto, surprised many of Zweig's growing army of followers.

In his declared war-time policy of being anti-political, anti-party, indeed anti-anything that smacked of politics, critics detected in his approach to the subject a desire to psychoanalyse, an activity regarded at that time with the sort of mistrust that produces witch-hunts. Yet despite the suspicions of the critics towards this relatively new and obviously to be reckoned with author, the public saw in his approach to eternal subjects, a reflection of its own many-sided image.

This biographical technique, while giving all the historic and salient facts and figures, had the temerity to probe into the minds of the characters involved. Zweig came up with some astonishing conclusions and the public reacted favourably.

Zweig uses the narrator in his short story *Amok* to describe his own attitude to psychoanalysis, 'Psychological mysteries have a positively uncanny power over me. My very blood tempts me to hunt for clues. Odd people can light within me, by their mere presence, a passion for grasping their secret no less violent than that kindled in us by a woman we wish to possess.'

Meanwhile he contemplated with astonishment the signs of success which were filtering through the ramparts of his mountain hide-out. Almost with distaste he viewed the masses of mail, much of it imploring him to ally himself to one political or social party or another, to lecture here on this subject, or to travel there to speak on that controversial theme or issue.

The emergence of *Fouché*, brought him face to face yet again with what he saw as a major problem.

In publicly giving tongue to his inner convictions, an author of necessity exposes himself both to acclaim and to criticism and; although Zweig accepted this hazard willingly, he could not reconcile himself to the responsibilities which followed upon such utterance. Much of his declared anti-ism, he felt, was deliberately misconstrued, particularly his attitude towards political corruption and military aggression. The floods of correspondence and personal visits from those in lofty and lowly places alike, the appeals to espouse himself to a specific cause, left Zweig in a state of bewilderment. Admittedly, he had sought to *expose* those evils, but with increasing stubbornness he refused absolutely to be drawn onto any rostrum of political or social reform.

All around him lay the effects of military achievement. Germany, with her inherent militarism, and Austria, her weaker partner, were now suffering the spoils of defeat. The miseries of hunger and inflation had caused national and political disarray; and through the insight of the prophet Jeremiah, Zweig, had predicted the outcome. Because he had seen fit to point out this folly with some clarity, and was even now releasing upon a war-weary public the products of his craft in such plays as *Fouché* and the biting satire of *Volpone*, he found it increasingly difficult to accommodate that public which was now making what he felt were such impossible demands upon him.

He was writing now with some power, and as his innermost thoughts dictated. He acknowledged his success, but with grave misgivings, and even twenty years later, he found it difficult to speak about it.

If the public thought it recognized a champion for all its causes, Zweig himself shied away with horror from such activity. His personality would, he suspected, be destroyed if he presented himself physically before those sections of the community demanding it. At that time, Zweig saw himself ideally atop the mountain hide-out, writing with the gusto of a well-oiled machine, reasonably insulated from outside interruptions and fulfilling at last the command from within. And yet why was he writing, if not to awaken public esteem, or at least active interest in the problems of life?

An author's public is as necessary as the air he breathes, but Zweig felt that his was somewhat unreasonable intruding itself too soon into his personal life; and so, with a growing sense of guilt, he tried to live apart, to withdraw into a desirable solitude which only a few of his most intimate and intellectual friends would be allowed to penetrate.

As things turned out, and because of the very humanitarian

and psychological nature of his work, the situation that resulted was exactly the opposite to that which he had envisaged. Despite, or because of, increasingly hectic conditions on the marital and social front, the house on the mountain became the recognized calling place for almost every Tom, Dick or Harry who had even heard of Stefan Zweig, the author. That public which Stefan longed to keep at bay, at least until he had had time to come to some sort of intellectually honest terms with himself, refused to accept his withdrawal, and proceeded to insinuate itself upon even the most intimate facets of his life. Some of his guests, however were welcomed by him with great joy—artists who had discovered his retreat, and longed to take up where they had left off when the war had broken out; and a gaiety almost reminiscent of the pre-war days would occasionally restore Stefan's good humour.

Increasingly, for he was besieged by many young and aspiring artists who felt that in this post-war champion of culture and personal liberty they would find a helping hand. In this their instinct did not fail them. Zweig, despite his natural reluctance, applied himself with a time-consuming zest and ineffable patience to the moral, mental and material encouragement of the youthful rank and file. In the furtherance of their craft and the encouragement of their toil Zweig was artist, father confessor and valued critic. Typically, the patience he bestowed on his youthful disciples wore a bit thin when it came to dealing with those nearest and dearest to him.

His attachment to Salzburg, at first so warm and uncritical, now waxed and waned with the seasons, and he frequently found excuses to 'get away' in order to complete some specific work.

On these trips to France and Italy, sometimes accompanied by Friderike, he continuously reviewed his emotional, domestic and literary life to date. Sometimes it seemed to add up, at others it fell desperately short—and yet to all outward appearances he was pursuing a dedicated and reasonably adjusted existence. He had made a very definite mark on the public, not only in Austria and

Germany, but in a growing number of European countries and as far afield as England and America.

Russia, too, despite the cultural darkness of the post-revolutionary era, displayed interest in his work; and Maxim Gorki, Zweig's revered contemporary, was instrumental in inviting the Austrian author in 1928 to attend the Tolstoy centenary celebrations in Moscow.

There was no valid excuse for Zweig to refuse such invitations; neither could he ignore for much longer the clamour of the outside world. The public, without which he admitted he could not exist and yet whom he still felt unable to confront, was even now hammering on the doors of his existence with as much determination as poor Balzac's creditors had hounded their elusive debtor over half a century before.

Only much later, when his wanderings and enforced periods of exile had reduced his spirit to a mere flicker, was Zweig able honestly to assess his attitude to that massive public which had attended him so faithfully during the years.

He makes it clear that although he genuinely desired to stand apart from the clamour of expressed opinion his later enforced endurance of a public existence, bound his destiny inextricably with the public's and provided him with the material he used so effectively on their behalf. 'In my personal life', he records, 'the most notable happening of those years [1920–1930] was the presence of a guest whom I had never expected—success. It is understandable that I do not feel at ease in mentioning the public success of my books, and in normal times I would have avoided even the most casual reference which might be interpreted as vanity or bragging. But I have a particular right and am even compelled not to pass over this fact—because this success, upon Hitler's advent nine years ago, passed into history. Of the hundreds and thousands and even millions of my books which had their secure place in the bookshops and in innumerable homes in Germany, not a single one is obtainable today . . .'

Zweig's guarded assessment of his own life and work becomes completely clear in the absolute dejection of these words, written only a short while before his death in 1942. It is a tragedy that he did not cling for a while longer to the mortal thread, if only to witness the fact that, even with the sum total of his work lying in ashes, and with the accumulated wrath of the Nazis mounted against the Jews, his work has survived the inferno of anti-semitism.

But now, a seed—barely that, more amœbic, was nevertheless moving towards its first definite formation. A study of Zweig's ensuing works, covering the production of a series of long short stories, and the *Adepts in Self-Portraiture*, in which the biographies of Tolstoy, Stendhal and Casanova, and of Mesmer and Freud are included, shows the beginning of his involvement with ways out of the human conflict. His analyses suggest a pattern of suicide; and frequently the subjects in his work are chosen by him to illustrate the effectiveness of this, the only conclusive weapon left to man in the exercise of his free will.

Chapter Twelve

If in his youth Zweig's thinking had been influenced by Goethe and Hofmannsthal, and later by Verhaeren and Rolland, the writing and now almost legendary personality of Leo Tolstoy appealed to him in early middle life, sometimes even to the detriment of his beloved Europeans.

This larger-than-life image of the Czarist aristocrat turned peasant, always intriguing to Zweig, was even more compelling now that he was actually about to meet Maxim Gorki, one of the Master's last and youngest confidants. In fact he felt much the same as when, many years before in Paris, he had gazed upon the elderly lady who in turn had gazed upon the all-mighty Goethe. He saw in Gorki not only an admired contemporary author, unafraid to show his true colours in both old and new Russian regimes, but also a physical link with yet another of the world's literary giants.

Zweig encountered considerable difficulties before setting off (in 1928) on his Russian safari, but they were mitigated by his inevitable enthusiasm for any project involving contact with those he admired.

Friderike, characteristically under the circumstances, remained relatively silent during the upheaval prior to leave-taking, but she became quite emotional when she discovered upon Stefan's return that he had apparently disposed of all expendable articles on his journey through the country now rejoicing under Josef Stalin's

New Order. Her spouse's generosity to the impoverished comrades he had met *en route* delighted her almost as much as receiving him safely back into the Salzburg fold once more.

He had been invited to Russia as a representative of the Authors of Austria, a position that he felt by no means confident to fill. Although Shaw, H. G. Wells and Andre Gidé were but a few of the eminent writers who had preceded him into the New Russia, his own belief that he should follow such illustrious men kept him on tenterhooks until the very moment of his meeting with Gorki.

Reports of the bloodshed and aftermath of the revolution of 1920 did not help and he struggled to keep his original image of the Patriarch before him. Tolstoy, with his single-minded conviction had invoked the act of excommunication, with all its hateful and frightening imprecations; and this demanded Zweig's slavish regard. He saw in Tolstoy's spectacular renunciation a demonstration of man's free will, an exercise in which he himself was becoming increasingly involved; although he realized with some envy that the often bizarre methods employed by the Russian author needed the flamboyance of the Tartar race if these nose-thumbing manoeuvres were to be carried out with anything like aplomb. The Russian approach to protest was singularly different from that employed on the more sedate and ascetic European front.

Zweig was probably well aware that neither he nor any of his companions would ever match, for example Tolstoy's ice-cold anger when, on learning that a guest at his table, a lady of noble birth, found the vegetarian food he offered not to her liking, he enquired what she preferred. Receiving the reply that a chicken 'would be rather nice', he ordered one brought to the table, complete with beating heart and feathers, and invited her to eat it. A singularly small incident when compared to public denunciation of the Church; but a message of encouragement to all those younger peace-addicts beyond the Russian frontiers.

The last time Zweig had seen Poland, it was lying devastated in the wake of the Austro-German assault. Now the train carrying him through those same areas represented in some way the escape he already longed to make, and he refers to the journey with a mixture of regret and hope.

There was to be a semi-official welcome awaiting him, and as usual the thought of any public appearance filled Zweig with a pessimistic anticipation. His dissatisfaction with titles or appendages of any sort, even the modest one of 'Austrian Authors' Delegate', made him restless. He would have preferred to make the trip in the anonymous, questing guise of his youth; but even he had to admit that a refusal would have been interpreted as ungracious by those who had organized the visit, and not least by Maxim Gorki himself.

Gorki had elected to write the introduction to the Russian translations of Zweig's books, including the recently published Tolstoy biography which was one of the reasons for the invitation. Zweig had been told that many of his books were now on sale in the Bolshevist version of the paperback, and that culture-hungry comrades of the New Order were practically fighting to obtain copies. But his first glimpse of Moscow hardly bore out this optimistic view. Acres of dilapidated buildings surrounded the station, and the seething masses of roughly clothed Muscovites looked anything but culture-hungry. The whole city and its inhabitants, barely recovered from the wounds of the revolution, appeared slightly unreal; and Zweig, who all his life had been content to live and work within the shadow of others, now found that he was to be plummeted into the hard light of public recognition, and under circumstances both extremely difficult and quite unlike any he had previously experienced.

The Tolstoy celebrations to be held in Moscow had attracted great publicity, partly because of the genuine affection in which the writer was held, and partly due to the fact that entertainment of any sort was pretty hard to come by in a country dedicated to the serious business of party politics.

But even revolutionaries need an occasional boost on the lighter side of life, and the authorities were quick to recognize this. Apart from the twin attractions of Lenin's rapidly shrinking and waxen corpse, displayed to the worshipping public in its glass coffin, and the hastily reassembled ballet company in the newly named Bolshoi Theatre, there was little a comrade could do with his free time. A somewhat dubious, but to the Russian, added attraction of these entertainments was the lengthy wait for admission; and Zweig saw in the endless shuffling queues for both box office and mausoleum an extraordinarily revealing facet of the Russian character. With the patience of forest bears the bulky, ill-clad citizens awaited their turn, munching stolidly on their sunflower seeds, ignoring discomfort and climate in a sort of universal belief that whatever it was they awaited, it would vindicate the self-imposed vigil.

If Zweig's already thinning idealism was not exactly bolstered by what he had so far seen in Russia, it is typical of him that on visiting the simple grassy mound at Yasnya Polyana, under which Tolstoy lies, his writing again became lyrical, as contrasted with his brusque reference to what he privately considered vulgar and theatrical in Lenin's permanent physical exposition. '. . . I saw nothing more magnificent', he recalls, 'nothing more moving in Russia than Tolstoy's grave . . . Away from the road and lonely, this noble shrine lies shaded in the forest . . . A small footpath leads to the mound, which is no more than a built-up rectangle of earth, guarded by none and watched by none, merely shaded by a few trees . . .'

In grappling with the unsavoury facts and grisly aftermath of revolution, the social and political inequalities which had set it off, and the part Tolstoy himself had actually played in the Czarist disaster, Zweig drew an unsatisfactory blank. Even now, some dubbed Tolstoy a revolutionary, an anarchist, others, a reactionary, and the remainder, more benignly, a sort of twentieth-century John the Baptist. Resting for a while in the peace of the forest at Yasnya Polyana, Zweig attempted to put the whole picture of war and peace, of love and hate, into some sort of recognizable perspective. The remains of the man who had preached peace lay beneath him; and if, as some claimed, he had been Lenin's pathfinder and his had been the call which set off the chain reaction of revolution, it only gave substance to the reasoning of the cynics who declare that a call for peace and equality invariably produces an outbreak of violence.

The impact of Tolstoy's presence, even in death, was more than disturbing now; and Zweig felt a greater urgency than before to talk with Maxim Gorki, once the excitement of the official celebration, the banquets and the speech-making were over.

At their subsequent meetings in Moscow, Zweig reports that the two of them got along so well that although neither knew the other's language they were frequently able to discuss many subjects without the assistance of an interpreter. Literary and intellectual rapport, it seemed, overcame such trivialities as the language barrier.

Zweig felt particularly privileged to obtain through Gorki's eyes, intimate glimpses of the ageing Tolstoy. Gorki was enthusiastically cooperative; he had had the presence of mind to jot down on scraps of paper many of the observations and aphorisms which Tolstoy, in benevolent or reminiscent mood, had let slip gratis during their conversations in the long summer evenings. Zweig, easily stirred by his imagination, visualized the bearded and booted figure as he sprawled easily on the garden benches, his gnarled fingers curling and uncurling with the flow of his thoughts.

'With her body woman is more sincere than man', Tolstoy had ground out thoughtfully one day, 'but with her mind she lies. And when she lies, she does not believe herself; but Rousseau lied and believed his lies . . .'

Zweig's mind went back to the tormented Vasya in Tolstoy's story *The Kreutzer Sonata*. The Russian writer, always concerned with the pitfalls of marriage, claims that the mere signing of the contract between two people does little or nothing towards maintaining a state of connubial bliss. Rather, it binds together those who are totally unsuited.

Vasya, the principal character in the story, is driven to the point of mental breakdown at the thought of his wife's infidelity, and confides his problems to a complete stranger during a train journey.

135

Here Tolstoy expounds his theories on the unsatisfactoriness of marriage, regarding as immoral the practice of contraception. 'To me it was disgusting,' Vasya says, 'I struggled against it, but she, with frivolous obstinacy, insisted upon having her own way, and I submitted. The last excuse for our swinish life—children—was then taken away, and life became viler than ever'.

Released from certain of her marital obligations, the wife's physical appearance improves, thus arousing her husband's jealousy. A subsequent affair with her music master only proves to Vasya the inadequacy of the marriage contract. He sees in its legal phrasing no safeguard against human fallibility. Eventually, he is driven to murder his wife, following upon a futile attempt at a reconciliation.

The Kreuzer Sonata undoubtedly reflects Tolstoy's own inability to accept the legal and emotional aspects of marriage.

Gorki's reminiscences of the other Tolstoy, the soldier, the gambler, the whoring young son of indulgent parents, followed. Once the words of a penitent Leo Nikolaevich show the author in yet another light: 'It is those caryatids who have kept all the magnificence and extravagance going. Not only by the labour of peasant men and women, not only by the taxes they pay, but in the literal sense of their blood. If the aristocracy had not from time to time mated with such horsewomen as she, they would have died out long ago . . . I was an indefatigable . . .' Here Tolstoy's lapse into the vulgar peasant idiom, affected even Gorki, according to his memoirs. Tough as he imagined himself, he flinched at the saintly old man's coarseness.

As during these meetings and conversations with Gorki Zweig learned more of the Russian's personal declarations, he found himself soaring to the heights of intellectual pleasure. He declared passionately: 'These people . . . half prophet, half peasant . . . I did not know their language, although it seemed to me I understood when they spoke.' The drabness and incongruity of the Bolshevik development, which had so depressed him at first sight, subsided as he went back in time, and saw again the Russia which had bred men like Turgenev, Lermontov, Pushkin and the others.

Through Maxim Gorki's devotion he recaptured the image of the country, not as she was in the late twenties, a united, impoverished and unlovely land with sprawling areas of concrete and communes, but as the all-embracing Holy Mother Russia who in turn begat such opposites as Tolstoy's Count Vronsky and Dostoyevsky's tortured Raskolnikov—a country vast and mysterious, as complex as the characters portrayed in her literature.

Many times during his life Zweig had been in love. In love with a moment of time—a passing cloud obscuring the moon. He had been carried to what he felt was the peak of emotional or spiritual ecstasy as in silence he had dwelt upon the observations of those gifted with intellectual insight. As with Tolstoy, the supreme moments of his existence were passed in exchanges of thought when mind reaches out to mind, and a bond of ethereal communication is forged, independent of more lowly relationships. Unfortunately for Leo Nikolaevich, as for Stefan Zweig and many of the others who wished to transcend the elementary level of development, their presence on the lower planes was not yet expendable; and those with whom they tangled en route were often wounded in this half-and-half process where the spirit competed with the physical, celibacy with sexuality.

Tanya, once so beloved by Tolstoy, and Friderike, already determinedly refusing to accept Stefan's occasional and deliberate periods of detachment, were only too familiar with the pattern of life which often demanded that they play second fiddle, sometimes not even that, to the tunes called by their self-absorbed, emotionally unstable spouses.

Already enmeshed in the characteristically disturbing Tolstoyian arguments for and against the indulgence of sex and its attendant problems, Zweig bemoaned the fate which had apparently seen fit to thrust him into such prosaic yet complicated marital conditions. In a wave of self-pity he felt that, like Leo Nikolaevich, he was destined to walk alone; and yet here he was with a ready-made family, domestic and personal responsibilities, frequently provoking open hostility, and innumerable demands from other members of society whom he could drop without even noticing it, if only he dared.

The visit to Russia was destined to leave an indelible mark on Zweig's thinking, and many of Gorki's memories sustained him in times of stress. Gorki's mourning for the adored Tolstoy set the tone for many of their conversations: 'He [Tolstoy] reminds me of those pilgrims who, all their life, long stick in hand, walk the earth, travelling thousands of miles from one monastery to another, from one saint's relics to another, terribly homeless and alien to all men and things . . .' The rapport between the two men increased, and although they did not record their reactions to one of the Sage's more cynical observations on marriage, they undoubtedly gave it considerable thought.

His views on sex and its problems caused a great deal of head-scratching and the daring inclusion in novels of accounts of the benefits and hazards of birth-control had already been tried out by Tolstoy himself and by his young disciple Anton Chekhov. 'Man survives earthquakes, epidemics, the horrors of diseases and all the agonies of the soul', Tolstoy had thundered out on one occasion, 'but for all time his most tormenting tragedy has been, is and will be—the tragedy of the bedroom!'

Of Tolstoy's death Gorki wrote: 'I do not wish to see Tolstoy a saint; let him remain a sinner close to the heart of each one of us. Leo Tolstoy is dead. It struck me to the heart. I cried with pain and anger, and now, half crazy, I imagined him as I know and saw him—I am tormented with a desire to speak with him. I imagined him in his coffin—he lies like a smooth stone at the bottom of a stream, and in his grey beard, I am sure, is quietly hidden that aloof, mysterious little smile. And at last his hands are folded peacefully—they have finished their hard task.'

Gorki's eloquence, despite its Slavonic gloom, the poetic use of descriptive phrases, puts Zweig's own at times somewhat extravagant use of language, his excessive admiration for fellow artists, into perspective.

These conversations with Gorki, typical of many sought by Zweig, illustrate the communal need for such communication between fellow artists. The interchange of correspondence, much of it of essay length and calibre, ensured a lasting and secure bondage between men of letters; and in the pilgrimages they undertook, exchanged and always faithfully recorded, there lay the added attraction of esoteric relationships. Their 'love' for one another fell somewhere, it would appear, between the youthful type of hero-worship and the more mature, non-physical form of homosexuality which had its roots in mutual admiration for creative work.

Tolstoy found it easy and natural to admire Chekhov—in fact Gorki claimed that he truly loved him, and records an incident where Tolstoy laid his heavy hand on the younger man's shoulder until Chekhov became uncomfortable beneath its weight. 'When he [Tolstoy] looked at him,' Gorki observed, 'his eyes were tender and seemed almost to stroke Anton Pavlovich's face. Once, when Anton Pavlovich was walking on the lawn with Alexandra Lvovna, Tolstoy, who at the time was still ill and was sitting in a chair on the terrace, seemed to stretch towards them, saying: "Ah, what a beautiful, magnificent man. Modest and quiet like a girl. And he walks like a girl. He's simply wonderful." '

Similarly, Zweig apparently felt no embarrassment when he recorded his love for Emile Verhaeren or for the tender and aesthetic Rilke. With naïve frankness these cosmopolitans reported their exhilaration at simply being together, their satisfaction in physical nearness and mental communion and their desolation when national or domestic necessity intervened to interrupt the relationship.

In their writing, all the full-blooded 'natural' behaviour patterns between the sexes is accurately and passionately observed; yet there seems little evidence to suggest that a comparable state existed within their own sexual spheres.

Since they were unable or, as yet, unwilling to live without at least the façade of marriage, this semi-ascetic attitude of the remnants of the post-symbolists frequently led to sexual confusion. Friderike, although she herself was continuously involved in the world of art, eventually discovered that no amount of worshipful admiration or maternal affection was sufficient to combat the restlessness which sought and discovered its outlet in an entirely different emotional state from that of conventional marriage.

Zweig's efforts to re-orientate himself after a trip were not always too successful, and after this last expedition he took even longer than usual to settle down to a reasonably ordered existence. However this did not prevent him enjoying the array of talent that came crowding into the house on his return: many influential figures in the literary and theatrical world came to visit him even during his absence, and Friderike made the most of these opportunities to act as hostess to such illustrious personalities.

Zweig had lost some of his shyness but he bewailed the fact that fate somehow had completely reversed the tables on him. His days of sallying forth in complete freedom to seek out his literary heroes and loves were, it seemed, gone especially as the Salzburg Festival was attracting more and more crowds each season.

It is difficult to extricate Stefan Zweig from the mass of talent and famous names surrounding him at that time. His friends and house guests read like entries from a Literary Who's Who. Bela Bartok, Maurice Ravel and Bruno Walter added their musical fame to that of H. G. Wells, Paul Valéry and Shalom Ash, all visitors to the house on the Capuchin mountain.

In the midst of the continual coming and going and the endless domestic preparation that such visits entailed, Zweig snatched anxiously at any odd hours to produce the work which somehow or other got completed during this era.

The biographies on Casanova, Stendhal and Tolstoy were now written and published. A collection of short stories which he titled *Kaleidoscope* was completed; initial drafts for the full length biography of Marie Antoinette were produced, and the two similar full-length biographies *Erasmus* and *Castellio against Calvin* were published.

Friderike adored the excitement and growing fame that Zweig's name continued to attract. No visitor was ever turned away, and no complicated rearrangement of domestic surroundings dismayed her or cooled her ardour for opening the doors to all and sundry.

Unfortunately her magnanimity, at first applauded by Zweig for its novelty, now produced in him an increasing irritability, as he discovered that perpetually playing host and working to a hard schedule did not mix too well. As fast as one guest departed another arrived; and with the exception of Romain Rolland, who was always in the special category of 'beloved friend', they triggered off wrangling with Friderike which usually sent Stefan off to his own rooms to dive feverishly into his work, declaring that if he could not find peace within his own house he would remove himself, lock, stock and barrel, to some resort where he would not have these incessant interruptions. And sometimes, Friderike reports, in rather more frank manner than usual, the situation between them became very unpleasant, occasionally ending in indelible insults.

Zweig had managed to avoid rows, both domestic and professional, until his middle life; but now everything seemed to descend upon him at once, and he hated it.

His desire for peace and quiet, his earlier loves, seemed to be receding even further into the distance. The frenzy of creative work and the resulting mass of administrative work, all of which was conducted from the house, were constantly interrupted by the social occasions (which he resented) and the intellectual conversations (which he enjoyed). The days were never long enough to fit in all their activities, and his work sessions were constantly rearranged, sometimes even shelved. Tempers ran high in all quarters, and still the procession of guests, relations, students, aspiring artists and hangers-on wound its way through all seasons to the house half-way up the mountain.

Meanwhile, beyond the confines of this once remote spot in Salzburg, political tempers were also running at a dangerously high level; and whenever Stefan had the time to reflect—something which, during this period of his life, was rapidly becoming a luxury he could ill afford, he felt the old apprehension grip him.

141

The peace of 1918 which had never been a peace, merely a sort of international wishful thinking, had often seemed in mortal danger; and from the increasing number of appeals and requests for support that he was receiving from all quarters and from many countries, it was obvious that throughout Europe there were people who mirrored his own unease. Inevitably, his name had become linked with any peace movement afoot and, contrary to his own inclination to keep out of the public and political eye, he was frequently roped in to lecture on this explosive subject in almost every European country. Obeying instincts often conflicting with reason, he travelled far and wide, expounding his theories of a Universal Brotherhood, the use of intellect as opposed to the use of violence, and, above all, the stimulation and utilization of what he considered to be man's finest human attribute—the exercise of compassion.

At times he felt that the force of destiny had him in so fierce a grip that he would never release himself; and yet the flow of work continued. Historical miniatures, short stories, plays and essays poured from him, almost, he thought at times, as if someone else were in charge, some other power than himself moving his mind and his hand.

Domestic problems there were in plenty, and Stefan's irritability mounted to outbursts of anger as he attempted to preserve his own choice of secretary (a young woman named Charlotte Altman) against the increasing hostility of Friderike's charge of the wretched woman's 'possessiveness'. It was one of destiny's quirks that this rather spiritual man, without too many of the masculine or physical attributes usually demanded by women, seems to have aroused their continual interest and often unwelcome and loving interference. Zweig felt rather like the proverbial dog's bone, tugged in all directions, as the ladies of his household laid their various claims upon him, and for a while, at least, his only concern, next to the one of fulfilling his self-imposed schedule of work, was to exist from day to day in the hope that somehow or other things would sort themselves out.

The turbulence of his life at this time was not without certain compensations, however. Much of Zweig's deepest insight into the problems of domestic and marital existence stems from his personal experience and does not depend, as does some of his earlier writing, on observation from without.

Like Ivan Turgenev before him, circumstances forced him to develop, almost against his will, 'the understanding that goes beneath the old delimitation of the novelist, hidebound by the law . . . male and female created he them . . .'

Chapter Thirteen

When he entered the artistic scene, Zweig had inherited a mixed bag of literary ideals, a goulash of somewhat self-conscious symbolism and that residual romanticism which, unwilling to evaporate completely, even enjoyed a brief renaissance somewhere midway between the period of the two world wars.

His involvement with the more realistically oriented French and Russian schools, however, marked much of his own style during the middle part of his life, as did his growing concern with the, at that time, somewhat suspect, Freudian system of psychoanalysis.

It was only with the publication of *Jeremiah*, his long-awaited declaration of spiritual awareness, that Zweig was able to obtain release from these restricting and conflicting influences. Zweig's essentially romantic preoccupation with emotion, already tempered by a realistic technique, benefited from Freud's scientific approach, but in time his special insight enabled him to overtake his friend's comparatively rigid classifications.

Zweig found many of Freud's dissertations and revelations in complete harmony with his own thinking; and although Friderike claims that her husband was never a wholehearted supporter of Freudian doctrine, many of his observations, and certainly the technique employed by him in the later biographies, suggest quite the opposite.

In tracing the pattern of Zweig's style, it would be futile to suggest that he ever dispensed entirely with the lyrical approach.

On occasion it even invades the most mature of his writing under the pressure of his overwhelming desire to convey to the reader a sense of compassion.

The Royal Game, the last of Zweig's stories and a product of much soul-searching, shows a lapse into lyricism so small as to be virtually unnoticed; yet insinuated between the polished technique of terse, almost biting dialogue, it nevertheless places the Zweigian stamp on this exposition of the use of psychology for destruction. His own comments on this story about a chess game carry one into a frightening area of mental activity: '. . . is it [chess] not a science, a technique, an art, that sways those categories as Mahomet's coffin sways between heaven and earth, at once a union of all contradictory concepts; primeval yet ever new; mechanical in operation yet effective only through the imagination; bounded in geometric space though boundless in its combinations; ever developing yet sterile; thoughts that lead to nothing; mathematics that produce no result; art without works; architecture without substance; and nevertheless, as proved by evidence, more lasting in its being and presence than all books and achievements; the only game that belongs to all peoples and all ages; of which none knows the divinity that bestowed it on the world, to slay boredom, to sharpen the senses, to exhilarate the spirit . . .'.

So much for the lyricism—the ensuing build-up of tension shows Zweig's ability to dispense with everything but the bare essentials. He commands the reader to remain witness to the nerve-wracking moves of two players, the illiterate Czentovic, a world chess champion and his opponent, the mysterious Dr B. Illustrating how acute mental exertion may assist the spirit to survive, Zweig uses chess to prove that survival is possible; Dr B. survives despite the disadvantages of racial inferiority and psycological victimization.

The style as well as the subject is atypical of Zweig. 'Czentovic never stirred. He meditated quietly, slowly, and as I felt, increasingly maliciously slowly—which gave me plenty of time to observe Dr B. He had just about consumed his third glass of water; it came to my mind that he had spoken of his feverish thirst in his cell.

Every symptom of abnormal excitement was plainly present; I saw his forehead grow moist and the scar on his hand became redder and more sharply outlined. It was not until the fourth move, when Czentovic again pondered exasperatingly, that he forgot himself and exploded with: 'Aren't you ever going to move?'

'Czentovic looked up coldly: "As I remember it, we agreed on a ten-minute limit. It is a principle with me not to make it less."

'Dr B., whose self-control diminished with the increasing period of waiting, could no longer conceal his tension; he was restless in his seat and unconsciously began to drum on the table with his fingers. Again Czentovic raised his peasant head: "May I ask you not to drum. It disturbs me. I can't play with that going on." "Ha!" Dr B. answered with a short laugh. "One can see that!"

'Czentovic flushed, "What do you mean by that?" he asked sharply and evilly . . .'.

As the minutes tick by Zweig lays bare the vulnerability of the mind to both positive and negative pressures, suggesting that ultimate release from such pressures may be achieved through attachment to an extraneous form of concentration. He infers that both men, by reason of vastly different circumstances, are on the borderline of madness, but are controlled by their dedication to a mental exercise which because of its tremendous demands, preserves an appearance of normality. Like Akutagwa, describing the 'Kappa's' of Patient No. 23's mind in *Kappa*, his terrifying story of mental illness, or Tolstoy, portraying Vasya's torment in *The Kreutzer Sonata*, Zweig relates the various bombardments to which the human mind can be subjected and yet survive.

The Royal Game represents the culmination in Zweig's life of the process of coming to grips with reality. Only at the end, does he jettison the romanticism which protected him from the truth. His subjects range from poor Boris in *The Runaway*, the exile from Russia who only wants to return there, to the guilt-ridden, alcoholic doctor in *Amok*. Zweig traces the excitement and misery of their lives by the use of vivid, sometimes extravagantly descriptive passages, which he allows to plummet to a few stark sentences once the end is in sight.

In *The Royal Game*, one of his last works, he scrupulously avoids concluding that death is the final answer, although he may already have been bent upon putting into action his own delayed plan of self-destruction. Obscurely, he rescues Dr B., the main character in *The Royal Game*, despite the suffering he allows him to endure *en route*, thus tacitly implying that the scales are ultimately weighed against the force of physical extinction.

The majority of Zweig's work, however, is permeated by the almost imperceptible thought processes which lead to the act of suicide, presented not as a method of escape but rather as a gesture of expiation when all other alternatives have failed. The deceptively peaceful tone of his earlier work, exemplified particularly in his lengthier short stories, tends to anaesthetize the reader against the final outcome; and it is with some shock that the reader recognizes his original intention to remove the subject from the scene via suicide or some other act of violence.

Very few of his characters survive this method of extinction (or release—depending from which side of the moral fence judgement is forthcoming) if they do, they are left with what was for Zweig personally, an even greater problem—a prolonged existence in a brutish or decadent society, the burden of senility or physical illness or, most unpalatable of all, the solitude of mental inadequacy. Rather than allow his characters to endure such humiliation, he challenges fate by wielding this remedy, confident that he can persuade the reader to follow the logic of his reasoning.

The drowning of the disillusioned rejected servant girl in his story *Leporella* is his solution to her timeless problem of unrequited love. In leaving Buch Mendl, the eternal refugee, to die of exposure and malnutrition on the street, and in directing Edith, the crippled heroine of *Beware of Pity*, to the terrace from which she throws herself, he approaches in different ways this central theme around which so much of his work is constructed. He is rarely precipitate, however, in suggesting suicide and allows his characters considerable time to explore every alternative before a final decision is reached. The sanity of the reasoning is never in doubt: it is possible to follow his thinking step by step as he himself ponders possible solutions, rejects them and finally seizes upon the only one that satisfies him.

For obvious reasons, it is biographically satisfactory to spotlight some particular dramatic happening or circumstance in the life of the subject and correlate it with his creative work. It is tempting to see in the blindness of Delius the resulting ethereal quality of *Walk in the Paradise Garden*, or in the madness of Baudelaire and Berlioz the rampagings of the *Symphonie Fantastique* or *Les Fleurs du Mal*. But personal tragedy should be considered separately from the work it may or may not have directly inspired; any creation must be allowed to stand upon its own merits. Conversely, it is arguable that most creative work is essentially the end result of conflicts between emotional experiences; and in seeking to find a balance somewhere between these precarious paths, a solution seems to lie in using Stefan Zweig himself as pacemaker.

His early emotional graph is reasonably steady, the periods of depression coinciding with the period of world conflict or personal bereavement. The later presence of more intermittent depression seems independent of exterior circumstances, and more attributable to the personality he has inherited. As his life progressed and he was witness to the calamaties of human existence, his theories on certain moral issues necessarily crystallized; and there is ample evidence from those who remember him that he expressed the intention of exercising his prerogative of free will in an act of suicide if and when his mortal existence became what he considered expendable.

Zweig, acutely sensitive to the opinions and reactions of those who surrounded him up to late middle life, took a firm grip on the reins of independent thought once his conscious mind finally accepted the fact of his Jewishness with the rise of the Nazis. Simultaneously with this clarification, his literary style emerged with a more sharply defined outline. Gone was the nostalgia which had haunted so many of his earlier characters, and on occasion weakened the structure of development. In place of such dedications as that prefacing, for instance, the Romain Rolland biography, referring to, 'the few, who, in the name of fiery trial remained faithful to our beloved home of Europe', Zweig lauds the power of patience in much more stringent fashion than hitherto in the *Biblical Legends*; and lucidly observes the passage of emotional time and his own relationship as a writer and biographer to it: 'Under the intoxication of destiny', he writes, 'the mind may traverse lengthy periods in a few days; whereas long years may count for nothing when life is void of momentous spiritual happenings. So, for the biographer, who is concerned with the inmost story of a life, only the pulse of passion counts'. Zweig, then, freely admits that he sees no cause for repentance in being more concerned with the passions than with the historical dates on which they were played out.

Again, it is noticeable that the things he wrote about did not always reflect his own and the world's condition, as *The Royal Game* and *Brazil—Land of The Future* bear witness. Both books, although widely different in subject matter and conception, emphasize physical and mental survival, and both contain a vigorous, even aggressive optimism despite the fact that they were written in time of war, when Zweig was in exile and contemplating suicide.

In spite of frequent reassessment of his views, Zweig's belief in the dignity of the individual human being never faltered, although his attitude to the various political and social structures devised by human beings was always one of suspicion. In these last two works however, both written in Brazil, whose political system he greatly admired, he dispenses with many of his old prejudices and concentrates his attention on the human element as the creative rather than destructive part of a political scheme.

At this, almost the eleventh hour of his life, he refuses his characters ultimate free will, and forces them to continue the struggle, even with all the cards stacked against them, and finally in some terms to survive. Dr. B. in *The Royal Game*, survives reasonably intact the refinements of psychological warfare, and in

Brazil his Jesuits become supermen in their defiance of nature and their victorious opposition to an effete imperialistic power.

The volume of work produced by him between 1921 and 1933 harvested a world-wide public, and reduced Zweig to inexplicable depths of humility. Sigmund Freud, toiling within the orbit of his own career and physical life in a no-man's land of mounting hostility, was an object of admiration for Zweig at this time.

Also, he was now well aware that the temporary routes of escape he had been using would cease when affairs in Salzburg came to a head under the Nazi régime.

Zweig was approaching yet another crossroad. The 'freedom' of which he continually spoke would shortly be in political jeopardy, and with his accursed foresight he knew it.

According to Friderike, he deliberately withdrew into a spiritual ghetto which was beyond her comprehension; and as she surveyed the backlog of domestic and professional responsibilities, she realized that she now had little chance of ever reaching through to him.

Meanwhile, between trips round Europe on a scale almost as vigorous as that of the Verhaeren days, his work continued. With a mass of unenviable complications lying ahead, and the apparition of political disaster and persecution branded on his mind, Zweig turned his eyes away from the Salzburg problem, and kept his finger, as a biographer, 'on the pulse of passion'.

Chapter Fourteen

After his fiftieth birthday Zweig's presence as an author on the European scene was important for two reasons, apart from his literary merit. At a time when involvement in politics and the doctrine of anti-semitism were offered as solutions to social imperfection, he became much more active in both areas, although he still withheld allegiance to any specific group.

His almost obsessive efforts to avoid publicity were more often than not negated by the public utterances which his conscience obliged him to make.

In this defence of the freedom of the individual to oppose a hostile regime, as in all problems, his behaviour seems on occasion inconsistent; and while he remained relatively immune, at least until the advent of Josef Goebbels, he was aware that his name was already on the suspect list in the early 1930s.

But emotionally, at least, he finally appeared resolved to embark upon the first of the two major events he saw as his destiny—the separation from Friderike; later, when he joined the ranks of the growing army of the stateless, a situation he already took for granted, the disposal of his own life was the second.

Even so, Zweig's connections and friendships with those in high literary and political places frequently thrust him into the limelight and compelled him to shoulder certain moral and racial responsibilities which he disliked intensely. Somewhat illogically, he refused to see why he was regarded in many circles as a champion of peace, a fact the public was now taking for granted, with the theatre, radio and cinema all offering adaptations of his work.

The rôle of peacemaker was entirely unacceptable to him, yet as his creative energy accumulated and each new publication was geared to this theme, his dilemma became increasingly acute. As European and world interest in his work increased, so did Zweig's disquiet. He looked back more and more often to his early post-war years in Austria. and wondered at the naïvety that had lulled him into thinking that Germany would ever be content to be a fifth-rate world power. The military humiliation and economic disaster of inflation had been overcome, but there still remained the bitter taste of defeat, and it was now not unusual to hear the radicals level their discontent at minority groups, and at the Jews in particular.

Walter Rathenau, Germany's Foreign Minister and Zweig's own lifelong friend, was assassinated, and he began to read into this act a motive far more sinister than the obvious one of political thug-gery put out by the press; and in the now rapidly growing national preoccupation with racism, he envisaged the most terrible future. 'Rarely have I sensed the tragedy of the Jew more strongly than in his personality', he wrote, 'which, with all its apparent superiority, was full of deep unrest and uncertainty'.

Rathenau had provided Zweig with a friendship beyond the usual confines of his acquaintanceship, and by virtue of his high Ministerial office had enabled Stefan to see into the labyrinth of political strategy—a revelation which did nothing to reassure him, in fact only confirmed the latter's morbid suspicions.

A short story, *Die Unsichtbare Sammlung—The Invisible Collection* written by Zweig shortly after the end of the first world war, enjoyed immediate success. It deals with the inflationary period and its impact on the lives of those who were struggling for economic survival. The blind and aged Herr Kronfeld, art con-noisseur and veteran of the 1870 war, has suffered, in common with the rest of the German population, as the mark is devalued; and when Herr Rackner, the famous art dealer, decides to pay him a visit in order to purchase, at what he hopes will be rock-bottom prices, some of the old man's *objets d'art*, he is horrified to learn that the entire collection has already been sold by members of his family in order to survive. Zweig recounts without sentiment but extreme pathos the appalling scene where Kronfeld handles the portfolios filled with cheap reproductions, meanwhile recounting the beauty of the Dürer woodcuts and Rembrandt etchings he imagines are there. Through the characters of Kronfeld's family Zweig illustrates the poverty of a post-war Germany and the unquenchable spirit of those who clung to life, often with only hope to sustain them.

As Zweig recalled his meetings with Rathenau, whose financial wizardry had temporarily rescued the country from inflationary disaster, he was forced at last to see the separating line between Jew and Aryan in a society he had always tried to visualize simply as 'European'. Rathenau himself had no illusions.

Outwardly, however, little had changed in Zweig's own life, unless it was the steady growth of the 'success' about which he writes diffidently; except that a definite melancholy would from time to time now engulf his thinking, taking him a further step down into the 'claustrophobia' about which he often complained.

Prolonged visits into Germany, France and Italy, and sometimes to countries beyond Europe, only served to confirm that the pipedream of his youth was forever dead. Chance remarks made by him at that time and on subsequent occasions foreshadow without too much doubt the presence of a severe anxiety neurosis, rooted equally, as he himself later confessed, in the human catastrophe preceded by the notorious Reichstag Fire, and his own mortal inadequacy:

'Shudderingly one learned of peacetime concentration camps and of secret chambers built into barracks where innocent people were destroyed without trial or formality', he wrote. '. . . already in those days I saw the first refugees. At night they had climbed over the Salzburg mountain or swum across the frontier stream. Starved, shabby, agitated, they stared at one; they were the leaders in the panic flight from inhumanity which was to spread over the whole earth. But even I did not suspect, when I looked at these fugitives, that I ought to perceive in their pale faces, as in a mirror, my own life and that we all, we all, we all would become victims of the lust for power of this one man.'

Many of his friends at home and in Germany, while bemoaning the fact of party bureaucracy, nevertheless realistically resigned themselves to the New Order; but Stefan still spoke out bitterly against the filing of human beings as so many numbers, as belonging to or completing this ethnic group or that; and as this political collectivization gained momentum, demanding that only *violent* reorganization could rescue Germany—and thus, automatically, Austria as well—from the lower echelons of the vanquished nations, the battle between his instinct and his reason alternately swung him from hope to despair.

The disastrous consequences of the Strauss opera *Die Scheigsame Frau* (*The Silent Woman*), proved that his hereditary and melancholy instinct, as exhibited in his story *Buch Mendl*, was the right one.

His choice of themes for the short stories, which were invariably at that time concerned with mental distress, shows a desire on Zweig's part to use his work as 'creative psychological investigations'. In *Buch Mendl*, the psychological spotlight reveals not so much the plight of the refugee as the inadequacy or apathy of the onlooker; however Friderike vehemently refutes any suggestion that the story is autobiographical, although a study of certain passages reflects many of Zweig's own comments on comparable situations in the 1939 war.

In growing concern and with some guilt, the reader follows Jacob Mendl's passive existence, from the Café Gluck to the internment camp. 'I have no information as to what Jacob Mendl suffered during those two years of internment, cut off from his beloved books, penniless among roughly nurtured men few of whom could read or write, in a huge human dunghill. This must be left to the imagination of those who can grasp the torments of a caged eagle . . . Of all the cruelties and wanton abuses of power during the war, the most needless and therefore the most inexcusable was this herding together behind barbed-wire fences of thousands upon thousands of persons who had outgrown the age of military service, who had made homes for themselves in a foreign land—and who, believing in the faith of their hosts, had remained.' Jacob Mendl somehow survives the rigours of internment, only to return to a society which sees his survival as an embarrassment. His killers are brash officialdom and the unwillingness of anyone else to 'get involved'.

More than a decade later, Zweig recorded a further, and no longer fictional, indictment of the racist system. 'The first ones, those who had been prompt to leave Germany and Austria, had still managed to save their clothes, their baggage . . . some even had a little money. But the longer one of them had placed his trust in Germany, the greater his reluctance to wrench himself from his beloved home, the more severely he had been punished. First the Jews had been deprived of their professional status, then they were forbidden the theatres, the museums—and scholars lost the use of the libraries. They had stayed because of loyalty or of indolence, cowardice or pride. They preferred being humiliated at home to humiliating themselves as beggars abroad'.

The 'spiritual ghetto' of which Friderike speaks was becoming more frequently the refuge into which Zweig withdrew, and this, plus his hopelessly overloaded programme of international engagements, forced her to accept a new situation which was at first utterly intolerable, then depressingly endured and finally recognized as inevitable.

A hectic although relatively pleasant interlude in the marital and domestic tension came with the arrival in Spring 1932 of Richard Strauss in Salzburg. The two men had first met about a year previously. Their relations were amiable from the first and Zweig was delighted when the composer invited him to collaborate on his new opera. Zweig suggested that it should be an adaptation of Ben Jonson's play *Epicoene, or The Silent Woman*, and they entered at once into detailed discussions. Jonson's play, a bawdy exposition of the male ego, designed to convulse audiences rather than to instruct them, was as far from political subversion as Hitler from God, yet with its emergence and its ill-fated appearance on the Dresden stage, the German leader and his Ministers fell upon the innocent old head of Sir Morosus and his creator, Stephan Zweig, the Jew, with disproportionate rage. No one involved in the turmoil of creation, least of all the composer himself, could possibly have foreseen that such a politically innocent theme, and launched upon the public at such a time, would precipitate the high-level discussions usually reserved by a Government for its world-shattering decisions—Zweig claims that Hitler himself was irrationally concerned that production of the opera should never take place.

At the time of the exuberant Strauss's arrival at the Zweig ménage, the government was practising political and racial persecution only on an experimental basis, and it had not yet become the declared policy for the control of non-Aryans. But by January 1933, when the opera was completed and Zweig's contribution as librettist finished, the entire picture of existence in Germany had changed, and so had many of his own attitudes.

The relationship between the two men (Strauss was sixty-seven and Zweig fifty when they first met) provided each of them with a new and provocative experience. Strauss, always the extrovert, and for long dutifully subservient to the demands of the stringent Hugo von Hofmannsthal, welcomed Zweig as his new librettist with some relief; and Zweig, having long desired to try his hand in the theatre once again, enjoyed the stimulation and artistic challenge the new work presented.

In a near-demoniac spurt of concentrated creative work, he finally produced the libretto in a little more than nine months. But when Strauss's congratulations arrived in February 1933, only weeks before Hitler's National Socialists took root in the German Chancellory, Stefan Zweig knew immediately that it was time for him to make the move that he had anticipated with dread and for so long. He knew his name was on Goebbels' list of Jews, and he came to the conclusion that he should not only accept but utilize his Jewishness and at the same time accelerate his move away from the house at Salzburg. The latter, as things turned out, proved far more complicated than the former, which surprisingly provided him with an unexpected relief.

Following upon the national boycott of all Jews in March of that year, Zweig called upon Strauss to withdraw their opera. This met with blank astonishment on the part of the composer, who referred almost humorously to his partner's 'Jewish egoism'; but there was little of humour in Zweig during those first weeks of open anti-semitism. A wrangle developed between him and Strauss, but the latter refused to withdraw his adored operatic brainchild, and went to extraordinary lengths in order to present it as planned at the Dresden Opera.

Zweig, now at last manoeuvred into a situation where he was forced publicly to acknowledge his Jewish origin, also realized, according to Friderike, that yet another of his artistic idols had feet of clay. The situation was reminiscent of an earlier one, in-involving Hugo von Hofmannsthal. The great poet had occupied a unique niche in Zweig's affection from his earliest schooldays—even Verhaeren's talent did not quite measure up to the perfection of 'Goethe's worthy successor'—and when Zweig discovered that Hofmannsthal had deliberately influenced Max Reinhardt against producing not only *Jeremiah*, but two of Zweig's subsequent dramas; *Volpone* and *Lamb of the Poor*, he was horrified. Friderike records his reaction in dutifully constrained terms.

'My husband, who had always revered this great poet, felt shocked by the discovery of a one-sided rivalry which his own truly naïve trustfulness would have regarded as impossible. After this, an association with Reinhardt seemed anything but tempting. And that with Richard Strauss seemed equally lacking a posthumous blessing from Hofmannsthal, the composer's former librettist.'

However, from a Strauss biographer, Norman Delmar, comes the contrary observation that Stefan Zweig not only grasped at the opportunity to succeed Hofmannsthal as Strauss' librettist, but even went so far as to humble himself unnecessarily, sometimes even embarrassingly. And from Zweig comes the fairly moderate comment: 'I have met many great artists in my life but never one who knew how to maintain such abstract and unerring objectivity towards himself.' Later, when the completed libretto was handed over, he wrote, 'Strauss did not change a single line in my whole libretto. Thus developed between us the most cordial relations imaginable.' If, as Friderike avers, Stefan was troubled by Hofmannsthal's jealousy, it appears that he soon subdued any personal prejudice he might have had for Strauss under the influence of their combined effort to produce the new opera.

Zweig's allergy to noise had produced frequent fissures in the marital stronghold; though Friderike rather quaintly attributes this abhorrence to her husband's long memory of incessant maternal chatter, rather than to the immediate one of her natural vivacity and that of Susanne and Elisabeth, her now teenaged daughters, their friends and the usual miscellany of guests and hangers-on. The house at Salzburg was probably no noisier than any other sheltering so many people, but noise had an exaggerated effect on Stefan at that time and contributed to his general 'malaise'.

The extrovert Strauss, on the other hand, seemed impervious to everything except his work, and even seemed to enjoy being dominated by his wife, Pauline. With understandable envy Friderike recalls how admirably Richard withstood the frequent demands of his one-time pupil, even, it seemed to her, thriving upon a diet of bullying.

The situation between Friderike and Stefan was now deteriorating rapidly, and the tension between them was at times almost tangible; it needed only a spark, a flicker of a glance, to plunge them into silence or even send Stefan hurrying from Salzburg. Their drawing apart was the more alarming to Friderike because she could not pinpoint the reason; and as the lines of communication gradually collapsed, her refuge was the traditionally feminine one of waiting and hoping. She was miserably aware that the burden of her love was unacceptable to Stefan in its present form, and she valiantly attempted to tone it down to provide him with the image of the partner that (she assumed) he now desired. But for Stefan the irritations of domesticity, which he had never really desired, only added to his preoccupation with the deteriorating political situation in both Germany and Austria and, as always, spurred him on to produce more and yet more work.

Regular commuting between Salzburg and Versailles, where endless hours had been spent in research for his biography *Marie Antoinette*, now shortly to be published, and the additional task of providing Richard Strauss with the *Silent Woman* libretto, left little time for him to pursue the 'idyllic' partnership that Friderike was so nostalgically to mourn.

Richard Strauss, Germany's acknowledged Master of Music, was uncomfortably aware that his own slight connection with Judaism—he had acquired a Jewish daughter-in-law—was sufficient to cause him trouble under the new anti-semitic laws; and although he had frequently declared his distaste for the Nazi Party's racial policy, his prime concern was only for his work. Nothing mattered to him except keeping himself and his compositions before the public, and he stifled any qualm of conscience he may have had when the Nazis objected to Zweig, the Jew, being his librettist.

He later accused Zweig of having a 'Moses-like' attitude about his heritage, and seemed deliberately to misunderstand the anxiety Zweig felt after the Nazi Party Ministers Goebbels and Goering and, it was suggested, even Hitler himself, had decided to ban the Opera, after personally boycotting the first performance.

The burning and boycott of Jewish books was now a regular and accepted spectacle in most of the public squares throughout Germany, and once the horror that he had so long anticipated had broken out openly, Zweig found that he could breathe more freely. At least the enemy had come out with a declared policy, however brutal. 'I regarded it more as an honour then a disgrace to be permitted to share this fate of the complete destruction of literary existence in Germany', he records, 'with such eminent contemporaries as Thomas Mann, Werfel, Freud, Einstein and many others whose work I consider of incomparably more importance than my own.'

Pillorying, the burning of books, public insults and repeated press attacks were already preparing the way for the concentrated effort which was to mark Hitler's political progress during the next few years, and Zweig, appalled but no longer surprised by the bitterness that marked daily life, took a long hard look at the sum total of his works and at the number of years he had lived, and felt that neither gave him cause for too much rejoicing. After only the second performance of the Opera, the first having been acclaimed enthusiastically by the majority of critics, it was withdrawn, and all public reference to it destroyed. Strauss was highly indignant but at this time helpless to do anything about the 'tainted' name of Zweig on the programme.

Later, Zweig claimed that the reported resignation of Richard Strauss from his post as president of the Reich Chamber of Music was a direct result of their association.

As the level of public insults increased, Zweig decided that he could take no more, and sought temporary refuge at least in a country which had seemed somewhat out of tune with his thinking so many years ago, but which now appeared to be the only sane place in a world gone mad.

Fog, damp and the enveloping, cloistered silence of the British Museum were in marked contrast to the fevered tempo of central Europe; his immediate concern with the Mary Stuart biography, already taking form in his mind, was second only to that of his anxiety for the future of his 'beloved homeland'.

Chapter Fifteen

Salzburg, once regarded by Zweig with nearly as much affection as his forebears reserved for the Promised Land, seemed in 1933 like the rest of Austria, too small to contain the inflammable, political situation, which he felt was already on the point of exploding. He found the apathy of the Jewish community there irritating to the point of stupidity in the face of such obviously hostile German policy. 'They acted', he commented fretfully, 'as if the cancelling of all rights of physicians, lawyers, scholars and actors was happening in China, instead of across the border three hours away, where their own language was spoken.' The house which had once enraptured him with its aura of decaying romanticism seemed now to suffocate rather than shelter; and with a premonition that no one else really shared, all he saw when he gazed at the magnificent view across the Alps was a threat to the entire, trustful Jewish population of Germany and Austria.

Several years before the actual declaration of war a chronic pessimism had gripped him, aggravated, no doubt, by his personal foretaste of the National Socialist anti-semitic policy. This fear was not so far shared by many of his friends, though, who preferred to see in the Strauss opera affair an isolated if unfortunate incident.

When, later on, Adolph Hitler occupied the house on the Berchtesgaden mountain, almost opposite to Zweig's own on the Salzburg mountain, it merely served to confirm the nightmare mental prophecies he had harboured for so long.

Most of his fellow Jews, although appreciative of his views at this admittedly tense period of political history, regarded him as something of a Jeremiah, and saw no reason yet why they should lose faith with the countries of their birth or adoption. But the description in his story *Buch Mendl*, written little more than a decade before as comment on the refugee tragedy of the 1914–1918 war, were to prove prophetic as well.

A comment made by Friderike after Zweig's death, although it refers to his handling of the Mary Stuart biography, is illuminating (and uncharacteristically succinct). 'The author [Zweig],' she wrote, 'although finding it onerous to make personal decisions, disliked hesitancy and lukewarmness.' Decisions were indeed always painful for Zweig, but he spent the major part of his life taking them; and there is more than a hint of masochism in this attitude which extracted such a toll from those involved emotionally in his life.

In examining the events which contributed to his vacillation, it is relevant here to refer to the *Biblical Legends*. They were published when racism was approved as a legitimate weapon of policy, and in them he extols the virtue of patience in the face of national and racial disaster, offering Benjamin, the eternal wanderer and epitome of tolerance, and Virata, the main character of the *The Undying Brother* Legend, angelic in his humility, as patterns for minority-group behaviour. His choice of subject and his handling of it reveal the contradiction of thought to which he succumbed. For while he was writing enthusiastically of the ultimate sanctity of staying put in the face of adversity, even of death, he was also feverishly contemplating the advantages of flight.

Several isolated but disturbing experiences had also added fuel to the despondency and conflicting thoughts which now occupied his mind for the greater part of the day. A life-long friend would avoid him in the street, or he would be asked to make personal meetings with non-Jewish acquaintances within the safety of his own house rather than in public, to avoid an official reprimand.

Although Zweig had just about weathered the unpleasant backlash of *Die Schweigsame Frau*'s disastrous début, the experience had left him shaken, and he had no more illusions about the devotion of an artist and a colleague. Richard Strauss, while doggedly defending his right to choose his own librettist, of whatever race or creed, gave Zweig public support only in so far as it ensured the safety of his own work; and Zweig, at last free of his tendency to envelop any friendship in an aura of romanticism, realized the limitations of such professional camaraderie.

If interest in the Nazi government's intervention had waned somewhat after the opera's enforced withdrawal, Zweig knew better than to allow his instinct to be lulled into a false sense of security. He had accepted the stigma placed upon him at the time, and nothing now would erase it. The shock waves produced by seeing his name bandied about as 'tainted' refused to level out, and the ever-widening schism in his mental outlook divided his conscious thought into two equally unattractive solutions.

If he remained he knew he would lose a physical and mental freedom that he valued obsessively. If he fled his homeland, an even greater spiritual loss awaited him; and as time ran out, and as he watched the straggling lines of refugees trickle through the mountain passes, the burden within him grew.

He reluctantly continued to accept invitations to lecture in many parts and capitals of the continent; and despite a massive German governmental brainwashing exercise large audiences there still listened eagerly to his plea for tolerance and compassion based on an understanding of people's physical and mental needs. Zweig's passionate anxiety for the fate of his own people in Europe earned for him at once the blessing of a devoted public following and considerable government displeasure.

About this time he suddenly became very much more introspective, he fell to examining the quality and texture of his own work with redoubled self-criticism. With nothing from publishers or public to substantiate his fears—rather the opposite was in fact the case—he pored over everything he had ever produced with clinical and microscopic care; and as his correspondence with Sigmund Freud increased, he saw in it a lifeline, and in Freud the only source of opinion to be trusted when his confidence in his own professional ability was faltering.

In talking about the Mary Stuart biography, Friderike observes that Zweig did not find Elizabeth, with her incessant intrigues and double dealings, a sympathetic character, and that he writes of her with only 'moderate respect'.

Because of its deep psychological insight and because it is a product of Zweig's maturity, the work requires a separate chapter of full analysis, but it is worth mentioning here because he fell upon the subject at a crucial time in his life, and in the thoughts and actions of Mary and Elizabeth he saw reflected his own dilemma.

Few if any of Mary's biographers can resist her femininity and Zweig was no exception; but Elizabeth was closer to home. In dealing with Elizabeth's vacillations, only too often culminating in irrevocably negative decisions, he also unconsciously reflects part of his own complexity. Like Elizabeth, he needed and waited for a very particular reason before taking final action on any issue; and it was a government order sanctioning the indiscriminate search of all Jewish or suspect private houses throughout Austria, that he seized upon as the excuse he needed to leave forever the land of his birth.

The chapter entitled 'Elizabeth against Elizabeth' deals in concise and disapproving fashion with the English Queen's indecision, but in some ways it outstrips in power the lengthy passion of Mary's calvary. 'Elizabeth was unable to sleep; she passed day after day in gloomy silence, her spirit obsessed with the intolerable problem of whether she should have the death sentence carried out. She tried to thrust aside the thought, as Sisyphus rolled his stone uphill, but always it rolled back again to crush her. Vainly did her Minister of State address her; she could listen only to the voice of her own conscience.'

Here Zweig's choice of words stabs swiftly and accurately to the heart of the matter; a writer, whether his explorations are fictional or biographical, unwittingly releases particles of himself through his subjects; and although Friderike saw in Zweig's presentation of Elizabeth only what she calls 'moderate respect',

164

the passages referring to the English monarch's periods of in-decision point to an acute understanding of the mood. 'Though Elizabeth had put a harsh gaoler in charge of Mary Stuart, she was herself in thrall to a yet harsher one, the most cruel on earth, her conscience. This struggle of Elizabeth against Elizabeth, this inability to decide whether she should listen to the voice of reason or to the voice of humanity, went on for three months, four months, five months, nearly half a year. Her nerves being thus overwrought, it was but natural that the final decision, when it came, should take the form of an explosion.'

As Elizabeth saw in the eventual disposal of her rival a way clear to pursue her aims unhampered and thus achieve a measure of freedom, so Zweig saw in casting off his marital partner and his allegiance to his homeland his way towards a liberty now denied him. Neither one was convinced of the rightness of such action, and Zweig, like Elizabeth, enjoyed little tranquillity once the step had been taken.

Simultaneous with his worries about political unrest came a revulsion of much that he had, if not taken for granted, then accepted without too much query.

His circle of friends, although continually widening, had some-how lost substance. Many of them were neurotically chary of the risks involved in attachment to non-Aryans, and while the gather-ings at the old house continued, even without the presence of the master, they now depended more often than not on social chatter rather than intellectual intercourse, lest forbidden subjects be touched upon. The gaiety was a little forced, but Friderike, with the desperation of one drowning, clung determinedly to this part of the life they had once shared.

Stefan's mind was occupied with preparation for the Mary Stuart biography, and he spent much of his time travelling be-tween England and France, and both countries drew him further away from Salzburg and for ever lengthening periods. Whenever he surfaced from beneath the mass of documents, papers and reference books, or forced himself away from the absorbing, near suffocating pressure of historical events at Fotheringay or Edinburgh, it was to learn of fresh disasters in Europe and increasing tension between Austria and Germany; and the frustration he had felt in Austria earlier was repeated in London, where again his seemed the only voice to speak out against the atrocities then just beginning. Complacency and non-interference seemed to him as criminal as the evil itself; but there was nothing he could do, there was nothing anyone could do, until, as happened in his own personal situation, and indeed in Elizabeth's, 'it was but natural that the final decision, when it came, should take the form of an explosion.' It would be convenient to place Stefan Zweig, now fifty-one, in the category of climacteric vulnerability, and to some small extent it would be correct, at least so far as his friend Richard Friendenthal recalls.

But the last decade of his life reflects not so much the image of a man imprisoned within the shackles of middle age, or even that of an exile lately deprived of material well-being, as a complete picture of one of his own fictional or biographical characters.

When Charlotte Elizabet Altman became his secretary, Zweig appears to have taken about as much notice of her as he did of Friderike when she entered his life. His work and the political situation tended to cloud out everything else, even a gentle-mannered, rather anaemic-looking young lady who was destined to accompany him on the last chapter of his earthly existence. It was to take Stefan, as always, a considerable time to realise that he was involved in a highly emotional entanglement and then, having reached a decision, to put it into action.

Meanwhile Austria mourned the untimely murder of her Chancellor, with about the same degree of sincerity as had been exhibited many years before at the assassination of Franz Ferdinand, the hostility between that country and Germany mounted daily, as did the straggling processions of refugees in whose pale faces Zweig had seen the reflection of his own image.

'The terrible state of homelessness had not yet begun', he wrote, recalling the months immediately before his own enforced exile, 'inexplicable to such as have not experienced it, that nerve-wracking sensation of reeling, open-eyed and wide-awake, through space, knowing that wherever one might gain a foothold one might at any moment be thrust back . . .'

Zweig's period of exile, the certainty of which had haunted him for so long, was about to begin.

Chapter Sixteen

Outside of his literary work, two of the main interests in Zweig's life were music and a fairly catholic, though discrimating, taste in art collection. His love of music developed in early life, later increased to a devotion second only to that reserved for his literary peers. Beethoven and Mozart were but two who challenged Goethe, Dostoyevsky and Tolstoy for his affection, and amongst his most prized possessions were a desk and a small cash box, once belonging to Beethoven, items in what became an impressive collection even when judged against those of international connoisseurs.

Assembled by Zweig over many years, and later bewailed by Friderike for its precipitate dispersal, the collection, comprising masses of literary and artistic documents and manuscripts as well as thousands of autographs, was later to become a dreaded responsibility. The cataloguing of autograph collection, a particular passion stemming from early boyhood vigils outside innumerable stage doors, had presented Friderike with a formidable task. Zweig, however, personally guarded items connected with Beethoven's death, which association made them seem especially poignant. A lock of hair, a laundry list written by the dying man, an invitation to his funeral, evoked in Zweig a tremulous sense of unworthiness: 'I never considered myself as owner of these things but only their temporary custodian. Not the sense of possession, of having them for my very own, enticed me, but the allurement of unifying, of moulding a collection into a work of art. I was aware that in this collection I had created something which, as an entity, was worthier of survival than my own works.'

One of the short stories in the collection *Kaleidoscope* gives the reader an idea of Zweig's interest and perception in the field of art and the excitement of an important auction. The furtive little hero of *Impromptu Study of a Handicraft* is as touching as all Zweig's underdog characters, but he probably serves more to indulge the author's own enjoyment in recounting one of innumerable excursions into dusty auction-rooms, where the supercharged atmosphere and aesthetic thrill of discovery provided him with a rare, uninhibited pleasure.

Associations formed and maintained over a period of years also brought Zweig into close contact with many of the stars orbiting in the musical sphere of that time; and in his friendships with such illustrious personalities as Arturo Toscanini and Maurice Ravel. already famous as a composer, and with Bruno Walter, a regular visitor to the Salzburg house and at fifty-eight, the general musical director of several Berlin opera houses, he found a unique opportunity to further his taste for music on the highest aesthetic and professional level.

In choosing Salzburg, itself the birthplace of Mozart, as his first real home, Zweig felt that he was associating himself even more closely with those whose genius in art excited him. Thus he was able to dwell as an observer in the hallowed atmosphere of a great musical past and the stimulating renaissance of that present.

By attending rehearsals, recitals and concerts—an effortless exercise in musically dedicated Salzburg—listening attentively to the never less than inspired conversations in his home and by mentally casting himself at the feet of these musicians an act of homage which always came naturally to him, he absorbed the musical colour and not a little of the technical skill abundant throughout the European scene and particularly in these surroundings.

With what was either instinctive or deliberately cultivated professional discipline, however, Zweig rarely became directly involved in the inevitable artistic personality clashes that from time to time erupted. He appears to have been relatively unmoved for instance, in the Max Reinhardt-Hofmannsthal affair, referred to earlier, although the latter's jealousy of Zweig's incursion into the theatre with his early plays is offered by Friderike as a possible cause for the various theatrical disasters that ensued.

On the other hand he records with amazement and delight the fact that he maintained the most coridial relationship with his publisher, Anton Kippenberg, a fellow art collector and founder of the Insel Verlag Publishing House.

This creation of an aura of professional geniality seems to indicate an extraordinarily benevolent attitude on his part; and in view of the substantial circle of internationally famous artists who gathered willingly, even eagerly around him during the middle part of his life, this absence of rancour or jealousy was undoubtedly part of the attraction. But very little of this geniality was exhibited by him in his domestic life at that time, indicating an increase in the divisiveness in his personality; indeed this seems to have worsened quite noticeably after his fiftieth birthday.

After much soul-searching and trying to come up with a conclusion to the contrary, even Friderike admitted that what she had called 'vagueness' was in reality 'the somewhat divided personality in Stefan Zweig.'

The desire to achieve what he saw then as 'freedom' had already become an obsession, and with the worsening political situation occupying much of his conscious thinking, he grasped at this as a reason for escape. Whether or not he saw in his intended flight a solution to both marital and political problems, is a matter for speculation, although his friend and fellow author Richard Friedenthal today recalls Zweig's acute uneasiness at that time just prior to the outbreak of war: 'Everything is hopeless. The war . . . my own situation. And I'm getting old, Richard. You know I have a horror of outliving my usefulness. Maybe one day soon, people will say, "There goes old Zweig", and I don't think I could bear that.' Friendenthal recalls Zweig searching for grey hairs, and his relief when he failed to find any.

If he seemed to those around him to be unduly pessimistic about the international situation, it is recalled by all who knew him that the periods of depression were unmistakably deepening, imposing an even greater strain on the task of maintaining the calm and munificent image he had publicly created, and steadily worsening his relationship with Friderike.

Geniality was again markedly absent in the persistent, almost childish outbursts of temper he showed whenever he was forced to observe family responsibility; and Friderike found herself in the unenviable position of go-between when he and his brother indulged in their frequent harangues over family finances, a subject guaranteed to produce a violent reaction in Stefan. His intense dislike of financial discussion threw everyone into disarray. He had already foregone his family inheritance in an effort to dissociate himself from the industrial aspect of his forebears, but even so his own lavish earned income, derived from a variety of sources—royalties from his books, translation fees, the sale of film, radio and theatrical rights—gave him cause for perpetual concern. He regarded money as an embarrassment, yet by accepting the generous fruit of his labour he steadily increased what was now a considerable fortune.

Filial attachment, never high on his list of emotional priorities, gets cautious airing when Zweig refers to his mother's death shortly after the German occupation of Austria in 1938. He elaborates on the persecution, and sees his aged mother, not as the irritating factor he had been forced—if only rarely—to tolerate nor as the central figure in discussions frequently descending into degrading squabbles, about whose financial responsibility she had become, but as a revered and tragic victim of Nazi persecution:

'Neither my brother nor I, her only children, was there, nor could we have come back, because a return to the deathbed of a mother would have been counted a misdeed by the representatives of German culture.' Zweig continues his denunciation of the Nazi system by explaining in some detail how Julius Streicher's racial edicts operated. His bitterness overflows, not so much at the thought of an elderly cousin and only remaining relative in

Vienna being ejected from the presence of the dying woman, ultimately abandoned to the care of an attendant Aryan nurse, but at the implication, now officially blessed by the government, that a Jew, given the opportunity, would immediately indulge in an act of so-called race defilement.

As in the withdrawal of the Strauss Opera and the public burning of his own books, he saw in this last indignity the Nazi persecution of the Jews reaching out to strike at him personally; his prediction of the course of his own calvary and exile was now becoming a certainty. These incidents served to impress on him the calamity rather than the privilege of his Jewishness, and in allowing this realization to obliterate all other issues he daily sank deeper into what became for him an endless nightmare.

During many subsequent conversations with associates in Austria and in England, he freely confided the terror he had felt as he lived through a re-enactment of traditional persecution which sought to reduce those who survived to a state of physical and mental cringing, which always seemed to him the most refined sort of torture, an unendurable humiliation.

An acute physical restlessness, more pronounced than any experienced before, gripped Zweig during the mid-1930s as he continued his familiar commuting between Europe and England. His biography *Erasmus* had just been published, and in portraying the spiritual conflict and material successes and failures of the sixteenth-century Dutch writer, humanist and internationalist, Zweig again follows the pattern of using his writings as a form of introspection.

Throughout the biography, he lays significance upon the achievement of spiritual freedom as a step towards universal compassion, and in summing up the brilliant but detached personality of the man he refers to as a 'great European', Zweig recalls yet again his own spiritual and humanist mentors:

'Schiller gave the message of world citizenship a poetic dress', he writes in the final chapter, and: 'Kant demanded everlasting peace, again and again, down to the days of Tolstoy, and later with Gandhi and Romain Rolland, this same ideal has been reiterated with logical force, and the spirit of understanding has claimed its ethical and moral rights as a counterblast to the club-law of authority and violence'.

Erasmus, as Zweig writes of him, emerges from beneath the dust of centuries, erudite but humanly fallible, disappointed but perpetually idealistic: 'For what the mind is capable of lifting from the narrow circle of the individual life and hurling forth into the realm of the universally human, that alone is capable of endowing us with strength beyond the strength of the individual. Men and nations can find their true and sacred measure only by making suprapersonal and hardly realizable claims'.

By the time his association with Sigmund Freud was established, his psychological objectivity enabled him to present what were then somewhat revolutionary methods in literary technique, resulting in his displaying an unerring insight into the female psyche.

This facility is demonstrated incisively in the short story *Amok* through dialogue between an anonymous and pregnant Englishwoman and an alcoholic renegade doctor, driven eventually to suicide by way of expiation for his medical ineptitude; but in this story, unlike others of Zweig's works concerned with the act of self-extinction, the reader's attention is concentrated on the plight of the woman and her arrogance, which later dissolves into an appalling mental and physical deterioration: 'You can understand, then, how thrilled I was by this woman, so haughty and fierce and reserved; so brimful of mystery, and gravid with the fruit of a recent passion'.

Zweig brings his tragedy into abrupt focus with the doctor's confession: 'One hundred thousand gulden? No, I won't do it for that'

'She looked at me, paling a little. No doubt she felt intuitively that the obstacle was not a matter of money. All she said, however, was: "What fee do you ask, then?"'

No romanticism, no superlatives when Zweig touches, as he so often seems to do, on the inner pulse of the female personality. Even when viewed in the light of a changing and now so-called permissive society, the eternal torment of a woman trapped by her own passion is presented with clarity and none of the sentimental trimmings often associated with such a situation.

If in *Beware of Pity*, Zweig's only full length novel, criticism can be levelled at the character of the sometimes too admirable Dr Condor, or that of the exasperatingly indecisive Lieutenant, it is unlikely that any female reader would query the behaviour that leads to Edith's ultimate decision.

So it is with the acute perception which portrays the two monarchs in *Mary Stuart*, Zweig assesses objectively and, from a feminine standpoint, accurately, their reaction to many violent and emotional circumstances.

1934 produced a crop of seemingly unrelated but vital happenings in Zweig's political, social and domestic life. With the assassination of the Chancellor and the increasing power of the Nazi administration in Austria came the edict, long foreseen and mortally feared, which gave the government unlimited power to search private homes on the suspect list—a new way of identifying Jewish citizens.

The horror with which Zweig greeted this proclamation can be measured by the hasty but irrevocable step he took immediately after his own house had been subjected to just such an official search. At the time Friderike found his fear abnormal, and his subsequent behaviour in surrendering his status as a resident of Salzburg incomprehensible; but Zweig, the moment of decision upon him, was deaf and blind to any reasonable approach. As far as he was concerned, all that he had previously imagined was now a reality, and only in physical flight could he see a glimmer of hope.

Compared with the drama of persecution, and the high degree of tension between the members of his household, the advent and presence on the scene of Charlotte Elizabet Altman, seemed almost irrelevant; and it is reasonably certain, according to several reliable sources close to Zweig at the time, that his concern with his work and with the desperate political situation tended to blunt his awareness of the impending marital explosion. Although for some time he had barely maintained even a façade of domestic bliss, it is doubtful whether, in his fretful search for the freedom he found so elusive, he would have become deeper embroiled in marital complications, exchanging one set of turbulent circumstances for another only slightly less turbulent, had not the political situation driven him into a spiritual and later, a geographical corner.

The picture of Zweig, then, between the years of the Nazi takeover and the outbreak of war in 1939 is one of negative preoccupation, a man so utterly caught up with his obsessions that he only rarely surfaced to the more prosaic levels where the time-honoured drama of two women competing for his affection was now being enacted under his own roof.

Lotte was competent, youthful, quiet and almost embarrassingly self-effacing, which latter virtue had gained her, initially with Friderike's approval, the position as Zweig's secretary. She was as unlike his wife, therefore, as it is possible to imagine, except in two significant respects. In her determination to penetrate the veils of introspection with which Zweig had surrounded himself, and her decision to dedicate her whole life to the man and his work, she was unknowingly following in her predecessor's footsteps.

Friderike, already well versed in this seemingly hopeless task, regarded her frail-looking opponent with astonishment, and her own stupidity at bringing the girl into the house to work for her husband, as now nothing short of lunacy.

Zweig's extraordinary facility, apparently unconsciously developed, for harnessing ardent and emotional feminine devotion, provided him throughout most of his life with substantial material and professional assistance, an equal quantity of the 'captivity and claustrophobia' about which he spoke, and an unwelcome amount of mental frustration.

Both Friderike and Lotte seem to have entered his life almost unnoticed by him, and when, on each occasion, he managed to wrench himself away from the period of retreat or detachment into which he had withdrawn, he found, to his amazement, a full scale emotional operation mounted in his favour. Over a period of three years, both women laid what they felt were presumably valid claims upon him, and the oft repeated but now almost childish longing to 'return to the days of student freedom' must have sounded empty even to Zweig. And as he battled to achieve this unattainable state, the bonds of personal and marital responsibility grew tighter and the more uncertain became his professional and social status within the country of his birth.

Work on *Mary Stuart* seemed to flourish under such adverse conditions, however, and while Zweig depended more and more upon the efficient and devoted Lotte for the professional aid he constantly sought, Friderike found herself playing out the rôle attempted by legions before her, though rarely with success, of the patient, loving, rejected wife.

Zweig, now working all out on the biography, indulged in what would seem to be more than an average degree of self-identification as he wrote of Mary's behaviour in the chapter entitled 'A Terrible Entanglement':

'In this cruel situation, Mary Stuart did what human beings are apt to do in such circumstances. She evaded decision, refrained from open combat, and took refuge in flight . . .'

And as Adolph Hitler's Party grew in strength, and millions in Europe quaked as they witnessed the only too familiar signs of impending persecution, Zweig immersed himself in the tragedy of the Scottish Queen, staving off the day when he, too, would be forced to choose between entering into open combat or retreating into total despair.

Chapter Seventeen

It is perhaps not inappropriate here to stop briefly and examine the singular character of Stefan Zweig as he was in middle life, a time when, in apparent contradiction of his expressed opinions, his behaviour seems to have been extraordinarily selfish.

The idealism of his youth, his persistent search for what he thought of as freedom and his unusually strong sense of compassion had now metamorphosed into an intolerable burden, eventually to drive his thinking towards a logical, predictable and long-sought solution.

It is unlikely that many of his literary or philosophical peers endured the rigours of the spirit in such comparative material comfort as Zweig. If it is desirable or useful to judge an author's output in terms of the conflict proceeding from his particular mode of literary existence, Zweig would probably be found wanting. The agonies of spiritual torture endured by Dostoyevsky, and recorded in his masterpiece *Crime and Punishment*; the frustrations born of Honoré Balzac's violent and largely unfulfilled sexual passion: these experiences were not Zweig's. Yet the evidence of the mental trials that he suffered places him alongside those whose deeds and proclamations are more obviously spectacular.

Correspondingly, he made no public confession of his short-comings and unease of conscience, which Ghandi found essential when he reached the physical point of no return; nor did he voluntarily surrender his social status, in emulation of Tolstoy's stirring of the sediment of guilt in his soul; the only way that Zweig could ease his mind was through the characters and subjects of his writing.

Paradoxically, he regarded his material wealth as a spiritual drawback, yet lacked the initiative to free himself from the burden; in a lifelong trial of his own conscience in which he was judge, chief witness and prosecuting counsel, he found much to enthrall his readers, but little to comfort his own soul.

It is of interest to compare Zweig's social conscience with that of Dostoyevsky, whose material circumstances were very much less prosperous. Take, for example, *Crime and Punishment*. Dostoyevsky stirs the hairs on the nape of the reader's neck when his impoverished hero, Raskolnikov, makes the decision to murder the old money lender for no other reason than that he sees her as unfit to live, on account of her profession, her reported cruelty, and his violent reaction to her unpleasant physical and mental make-up. Yet no judgement is forthcoming as the author investigates every aspect of the logic or insanity of such an act. At the same time, he provokes the reader and invites him to follow and to share his analysis as he switches the spotlight of hate, compassion and despair on each character in turn

In placing Raskolnikov near enough to overhear a conversation which, with its deceptive insouciance, provides both motive and final judgement in the story, he stabs directly at similarly innocuous factors which have proved instrumental in the miscarriage of justice, or even in sparking off world-shattering events.

' "Now look here," ' Raskolnikov hears the student say, as he expounds his theory to his officer companion.

' "I was joking, of course, but look at it this way; on the one hand we have a stupid, senseless, worthless, wicked and decrepit old hag, who is of no use to anybody and who actually does harm to everybody, a creature who does not know herself what she is living for and who will be dead soon, anyway . . ." ' Thus, in Raskolnikov's hypnotized presence, Dostoyevsky's two minor characters discuss the logical reasons why the old woman should be forcibly removed from the scene, without having the slightest intention of carrying out their suggestion.

' "Here you go on talking and making speeches at me, but tell me, would you kill the old woman *yourself*?"

' "Of course not! I was merely discussing the question from the point of view of justice. Personally, I'd have nothing to do with it." '

And so, in one short sentence, Dostoyevsky presents his brilliant denouement: ' "Well, in my opinion, if you're not ready to do it yourself it's not a question of justice at all . . ." '

On the simple exchange of a few chance remarks the Russian author hangs the whole of his ponderous story, and as the reader follows the tortuous debates that ensue between the various personalities, the quality and weight of the writer's lifelong involvement with the problem of survival in a hostile society is revealed.

Reaching into the depths of the subconscious, Dostoyevsky pulls out the nightmarish experience of a desire to inflict some frightful injury on the part of an essentially civilized person whose mind has been distorted by a sense of injustice:

'His [Raskolnikov's] hands were terribly weak; he could feel himself how they were growing more and more numb and lifeless every moment. He was afraid he would let go the hatchet and drop it. Suddenly he felt his head beginning to spin. There seemed no strength at all left in him as he aimed the blow . . . but the moment he brought the hatchet down all his strength returned to him . . .'

While Dostoyevsky struggles with the problem of social injustice and the eternal combat between the desires of the subconscious and the discipline of the conscious mind, Zweig importunes his readers to examine with him and through the eyes of his characters, the divine virtue of compassion, and to mourn when its absence plunges the innocent into humiliation and disaster.

Zweig's style, lighter in texture than that of Dostoyevsky, and without the occasional earthy humour that spikes Balzac's tragedies, produces none the less similarly disturbing reactions. He opens his short stories almost perfunctorily, and moves the reader swiftly into the main action, much after the fashion of Tolstoy or de Maupassant.

In *Letter from an Unknown Woman*, published as early as 1924, the story is presented through the medium of the feminine first person. Here Zweig accurately depicts the highly emotional behaviour also manifest in so many of his later character studies, both biographical and fictional.

' "My boy died yesterday. For three days and three nights I have been wrestling with Death for this frail little life . . ." ' Zweig moves the pen of a woman recalling her infatuation for an adored and thoughtless lover, who reads with growing horror of the dire results of his passion, ending with the death of a son he never knew.

Laden with romanticism, the story still fulfills the author's purpose in that both characters are portrayed with a compassion which enables the reader to see their respective actions in the most sympathetic light.

Zweig's *Unknown Woman*, similar to the anonymous character in *Amok*, is the picture of eternal woman, and as in the case of all his feminine subjects, his style is full of expertise and frequently exhibits more than the usual ring of truth:

' "But the child was all in all to me. It was yours; it was you reborn. But you must not suppose that the months of waiting passed so happily as I had dreamed . . . They were full of sorrow and care, full of loathing for the baseness of mankind. Things went hard with me . . . I had to go to the maternity hospital. The child, your son, was born there, in that asylum of wretchedness".'

And as Zweig allows the woman full emotional rein in this, her first and last letter to her lover, she swings from hasty recrimination to declarations of passion, feverish fantasy and a pathetic jumble of irrelevant reminiscences which end in a denunciation of God. R, Zweig's cautious pseudonym for the narrator, a supporting character in the story, is shown as guilt-stricken after a lavish and uncaring existence, and is left to brood over his inadequacies and to subdue what must have been an intolerable load on his conscience: 'The letter fell from his nerveless hands. He thought long and deeply. Yes, he had vague memories of a neighbour's child, of a girl, of a woman . . . He shuddered, feeling as if an invisible door had been suddenly opened, a door through which a chill breeze from another world was blowing into his sheltered room. Something welled up within him; and the thought of the dead woman stirred in his mind, bodiless and passionate, like the sound of distant music.'

Countless cinema audiences choked back the tears and sniffed their way through an adaptation of this story, without his interconnecting descriptive passages it was forced to rely more on the obvious tragedy than on the underlying emphasis of universal weakness out of which is born what he calls 'deathless love'.

Almost fifteen years after the emergence of *An Unknown Woman*, his novel, *Beware of Pity*, later to be another successful vehicle for the cinema, was published. This book, a product of the years when Zweig's own life was reaching a critical period of change, again deals with the development and dispensation of pity as opposed to the greater and more objective virtue of compassion.

Friderike had more than adequate reason for damning its advent with faint praise. Unable to dispose of the loyalty and admiration she had experienced for over twenty years, she found it difficult to accept a work in which her rival had taken so active a part. Lotte, frail but trained to competence as a secretary, and desperately keen to overcome the physical deficiency of occasional asthma attacks, typed out the entire manuscript; and Friderike would have been less than true to herself if she had not let off a few rounds of destructively critical ammunition once the novel was published.

'. . . this novel was my husband's first work whose growth I had not seen from day to day', she commented. And later she refers with some acrimony to 'the sudden conversion of the half-baked Lieutenant'—the self-declared coward who is Zweig's hero in this story of agonizing indecision.

But Lieutenant Hofmiller's attitude seems anything but 'half-baked', as he makes his passage through a web of torn loyalties. Drawn by a series of chance circumstances into the household of the wealthy landowner Herr von Kekesfalva, the young Lieutenant, garrisoned in a nearby town, becomes hopelessly entangled with Edith, Kekesfalva's crippled daughter, thereby ensuring almost certain tragedy for everyone concerned.

The theme and the timing of publication seemed inevitably to point to the association between Zweig and Lotte. The peg was there and it was easy to hang the literary work on it; and Friderike makes the statement that 'Zweig, it can be assumed, would not have chosen this theme had he foreseen the future role of the girl who had indirectly interested him in it.'

However, it will be seen that the subject of *Beware of Pity* repeats yet again Zweig's concern with physical frailty and moral weakness, and the conflict and indecision which results. The subject and his approach to it point strongly to a progression of his thought along these lines.

In the young Lieutenant's horrible predicament he again turns the light on his own disaster, and in describing how the burden of another's love and dependence can destroy personal freedom he uses Hofmiller as his mouthpiece; when, for example, the young man reads a letter declaring the helpless Edith's undying love:

' "Forgive me for the last few days, but I was distracted by the fear that I was a burden to you. Now I know for *what* and for *whom* I must get well. Never have I awaited your coming with more impatience. Always, your E." '.

' "Always." I shuddered as I read that word, which binds a person irrevocably and for all eternity. But there was no turning back now. Once more my pity had been stronger than my will. I had yielded myself up. I no longer belonged to myself'.

There are still two schools of thought on the subject of this work. Those of his acquaintances who see it in the reflection of Lotte's image and Zweig's own state of mind concerning her, declare that on both counts there was sufficient reason for its production; and those who maintain that the author's concern with what he saw as a universal rejection of the humanities reached a peak about this time, thus igniting in fictional form, the self-debilitating round of conscience-analysis to which he was interminably prone.

In Zweig's sombre introduction to the book he gives more than a clue to the factors he himself regarded as vital:

'There are two kinds of pity. One is the weak and sentimental kind, which is really no more than the heart's impatience to be rid as quickly as possible of the painful emotion aroused by the sight of another's emotions or unhappiness, that pity which is not compassion, but only an instinctive desire to fortify one's own soul against the sufferings of another; and the other, the only kind that counts, is the unsentimental but creative kind, which knows what it is about and is determined to hold out, in patience and forbearance, to the very limit of its strength and even beyond . . .'

Viewed with as much objectivity as is possible when examining a work of such disturbing emotional content, it would seem that Zweig's inherent ability to absorb and even endure the pangs and humiliations of others was approaching its climax. With each developing situation, and more especially in the period of his middle life, whether personal, political or international, he involved himself to a degree where his own psyche inevitably suffered.

As he battled to regain what had been lost, the necessary ability to manoeuvre within himself became less, and as he drew blank after blank in this fearful quest, he appeared to lose sight completely of his own spiritual and emotional freedom. Dr Friedenthal aptly describes Stefan Zweig at this time as 'over-refined—over-sensitive—thus he was a man carrying a heavy burden'.

The international reading public, or at least that part of it still unmolested by restrictive Nazi edicts, fell eagerly upon *Beware of Pity*; and it has lost little of its impact today. If the subject has the effect of discomfiting those readers who prefer neatly categorized situations that fit into a black or a white compartment, then this essentially 'grey' literary vehicle of duality and indecision will produce in them some impatience. Its semi-romantic setting—it is set in 1914—is, however, calculated to capture the unwary; and Zweig's technique, invoking an intimate revelation of a magnificent but rapidly decaying mode of European existence, invariably achieves what it sets out to do, in that the casual reader and the sceptic alike find that they have been caught up with the author's delicate literary approach and humane concern for his characters.

The final decision to leave Friderike and the Salzburg house was not accepted by Zweig as a *fait accompli* until he had subjected himself and those around him to endless soul-searing examination. Plans were made, scrapped and fresh ones begun, as he attempted to come to what could never be a satisfactory compromise for any of the three involved.

Working visits to London and to Paris, an almost impossibly strenuous literary programme (undertaken now with Lotte as companion), insulated him for a short while from the double problem confronting him. But whenever he returned briefly to Austria, the situation crystallized, for though the frontiers were not yet finally closed he knew his days as a citizen of that country were numbered.

In allowing his imagination to run riot along these lines, he saw himself already joining the increasing tribe of refugees he had watched with such apprehension only a year or so before.

The sensitiveness of the Jews to possible danger, which he later described as having increased sevenfold, was almost at saturation point in his own case. Yet still he waited, observing with no surprise the various calamities as they occurred.

Finally the nightmare of statelessness became a reality: his Austrian passport was declared void, thus making a mockery of his earlier and voluntary statement regarding the relinquishing of his Salzburg citizenship; and his attention was now split between the imbalance of his official non-existence and his doubly involved emotional life.

England, still poised politically on the brink of peace at any price, seemed like a haven in a world gone mad, as Zweig, now the owner of a temporary visa, the dreaded piece of white paper that was his 'passport for the stateless', attempted to make some sort of plans for the future.

Chapter Eighteen

Lotte Altman was of so retiring a nature, and she came into Zweig's life at so late a stage—he was after all in his sixth decade—that the association might be expected to have little effect upon him. But the events that ensued belie this supposition, and their relationship cannot be ignored in any consideration of his life and work.

It has been suggested by a close relative of Lotte (Mrs Eva Alberman), that the association between Zweig and Lotte progressed 'naturally' rather than explosively (as is frequently the case where an older man sees the opportunity to recapture a measure of his lost youth in the arms of a young girl), and in some respects the explanation would seem to account for at least part of Zweig's actions.

He was, on his own admission, seeking a refuge from an overdose of demonstrative affection and an increasing invasion of his privacy.

His lethargy had been apparent for some considerable time, and his longing to withdraw from all that Friderike had so painstakingly built up around their lives had already driven him to seek out the silence he craved in a variety of different ways. His mood at this time would appear to preclude any suggestion of a grande passion and this, together with Lotte's far from robust physical make-up, lends substance to the view that whatever her deeper emotional feelings were for Zweig, the sexual relationship between them was probably less than satisfactory.

Formed when Lotte's work as his secretary brought them into

close contact, the attachment between them appeared to move almost unnoticed into the stage where neither one saw sufficient reason to alter it course. It cannot be denied that this 'natural' progression nevertheless culminated as violently as any natural event, despite the perhaps rather defensive view that Zweig's defection and Lotte's absolute devotion to him were relatively unimportant: that neither had too much bearing on his life as an author, or on hers as the woman he eventually married.

Again, it is pointed out that such marital complications are today so commonplace as to make this particular one seem insignificant; and that with the passage of time it will seem so much more unimportant that Lotte's life can remain inviolate.

But any sequence of emotional entanglement manufactured by a group of intimately connected human beings must, in whatever age and at whatever stage in an existence it erupts, seriously affect all those concerned; and Zweig's ultimate decision to sever the connections that had bound him to his earlier life was not reached lightly, nor, when it was accomplished, was there too much rejoicing in any of the camps.

The circumstances responsible for the collapse of Zweig's first marriage seem trite enough; such situations have been the hook on which so many playwrights have hung their fictional eternal triangles that the real-life thing starts to seem like a play.

But the secretary engaged for Zweig by his own wife was not a good-time girl out for an emotional fling. On the contrary, Charlotte Elizabet took life very seriously, and her relationships even more so.

The coming together of Zweig and Lotte at such a time would seem to prove that human lives follow a predestined course, and when the socially external conditions are finally separated from the emotional, it is relatively simple to see here how one partnership dissolved in the light of another.

One can easily sense and even sympathize with Friderike's anger and rejection of Zweig's explanation that he desired to exchange his marital freedom for a 'student's freedom'. Even Zweig himself, plagued as he was at that time by a terrible sense of foreboding

186

over the future of Europe under the domination of Hitler, must have detected the hollowness of his excuse.

His interminable wanderings—he made several extended lecture tours across the United States and to many countries in South America during the immediate pre-war years—were, according to him, a flight from the hell he saw yawning before him in Europe. But 'no matter how far I withdrew from Europe, its fate accompanied me', he wrote. So it would appear almost fatuous of Zweig to offer such a lost cause as 'the freedom of youth' as a reason for his regard for Lotte. Herself a refugee from the very cause responsible for Zweig's haunting, she could no more give him freedom than Friderike, with her energetic social round and her aggressively mature outlook on life, and Zweig must have known this.

Ideally, at least from his own point of view, his existence would probably have been uninvolved by any permanent association with women. He had all the makings of an aesthete, and in his complete dedication to work, not a few of the attributes of the ascetic. Neither virtue is exactly conducive to a successful marriage, although Lotte's uncritical acceptance of all that he was or that which he lacked, would have simplified that problem. From many who remember them together comes the same comment in a variety of guises: 'You would forget that she was there . . . she seemed almost non-existent'.

If her rather plain mien and excessively quiet manner brought to mind a shadow rather than substance, Lotte's emotions, as she was later to prove beyond all doubt, were as deep and as fathomless as those of Zweig himself. It seems, therefore, that any passion in the relationship was manufactured by Lotte shortly after their first meeting, when she was overcome with an almost compulsive desire to serve the man whom she so greatly admired. This, as I have remarked, was the only quality she shared with Friderike. The difference between their characters was utterly to Lotte's advantage: while Friderike had allowed her love to become too obvious and eventually too heavy a burden for him to support, Lotte avoided that trap by modifying to some extent the depth of her natural feelings.

Zweig had been complaining for some time about the tedious social obligations with which he seemed to be surrounded whenever he made appearances at the Salzburg house. During the early 1930s these had become increasingly rare, and after the indignity of the official search in 1934, practically non-existent, although Friderike stubbornly stuck to her guns and maintained her adored 'open house'.

To be in Lotte's presence, then, with her physical and mental humility, her anonymity and preference for the background and her willingness to exist in almost total silence if this was demanded of her, must have seemed to Zweig rather like being left alone in a deserted theatre foyer once the performance has started.

His own desire to participate in any social affair was lessening; and although he frequently and dutifully appeared at the various literary and diplomatic functions to which he was invited in London or Paris, he did so with much misgiving.

From a fellow Viennese, a young doctor then studying in London, and himself shortly to be caught up in the consequences of Hitler's policies, comes a striking assessment of Stefan Zweig at that time.

With typically misplaced optimism in the face of almost certain disaster, the diplomatic functions at the Austrian Embassy in London were still operating at their usual brilliant and intellectual level, and when Baron Frankenstein, the Austrian Ambassador, summoned the faithful to attend, some of the country's old magnificence was relived, although those who attended probably knew in their hearts that they themselves would shortly be adding to the numbers of the ever-lengthening queue of the stateless.

Robert Kahane, along with the majority of his fellow Austrians, was a devotee of 'Vienna's man of letters', and was thrilled at the prospect of meeting Stefan Zweig at one of the Baron's international gatherings. As he was introduced to the excessively quiet, ultra-polite, middle-aged man, his mind flashed back to the characters and the stories, so vital and tense, which had captured his imagination from the first.

As he made the requisite noises and tried to digest the fact that he was really face to face with the author whose works all Europe had come to know either through the medium of his books, plays or cinema adaptations of his short stories, he felt that beneath the polite exterior there lay a great unrest, so deep a preoccupation that it needed only a little added perception to see that Zweig's spiritual self had even then apparently some difficulty in remaining within its mortal frame.

Kahane, separated from Zweig by almost three decades, but bound to him by the deeper ties of race and heritage, seemed to glimpse in that lonely figure—he always appeared on the fringe of a gathering rather than in its midst—the entire panorama of Europe's past, its tragedies and splendour, and in dark and sombre outline, the picture of the years to come.

It was as if Zweig's presence emphasized his own impending exile; and today he recalls, much as Zweig himself was to recall on many subsequent occasions, the optimism and brilliance of Europe's diplomats and intellectuals, who persistently turned a deaf ear whenever the name of Adolph Hitler had the temerity to crop up.

During the inevitable and endless discussions and harangues between himself and Friderike, he had already asked for a divorce, but had not yet pressed the issue too strongly; he was still teetering on a middle course which only proved its uselessness with the passage of time.

'There came three years of indecision,' Friderike records, 'during which Stefan wavered in his desire to spare one or the other woman.' Events, time, circumstances, all had changed, but Zweig was unchanging in his lifelong indecisiveness; he wanted, and at the same time he did not want.

Friderike gives the impression that the ashes of a great passion lay behind them, and that in Zweig's association with Lotte she saw a rekindling of the flames—though, to salve the remnants of her own pride, she implies that the new fire would necessarily be of lesser intensity. In her grief or, even worse, her disbelief of what had happened, she tends (like any woman in such a position) to overdramatize the delights of her married life with Zweig.

189

It had in fact been some time since her husband had shown any real affection for all she held so dear, although his friendship undoubtedly persisted to the end. Perhaps Lotte, though she ultimately married the man she worshipped, was the loser.

Zweig's attitude to marriage in middle life appears to favour a working partnership rather than the fulfilment of the many obligations of nuptial responsibility. The companionship of a woman was obviously desirable to him, although, as Friderike had discovered, even this was governed by his limitations. The compassion to which many people attribute his attachment to Lotte may well have been subliminal; what is certain is that he discovered in her professional efficiency an answer to the many problems connected with his working life.

Did he, then, ever realize the true extent of her giving? Did he perhaps take for granted the final gift of her life—to which he does not refer in his Declaration, written just before their suicide. Did he see in Lotte a fortuitous gift to the domestic and literary scene, someone who could quietly and efficiently take over from previous secretaries, several of whom had crossed swords with Friderike, making life intolerable for the peace-seeking Zweig. His tyranny where work was involved was notorious. The mildness and humility were absent if plans and work projects were upset, and during the early thirties this was more often the case than not. His official commitments took him travelling ceaselessly around Europe, avoiding Salzburg like the plague, and only returning when specific family matters demanded his attention. He found disorganization intolerable, and his fretfulness and irritability increased. It was only after he had turned with relief to this quiet girl who seemed to anticipate his every thought that he was forced to acknowledge that the situation in which he found himself was not a literary compromise but an emotional one, involving the lives of two women.

Friderike, in her youth, had fallen madly in love and had deserted her husband for him. Lotte had repeated the exercise and ultimately was to surrender her life up to him; yet in accepting the devotion of both women, Zweig had blindly followed his own earthly existence as he saw it, grateful no doubt for the substantial material assistance each had given in her different sphere: inordinately resentful when official and social objections to his union with Lotte were raised; and possibly ignorant of the exact depth and enduring quality of the love each woman held for him.

If Lotte's devotion to Zweig seems exaggerated, subsequent events prove that in this respect, at least, she was unique. So long as Zweig breathed, Lotte lived, and when he arrived at the decision to end his life, hers ceased simultaneously.

Chapter Nineteen

For almost three centuries biographers, seduced by the personality of Mary Stuart and the web of intrigue surrounding her, have sought to reconstruct her personal and historical drama. So powerful an effect indeed does her life have on any author whose imagination it captures, that one of her most recent biographers (Antonia Fraser) confessed unashamedly that the tears were pouring from her eyes as she studied the letters and documents concerned with the last years of Mary's existence.

Working on this particular subject appeared to have a profound effect on Zweig. Emotionally, his own life was at a crossroads, and although he had decided to abandon, at least temporarily, any further historical studies, declaring 'I had had enough of biographies', his decision was reversed without further ado once his mind had seized upon the Mary Stuart project.

Begun shortly after Lotte arrived in 1933, and completed partly with her professional assistance as secretary during the following eighteen months or so, the work appears particularly significant on several counts.

As a study in feminine psychology it reveals Mary's entire personality at all levels of her emotional development; it also shows the author to his biographer as having an almost uncannily correct insight into the behaviour patterns of a woman under the various stresses to which she may be subjected. At the same time, the writing discloses much of Zweig's own attitude to the passions governing the actions and reactions of human beings.

Social, political and emotional crises are reviewed with strict objectivity as he examines the conditions which govern them. With perhaps less objectivity and considerably more compassion he observes the results when such conditioning breaks down before what he 'calls an elemental emotional force'. 'When mental states are thus intensified', he writes, describing the passion of Mary and Bothwell, 'it is foolish to scrutinise, for logic and rationality, the actions of those in whom they rage, since it is of the essence of uncontrollable impulses to be irrational. Passions, like illnesses, can neither be accused or excused; they can only be described with ever renewed astonishment not untinged with horror in face of the elemental forces which disclose themselves from time to time in nature and not infrequently in human beings, violent discharges of energy which are not amenable to the measuring rod of customary human laws . . .'

This biography is a product of Zweig's maturity, and is handled with a degree of sensitivity even deeper than that employed in many of his previous works. While carefully assessing the circumstances surrounding the central personality of the drama, and allowing for the often necessarily extreme political, diplomatic and human manoeuvring practised at that time, he returns compulsively to the original theme of an overriding compassion which had begun to dominate his thinking.

Of Mary's uninhibited sexual passion for Bothwell and the latter's reaction to it, he writes, 'Their expression does not belong to the realm of conscious but to the subconscious impulses of man, and is quite outside the circle of his personal responsibility. It is just as senseless to sit in judgement upon an individual who happens momentarily to be a prey to an overwhelming passion, as it would be to call a thunderstorm to account.'

Where Friderike saw as irrational Stefan's decision to leave Salzburg and dispose of everything connected with their life, so in the Mary Stuart biography, Zweig unhesitatingly rationalized the Scottish Queen's actions: 'With eyes closed and ears stopped, drawn on as it were by a magnet, Mary moved along her path towards disaster . . .'

His deepening understanding of the psyche and the whole range of emotions controlling it tempted him to explore his subjects from this angle, and in this vehicle he found abundant material, not only in the principal personalities of the two queens, but in those he refers to as the 'darkling characters' surrounding them.

By and large Zweig's works seem to be chronologically in step with own conscious progression from the mechanically psychological to the wholly spiritual. *Mary Stuart*, for instance, deals specifically with the mutilation of the self through elemental emotional forces; whereas the indefatigable Benjamin of the Biblical Legend *The Buried Candelabrum* trudges on relentlessly, all passion sent, towards his spiritual goal. At the time of his absorption with *Mary Stuart* Zweig's passion, whether mental or physical, was as much a part of him as his own hand. It was perhaps only after the completion of this work that a refining process from the emotional to the spiritual took place. His approach to the complicated human issues in *Mary Stuart* and his observations on the results bear witness to the image and personality he himself projected at that time.

While, for example, he found himself appalled at the thought of tyranny, fear and humilation, he concentrated on the problems of those caught up in their backlash. Similarly, in expounding his theories and beliefs on the tragedies of sexual and emotional entanglements, he identifies himself still as one of society's moral delinquents.

With so accurate and sensitive a touch that he could well have been reflecting on his own problem, he declares, '. . . so at length Mary Stuart threw off her intolerable inertia. No longer did she care what the world thought of her, or whether her actions were wise or foolish. Movement had become essential to her, speedier and speedier movement, to outrun the warning, and the threatening voices. On! On! Anything now but stillness and reflection, for self-communings forced her to recognize that no skill could save her. One of the mysteries of the human mind is that, for a brief time, speed can overcome anxiety. Just as a coachman, who feels and hears the bridge breaking down beneath his carriage, flogs his horses into the gallop which can alone rescue him from the danger, so Mary Stuart spurred the black charger of her destiny into despair, hoping to outrun her thoughts, to escape from her own criticism. Neither to think nor to know nor to hear nor to see any more; only on and on into frenzy!'

It was Zweig's own increasingly obsessive desire to run, and the continual nightmare of a horror that only he could perceive, that kept him physically on the move even then, and his mind perpetually restless as it grappled with the images it produced. Just as in Mary Stuart's case, these mental pictures were not figments of their owner's imagination, but positive constructions of future calamities.

Much of Zweig's own foreknowledge is reflected in his lucid description of Mary's appalling dilemma; and the Jungian 'black charger of her destiny' was a familiar enough figure to him during this period of his life.

Describing his thoughts as he awaited the long anticipated news that a state of war existed between Germany and England, he wrote: 'My destiny lay in their hands, no longer in mine. They destroyed or spared us helpless ones, they permitted freedom or compelled slavery, and for millions they determined peace or war . . . And there in my room I sat like everybody else, defence-less as a fly, helpless as a snail, while life and death, my innermost ego, and my future were at stake, the forming thoughts in my brain, plans born and unborn, my waking and sleeping, my will, my possessions, my whole being . . .'

Here, although his words convey a passivity he clearly did not fully experience, he unconsciously repeats the manner in which he had described Mary Stuart's lengthy imprisonment following upon the comparatively short years in which her emotional and sexual passions had free rein, he writes: 'The monotonous procession of the days, the weeks and the months was marked by the circling of the sun, the moon and the stars. Night followed day and day followed night, summing up the months and the years. Kingdoms passed and were renewed; kings rose and fell; . . . Women grew up, bore children, and withered. Only this one life was perpetually in the shadows, cut off from its roots, no longer bearing blossom or fruit . . .'

In dealing with Mary Stuart's involved and at times almost incredible affairs, Zweig's observations of a woman in thrall to a lover are accurate enough to produce a mental squirming in any feminine reader if she is honest with herself. Of her flight from Edinburgh with Bothwell, her newly acquired husband and murderer of the youthful Darnley, he writes: 'During the night, hastily dressing herself as a boy, she mounted her horse and, soon joined her husband, rode with him to Dunbar, leaving all else in order to live or die with Bothwell'. And on the desertion of Lething, Mary's last loyal follower, Zweig comments: 'Mary was unteachable; she could be neither intimidated nor warned. In this astonishing woman, danger served only to intensify the courage that gave her greatest follies a romantic glamour . . .'

With a penetration rarely forthcoming from any member of the male species, Zweig records the behaviour of a woman caught between discipline and passion; and Friderike, who was at the time of publication caught up in her own great disillusionment at Zweig's defection, was later to write: 'He strongly emphasised Mary's womanhood, dominated by an elemental indomitable natural force'. A commendably restrained comment in view of the situation between them at the time; although the clarity of Zweig's understanding of the passionately involved characters in the work must have stung her *amour propre*.

She was essentially a woman who followed her own heart; her husband's grasp on this specific subject and at such a time in their own lives, could only have added to the irony which moved her to write: 'He could fortify others . . . but he could not fortify himself'. Zweig, the observer and biographer, objectively capable of appraising the cause-and-effect process responsible for the entanglements that came under his scrutiny, was as helpless 'as a snail' where his personal life and relation to society were concerned.

Time, as he well knew, was running out. Political events were rapidly reaching a climax, and it was now a foregone conclusion that Hitler's demands would prove insatiable, despite the go-slow methods of British politicians. Austria would inevitably be annexed by Germany. Many of Zweig's own circle had already left for America; and after several hasty visits to Austria, sandwiched between working spells in London and France and a hectic tour of South America, he had for once brought his lengthy deliberations to a conclusion, and practically demanded that Friderike should sell the Saltzburg house, lock, stock and barrel. Her reaction to this sudden and she guessed, final decision to break away, was one of horror: 'And yet it had to be sold, like a bit of junk, to anyone offering an acceptable price . . .', she moaned, and indeed her nostalgia, though heavily laden with sentiment— 'untouched our bed from which we had listened to the rustling leaves in the ancient ash-trees outside'—seems justifiable, as the old house, with its romantic and exciting aura of artistic fame, representing the sum total for which she had gambled her entire existence, was knocked down to the first bidder.

They were manifestly at opposite mental poles now; Zweig's melancholy anticipation of catastrophe saw a partial solution in physical flight and mental detachment, whereas by that time Friderike's down-to-earth attitude recognized the writing on the wall as clearly as any politically insecure individual, and it dictated that she should stay put to watch developments. Yet her refusal to believe that such national disaster could separate, rather than weld even more firmly together, the lives of her husband and herself, was perhaps typically, romantically naïve. Even Lotte's presence was not yet fully recognized as a direct threat to her marital security; and she later went so far as to countenance an extraordinary suggestion of Stefan's that the three of them should live together in a sort of aesthetic benevolence.

The experiment, doomed under any circumstances, took place in London, where Stefan and Lotte had embarked upon what was to prove a perpetual house-moving process. Friderike decided to tolerated the situation but on a temporary basis only.

Next to Zweig vacillations and Lotte's ethereal endurance Friderike erupts as full-blood and female, and hopelessly ill-equipped to deal with these two, drawn together by the obscure strands of their introspectiveness.

The circumstances and personalities of this situation while differing widely from those in Zweig's biographies of the time, nevertheless find a parallel in the obsessive behaviour of the characters whom he chose and the sometimes incomprehensible manner in which their plans are followed through.

Over all lies the shadow of disaster, and Zweig's comments on Mary Stuart show more than a hint of his usual prescience. While writing of the Scottish Queen's unbridled emotions, he suggests that her devious means justified the end as she saw it; and in describing her type of love, so violent that it casts out fear, he may well have utilized what he had already discovered in Lotte's singular attitude to him and to his own now negative philosophy. 'Such women's love and passion is a concentrated extract, their ardours are compressed into one convulsive episode, they drink the cup to the dregs, and for them there exists no salvation and no way back. A supreme example of this kind of love, of love that is truly heroic, that allows passion to have its fullest range, and to exhaust the emotions even should this lead to self-destruction . . . '

In the light of such statements and of Lotte's proven and 'truly heroic' love for him, it still remains a matter for speculation whether Zweig recognized the magnitude of her offering, or whether he had withdrawn so far from reality that he merely accepted it.

Mary Stuart, the precursor of *Beware of Pity*, appears to be a direct literary product of Zweig's weighty and personal intro-spection, and in dealing with the ill-fated characters, he reveals even more plainly than through the words of the novel his inner-most thoughts on the questions of life and love and death.

There is no opposition to the suggestions that Zweig was continually flirting with the idea of suicide, and the German troops who overran the Austrian border in 1938 provided ample reason for considering it, if indeed he needed one. Even so, the final decision was delayed long enough for him to savour to the full the bitterness he had for so long awaited.

To be dubbed, first, 'stateless', then 'enemy alien'—these signs of political stigma were for Zweig as inevitable and as final as any martyr's stake, although he always abhorred the use of such words in connection with his own existence.

With the same masochistic relief that he had experienced when his books were publicly burnt in the streets of Germany, he now embraced the hateful condition of being homeless. The fact that, shortly after arriving in England with Lotte, he purchased a lovely old house on Lyncombe Hill, in the city of Bath, was a relatively empty gesture which only served to emphasise in his mind the futility of his own life.

As he attempted—with, on his own admission, only half his consciousness—to settle down in this relatively remote spot, the agony of depression closed in upon him, divorcing him from hope, but at the same time providing the energy which was to produce *Beware of Pity* and several other of his more notable works.

Chapter Twenty

The period of extreme mental turbulence and political pressures in which Zweig was caught during the years between 1934 and 1939, sought expression, as always, through the medium of his work. After the publication of *Mary Stuart*, in 1935, came *Castellio against Calvin*, a shorter but pungent indictment of religious dictatorship. The bitterness that shows through some of the writing here is undoubtedly a reflection of his attitude and reaction to the racial strife currently surging around him.

As in *Mary Stuart*, he expresses an intense sympathy with those caught up in the uncontrollable impulses of sexual and emotional passion, so in this less well-known biography of two men destined to champion opposing causes he draws a parallel between conditions in sixteenth-century Switzerland under the domination of Calvinistic hypocrisy and righteousness, and the suppression of free thought in Germany under Hitler.

Personal and political insecurity influenced him in the choice of many of his subjects, and while he suggests that the reader's tolerance be exercised in favour of all those bedevilled by extremes of passion, he condemns out of hand any situation that results from an emotion directed purely towards the exercise of political or militaristic power.

Mary, Darnley, Bothwell, even Elizabeth, all received a partial dispensation from Zweig for their fallibility. Whereas Calvin, for all his theological brilliance, obviously horrifies his biographer as creature less than human; and Zweig can find little in the French reformer's logical appraisal of the Gospels and harsh application of religious dogma to offset the violence perpetrated in his name.

As he describes Calvin's dissimulation, the reader senses the nausea and loathing he felt for a man who could climb into the pulpit and raise his eyes to God after submitting the pathetic Servetus, his declared opponent, to roast by inches at the stake. Zweig's words almost tumble over themselves as he relates one of the most horrible of all recorded public burnings, and incurring, no doubt, scholarly disapproval he does not baulk at dramatic presentation, which produces a powerful reaction in even the casual reader, when describing events leading up to and resulting in tragedy and disaster.

With the same degree of intensity that he used to record his revulsion of all tht dictatorship meant to him as Hitler swept to power in Europe, he censures the mental servitude in which the public was held by Calvin's fanatical preaching; and the unrestrained writing devoted to the ghastly murder of Servetus is reminiscent of his style when recalling the treatment meted out to the Jews under Nazi rule: 'I thought that I had foreboded all the terror that would come to pass when Hitler's dream of hate should come true and he triumphantly occupy Vienna, the city which had turned him off, poor and a failure, in his youth. But how timid, how petty, how lamentable my imagination, all human, imagination, in the light of the inhumanity which discharged itself on that March 13th, 1938, when Austria, and Europe with it, fell prey to sheer violence.'

The subtitle *The Right to Heresy* of the original version of *Castellio against Calvin* indicates clearly that Zweig regards the right of free thought, even if it labels a man a heretic, as fully justified when oppression reigns; and when any dogma associated with the evils of racism is rampant, he elevates this basic right to the indestructible realm of the spirit.

His absolute damning of Calvin's edicts discloses yet again what has already been established, that he considered material or political gain worthless when achieved by the impoverishment of the spirit.

If, as some maintain, Calvin's presence in Europe in the six-teenth century provided succeeding generations with certain mater-ial and religious benefit, Stefan Zweig, for one, failed to recognise their existence.

The iron grip in which the Calvins and the Knoxes and the Luthers had held Europe was again evident in the twentieth century; and just as a Calvinistic God or a Lutheran God demanded eternal salvation for His chosen subjects and eternal damnation for those opposing Him, so did Adolph Hitler separate people, pro-pounding the theory of eternal damnation for those he styled 'non-Aryan'. The same song but with a different tune; and Zweig, acutely and inherently sensitive to historical persecution and racism, turns his pen on Calvin's gross egotism and inhumanity with almost as much violence as the reformer himself exhibited in his dealing with 'heretics.'

In describing the appalling death of Servetus Zweig seems deliberately bent upon producing a horror reaction in his readers; and that such an atrocity is made the focal point of this biography confirms the opinion of many who knew him that he was obsessed with the historical barbarity of mankind, while yet clinging to the belief that ultimate salvation might be achieved through individual acts of compassion.

The Right to Heresy portrays much of Zweig's attitude to twen-tieth-century European political and racial dogma. He precedes the Introduction to the book with a quote from Castellio's writing: 'Future generations will wonder why, after so splendid a dawn, we were forced back into Cimmerian darkness'—which echoes, almost word for word, his own cry from the political wilderness of 1939: 'Only now, since they were swept up like dirt in the streets and heaped together, the bankers from their Berlin palaces, and the sextons from the synagogues . . . the philosophy professors, the baptised and the semi-Jews . . . Jews forced into a community of interest . . . They were driven out of lands but without a land to go to. They were held balmeful but denied means of expiation. And they stared at each other with smarting eyes: 'Why me?' 'Why you?' 'Why any of us?' And none could answer.'

The burden the Zweig carried within him was daily increasing; and Lotte's companionship, purchased at a high emotional cost, tended to increase rather than dilute his pessimism. Despite the decline in his affection for Friderike he felt acutely guilty now that he had come to the point of leaving her.

Friderike, with her more earthy approach and animation, would seem to have been ideally equipped to survive the disenchantment of a lengthy marriage; but her zest for life and, as Stefan saw it, misplaced optimism, eventually wearied and drained him. He did not *want*, nor would he accept, the comfort of those around him, whom he saw foolishly geared to a state of perpetual hope. In Lotte's physical nearness he found nothing to intrude upon his daily working life, which occupied him now to a near fever pitch of activity; nor did he meet with opposition or interference from her, whatever his mood.

If Lotte had set out to become Stefan's *doppelganger*, she certainly fulfilled her mission. After the turmoil accompanying his break with Friderike had gradually subsided, it seems possible that Zweig's clamour for the freedom he desired was in part granted, although it now becomes apparent that freedom meant for him the absolute right to pursue his expressed line of thought, even if this lay contrary to the majority of determined optimists, and to exercise his free will in determining the span of his own existence. In every respect Lotte have her partner *carte blanche* to follow his star. If a state of melancholy seized him, or a feverish bout of uninterrupted work threatened his health, he was now confident that he would not be overwhelmed with good advice or belaboured by unwelcome bursts of hearty encouragement. She accepted every variation in her partner's physical and mental behaviour and although her own health was far from robust she appeared to gain renewed vigour as she accompanied Zweig on his interminable wanderings, or sat beside him hour upon hour in her capacity as secretary and literary assistant. Stoically she survived incredible stints of fatiguing travel and prolonged working sessions, while developing the ability to accept what even then she must have recognised as inevitable personal disaster.

The partnership (eventually cemented by marriage), was evidently a period of treading water for both of them, and it was their acceptance of this state which enabled them to survive in a physical contact whose closeness only contributed to the production of some of Zweig's finest work.

Before deciding on Bath for their *pied à terre*, they had wandered and lived, as Zweig himself describes it, 'spatially' in various parts of Britain. And as Adolph Hitler's storm-troops violated the peace and the people of Poland, and Benito Mussolini added to his dictator's laurels by intervention in the Spanish Civil War, now in its third disastrous year, Zweig withdrew uneasily into the relative calm of the Somerset hills. Recent memories of Franco's Spain, glimpsed en route during one of his trips to South America, had convinced him that here, as elsewhere, mankind was following a policy of hate set out by an almost unprecedented number of self-styled dictators. Francisco Franco, Benito Mussolini and above all, Adolph Hitler, were the devil incarnate and in triplicate, as he saw it; and nothing could save the human species from self-extermination under such men.

As friends tried to reason with him he would brush aside their arguments impatiently. 'Ah! You don't know. You haven't seen these people as I have . . . it's hopeless.!' he would counter any suggestion from his friend, Richard Friedenthal, whom he had met again in London. 'But, Stefan, wait. Don't do anything hasty. Just wait to see how things will turn out. It may not be so bad as you imagine', the philosophical Friedenthal, himself later to be a victim of Nazi bombing, would say trying to calm down the agitation. But Zweig was not even listening, seeing yet again the visions of humiliation and horror that continually passed before his eyes.

And so, while the others dug in mentally and prepared to wait and see which way the fanatic in Germany would leap, Zweig moved with Lotte and those few worldly possessions that he had rescued from Salzburg, into a temporary lodging in Lansdowne Terrace in the elegant city of Bath.

Meanwhile history had been unpleasantly repeating itself in the length of time, the volumes of official correspondence and the nerve wracking indecision that accompany any legal breaking and re-making of marriages.

The long and involved haul Friderike had endured before officially becoming Stefan's wife had now to be lived through again; and although she had once wrung from her husband the promise that he would not remarry if and when she granted him his freedom, she must have known even then not to trust such a declaration.

Stefan and Lotte, resembling Mary and Bothwell in their singleness of purpose, stopped their ears and shut their eyes to any recriminations that might follow; and Zweig himself, far more concerned with the international disaster unfolding in Europe, appeared to regard his remarriage as a necessary move in the pattern as a whole, a completed step in what he now saw as the final stage of his mortal journey.

In reviewing the output and content of Zweig's literary work, or at least that part of it which illustrates specific areas of thought, it has been possible to compare it to a large extent with the circumstances and mental development controlling his life. But with what was now an acknowledged self-awareness of his own spiritual being, Zweig's moral behaviour pattern, that is, the depths of melancholy into which he sank, refusing to see or unable to envisage a glimmer of hope, contradicted both the style and chosen subjects of his work at this time, as well as presenting a conflicting picture of his own personality.

A man without hope, who could effortlessly forecast today's events yesterday, so vivid was the sense of his precognition, he figuratively canonized the subjects of his Biblical Legends for their virtues of faith and endurance. Faith in God, and in the spirit of God in man, occupied much of his thinking, and was responsible now for rescuing many of his subjects from extinction. It will be remembered that Dr B. in *The Royal Game*, one of Zweig's last works, epitomizes spiritual survival, and contrasts with extermination of others whom the author allowed to perish under incomparably easier circumstances.

After the emergence of *Beware of Pity* in 1939, Stefan Zweig captured his reading public by preaching the gospel of hope though endurance, while personally practising a see-saw of conflicting and contradictory philosophy. *Amerigo—Comedy of Errors*, one of Zweig's last works, illustrates this point. The book is written in forthright style, even daring to be mildly humorous on the somewhat ridiculous mix-up of names and claims of the New World discovery by so unlikely a person as a 'grocer'. Amerigo Vespucci and his casual voyage across virtually uncharted oceans obviously amused Zweig by the sheer inconsequence of such an undertaking; and in the final naming of the huge continent after so lowly a personage as Vespucci, he finally allowed a scarcely recognizable levity to show through his writing.

The English and their philosophy were alternatively disowned and embraced by Zweig. He regarded as utter stupidity, as did Lotte, their inability to see the moral danger which confronted them; and yet, as he permitted himself, often somewhat grudg--ingly, to witness what for him was a completely alien attitude of 'wait and see' and 'there'll always be an England', he found himself longing on occasion to become part of this absurd, heroic and slightly phlegmatic army of civilians-cum-soldiers.

But the pattern of ancient knowledge was unalterably set, and Zweig and his adoring Lotte, could find only temporary respite in the midst of a rural city unwillingly geared to the activity of world war.

As the Prime Minister of England, Neville Chamberlain, broadcast to the nation on the 3rd September 1939, on the breakdown of his 'peace at any price' talks with Adolph Hitler, at the same time declaring that a state of war existed between Germany and England, the whole western world trembled.

Three days later, on the 6th September, Zweig presented himself with Lotte at the Register Office in Bath, armed with a special licence and the now positive foreknowledge that he would complete, if possible, the literary programme to which he had committed himself and then, with his young wife, make preparation to sever the threads of what he considered to be a now useless mortal existence.

206

It is not unreasonable to assume that the fissure in his personality was now established and operating beyond his conscious control. That where before he was able to discipline negative thought patterns, the authority to do this had now been withdrawn.

Stefan Zweig, now aged fifty-seven and his bride, Charlotte Elizabet, thirty-one, returned to 'Rosemount', the house on Lyncombe Hill that Stefan had spotted during his earlier travels through Somerset and that he had just purchased in Lotte's name. The time they were to spend in Bath was a peaceful one but both knew it held the promise only of a temporary refuge.

Chapter Twenty-one

As far as Britain was concerned, the ersatz peace—or war—which followed upon the heels of Chamberlain's announcement, came as something of an anti-climax to all those who had heard the solemn pronouncement.

As night followed day and weeks became months, and still no warning sounded the approach of enemy aircraft, the tension inevitably lifted, although everyone realized that the pause could only mean a breathing space before battle between English and German troops was actually joined.

With horror the British public digested the facts as they were revealed now through many official sources. Chamberlain's appeasement policy, which had deluded into a false security all those who believed that Hitler would call a halt to his demands after the occupation of Austria in 1938, was flung back at the seventy-year-old-Prime Minister. After German troops had overrun the independent republic of Czechoslovakia in the spring of 1939, even those still loyal to Chamberlain's policy felt unease at the contempt with which the Nazi leader had first broken the Munich Agreement of 1938, in order to 'legalise' the occupation of that country, then violated the non-aggression pact signed with Russia in 1939, by occupying Poland.

The full impact of Hitler's militaristic demands was barely realized, before German troops, shortly aided and abetted by the Italian army under Benito Mussolini, had swallowed up vast slices of Europe.

France's so-called 'anti-aggression' front, a hasty but inadequate build-up of weapons and armed forces, was now assembled. This, plus an almost blind faith in the hopelessly out-of-date fortifications of the Maginot Line, its original strength reduced by expansion and lack of adequate military support, to the slenderest of defences, was destined to crumble almost as soon as the Nazis set their sights on France.

The news coming out of Poland was now almost unbelievable. To the majority of those caught up in the beginning of hostilities, war was one thing, but racial annihilation, which was now unleashed by Nazi atrocity, was another.

Reports of the establishment of ghettos, and the herding together of vast numbers of Jews throughout Poland for shipment to concentration camps and medical experimental centres, went far beyond any of the so-called permissive laws of war.

Hitler's policy of creating a race of Aryans throughout Europe was now fully declared. What had begun in Germany and Austria in the early thirties, the burning of Jewish literature, the sporadic arrests and humiliations, had been an indication of what was to follow; although even the most sensitive observer probably never imagined the lengths and the horrors to which Hitler and his ministers would carry out the policy of racial purity.

Already the word 'refugee' was part of the everyday vocabulary. Those who had managed to escape from Czechoslovakia were already recounting to an incredulous British public the establishment of such machinery as the concentration camp and the gas chamber; and with eyewitness accounts of the razing of Warsaw and appalling stories of mass extermination of the population, British phlegm underwent a dramatic change. This man, Hitler, parodied in song, lampooned by cartoonists and largely ignored by the English as a crackpot, had at last shown his true colours.

The wave of anger that swept through the nation, gearing it at last into violent action, was marked by Zweig, as he worked and moved amongst the people, with something like pity. What he had foreseen for so long had come to pass; and the western world was set back on its heel in shocked surprise and military unpreparedness.

A last-minute decision took Zweig to France, just before the final blow of occupation fell. Words failed him as he recalled the inefficiency and haphazard fortification, evident even to the layman, and doubly so to his discerning eyes. 'These French troops—they are all there, lounging around, smoking, laughing. They simple do not realise that this is no ordinary man, this Hitler. He is evil. And the Maginot Line . . .!'

An attempt to counter the mounting apprehension was again met with a rebuff, as Richard Friedenthal once more strove to calm his friend's obvious terror; but he knew that he could offer no other consolation than that they were all virtually in the same boat; and the lucky ones, those who had managed to get out before the Nazis consumed all of Europe, must somehow try to weld themselves together and combine forces with the British and French in an effort to combat and finally overcome such evil.

Geographically, their situation in Bath was more than appealing, and as yet none of the ugliness of war had touched the city or the surrounding countryside; and as Friderike remarks, the city must have reminded Stefan in many ways of Salzburg. The rolling hills and cluster of Georgian houses nestling in their folds, reflected a peace which Zweig longed to accept; but he realized that he must not be seduced by such calm and beauty. He knew that Somerset, for all its rural detachment, was destined, with the rest of England, to fall beneath the Nazi war machine, just as the lovely towns and cities of Austria had done. In imagination he saw it all happening, and the nightmare of knowing rarely left him.

Rosemount, with its mellowed stone and spacious rooms, accepted its latest owners with the philosophy born of long entry. The two rather oddly assorted individuals who were to take up residence had caused a minor flurry in the local community, and in between the unpleasant duty of reading press reports and listening to radio communiqués, the name of Stefan Zweig was heard on all the local lips. '. . . Very famous, you know . . . the Austrian author—a refugee—probably Jewish . . . Wonder why he's come to live here . . .' '. . . And the girl. Very quiet. Looks ill. . . .!' Then, with typical British summing up of a barely guessed-at situation: 'Ah well . . . they seem a very nice couple. Hope they'll be happy here . . .'

Not until after the actual marriage ceremony, however, did the residents of Bath, and specifically those around Lyncombe Hill, realize that the rather quaintly attired middle-aged man and the pale, excessively shy girl had only just then become legally man and wife.

Was it now in order to offer congratulations—to rejoice, if indeed the opportunity arose . . .? But this is one time when British reserve met its match. Stefan and Lotte invited no expression of rural enthusiasm or county celebrations to mark their wedding day; and it was only when a few paper rose petals were discovered by chance beneath some cushions that word went out that what had until then been suspected was apparently true.

The rustle of excitement was soon dampened by the increasingly depressing news of the war situation; but as Stefan and his wife settled into the house, their presence was treated as something of an honour, while bringing home to the local people the desperate situation of refugees now pouring into England over the borders of occupied European countries.

Zweig recalls with immense nostalgia those first few months in England. 'I withdrew to Bath, and to Bath in particular, because that city reflects more faithfully and impressively than any other in England a more peaceful century, the eighteenth, to the reposed eye; it is the city, too, where many of the best men of England's glorious literature, Fielding above all, achieved their best . . . But how painful the contrast between this gentle countryside, endowed with a mild beauty, and the growing unrest of the world and of my reflections . . .'

The longing to return to the earlier days of his life, and the knowledge that nothing past can ever be recaptured, permeates his reminiscences. Just as July of 1914 was the most beautiful that I can remember in Austria, so challengingly beautiful was this August of 1939 in England. Again the soft milken-blue sky like a heavenly tabernacle, again this benign sunshine over meadows and woods besides an indescribable splendour of flowers—the great equable breathing of peace over the earth while mankind girded itself for war. The madness seemed as unbelievable as at that former time in the face of this quiet, persistent exuberant flowering, this rhythmical calm that seemed to take joy in itself, in the valleys of Bath, whose loveliness reminded me strangely of that Baden countryside in 1914.'

The same sun that bathed the meadows and hills of Somerset during the late summer and early autumn of 1939 was to glint off the steely bulk of the barrage balloons floating above the coast of England and cross-crossing the 'gentle countryside' with their comical, ominous presence.

British troops joined their French allies in preparing to dig in behind the now publicly maligned Maginot Line; and theatre audiences rocked with laughter as comedians sang out the rollicking choruses of 'We're going to hang out our washing on the Siegfried Line'. The British mentality was becoming more of a mystery to Stefan Zweig with each day that passed; and yet even he, plagued by a mental agony that few are called upon to endure, found himself observing with grudging admiration this seeming idiocy in face of mortal crisis. Alien, misplaced as it was, he admitted to those few with whom he shared a confidence that he realized its ultimate qualities while abhorring its apparent initial slowness to react. 'Once more I wandered down to the town to have a last look at peace. It lay calmly in the noonday sun and seemed no different to me from other days. People went their accustomed way in their usual manner. There were no signs of hurry, they did not crowd talkatively together. Their behaviour had a Sabbath-like quality and at a certain moment I asked myself: "Can it be that they don't know it yet?" But they were English, and practised in restraining their emotions. They needed no flags and drums, clamour and music to strengthen themselves in their tough, unemotional determination.'

Zweig, oddly, came to terms with British restraint and dogged determination, and it did much to fortify him in the hours of his deepest melancholy.

He turned now with some eagerness to plans that had long been shelved, to complete the work on his Balzac biography. The garden at Rosemount, brilliant with early autumn flowers sloping away to the hills of the valley below, was like balm whenever he managed to turn his thoughts from the tragedy of Europe.

And as he immersed himself, this time with Lotte's continuous help, in the familiar pattern of research and planning, he applied himself to what he then regarded as his remaining literary task.

Chapter Twenty-two

Beware of Pity, Zweig's only full-length novel, must call to mind the circumstances under which many of his devotees declare it was written.

Those loyal to his work and memory regard the emergence of this particular book as particularly significant, and certainly an obvious explanation for it could lie, as has been stated, in his meeting with Lotte and his concern for her frail physical and social state. But in the complexities of Zweig's personality, obvious reasons are seldom to be associated with any of his actions or reactions.

By virtue of its somewhat unusual content the story seems to fit neatly into the comparably unusual situation in which the author had entangled himself. It would not have been unnatural for him to adapt the circumstances of his own life into a work of fiction; and there is undoubtedly plenty of Zweig's own contemplations in the portrayal of successive crises.

But in considering here all that has been disclosed of his earlier life, his experience and relationships, and setting these against the specific circumstances under which he and Lotte met and became intimate, it does not always add up to a picture of the kindly and understanding benefactor, dripping with pity for the young girl who is so obviously in love with him.

In his rejection of Friderike, Zweig was fully aware of the unhappiness he was causing; and in reaching for Lotte, his admiration for her working efficiency and subdued personality certainly matched his concern for her health and precarious background—she and the members of her family were early refugees from the Nazi pogrom in Germany.

Therefore, while it is tempting to make the material fit the pattern, it seems unlikely that the affair and ultimate marriage between Stefan and Lotte is attributable, as some commentators claim, solely to his overwhelming pity for her.

The *quality* of Zweig's compassion, which infiltrates all his writing and which, on his own admission, embraced universal suffering, would appear to operate on entirely different planes from any emotion which dictated, against all odds, contracting a second marriage and at such a time.

Beware of Pity was launched at a time when it could expect at best a swift and possibly even unsympathetic passage, yet contrary to all expectations, and not least to Zweig's own typically cautious opinion, the book enjoyed an enormous success. Its impact was possibly greater and of longer duration than that of any of his previous works. The refinements of his craft and an unerring sense of timing reached through to stolid but always accessible British hearts.

To what lengths he personally was prepared to go in the pursuit of freedom is manifest in many of his works and in the facts of his life and death as they are known. The compassion about which he speaks so persistently, and which he strove for so vehemently, could not be put into practice where his own emotional and specifically his marital circumstances were concerned; and while that section of the public which interested itself in his intimate background saw a ready-made reason for the writing of *Beware of Pity*, the unusually forceful style in which many of the passages are written reflects yet again, but in more mature vein, his heavy burden of pessimism.

Man's ability to initiate a state of war, and his own revulsion from its terrible consequences, were of paramount importance to him. On any subject and through the voices of innumerable characters, this thread always emerges to connect his works and establish his authorship.

Remote as the gentle Edith seems from the disasters of war, Zweig uses Lieutenant Hofmiller to sum up the entire story when, after her suicide, he flings himself into battle and what he hopes may be forgetfulness or death: 'To have the death of a human being on one's conscience no longer meant the same to a man who had been to the front as to a man of the pre-war era. In the vast blood bath of the war my own private guilt had been absorbed into the general guilt. Thousands upon thousands of those who went to the war with me did the same, with rifle, bayonet, hand grenade, machine gun and naked fist.' '. . . hundreds of thousands, millions of my generation, in France, in Russia and Germany—of what moment, then, was one murder more, what mattered private, personal guilt in the midst of this thousandfold, cosmic destruction and wrecking of human life, the most appalling holocaust history has ever known?'

Whatever the subject matter, era or background, the tirade against bestiality and war is there. Edith's personal tragedy seems merely to subscribe to the message which Zweig was determined to reveal throughout all his work.

Seeking constantly to illustrate the fissures into which human lives can fall, he was now consciously or unconsciously revealing the irreparable damage within his own mind.

Chapter Twenty-three

For all the despondency and growing depression, there were some heartening interludes during the time Zweig and Lotte spent in Bath. His prompt establishment as a member of the local community gave him great pleasure, and although he was rarely joined by Lotte, he became a familiar figure as he set forth on what became known as his 'walks'.

To his astonishment, he discovered that what he had previously condemned as 'stolid' or 'unemotional' in the British mentality, proved to be merely disguise for a concern and righteous anger against injustice, second only to his own. The people of Bath, although seemingly detached from the centre of military activity, were in fact caught up in the war as surely as anyone else.

As 1939 drew to a close and still the uneasy wait for air attack continued, the cities, towns and villages of England were rapidly converted into what was hoped might prove a united bastion of civilian defence if German invasion actually took place.

The whole country was plunged into a stygian darkness as the order proclaiming the blackout was enforced. At first taken with the usual British pinch of salt, the populace was left in no doubt about dire consequences to individuals and country alike, if the order was flouted. The now all powerful Air Raid Warden, custodian of civilian welfare under attack, pounced like an eagle on its prey whenever the tiniest chink of light showed through hastily and sometimes incongruously draped windows.

Bath, with its maze of crazy winding streets and tortuous hills and byways, proved more hazardous than most cities under this latest proclamation; and although Zweig saw in the lovely country-side and in the elegant Georgian buildings a reflection of the past which so attracted him, he was left in no doubt that war had reached this ancient west-country city as surely as it had touched and then swallowed up Salzburg.

The Conscription Act was now in force; and as Britain denuded herself of huge sections of the male population, others, military refugees from German-occupied Czechoslovakia and Poland, took their place.

All over England hastily-erected camp sites housed bedraggled-looking soldiers who had somehow managed to get out from beneath the very heels of the occupying Nazi troops; and their appearance amongst the British people possibly did more than any press, radio or cinema report to bring home the fact of this latest conflict between nations.

Eduard Benes, president of Czechoslovakia, and his Foreign Minister, Jan Masaryk, had set up a National Committee in London, and those members of the Czech armed forces who had found a temporary oasis from the disasters in Europe were now already divided between themselves on questions of political loyalty.

As the winter of 1939 melted into early spring, British and French troops were still hopefully manning the Maginot Line, the fortification reviled by Zweig as utterly useless long before its collapse under German assault in April; he would have been more than justified in saying 'I told you so' to those of his acquaintances who had brushed his predictions aside as unduly pessimistic.

Events of the war in Europe were now unfolding in conformity with Zweig's predictions, and he was desolate, but not surprised, when Paul Reynaud, France's Prime Minister, succumbed to un-bearable pressure from his cabinet and made way for Marshal Pétain to sell out the country to Germany. As he had foreseen, France had psychologically lost the war as soon as the Maginot line, the defences in which she had placed her entire faith, had given way.

With the country under the domination of the German-controlled Vichy Administration, the might of Hitler's Nazis moved a fearful step nearer to the ultimate purpose of its exercise —that of occupying Great Britain. Yet Lyncombe Hill seemed remote from the urgency of war. The rolling countryside and amiable hills provide Zweig with his favourite pastime of walking; and as he set forth on his rambles, wearing a preoccupied expression and the curious outfit of brown jacket, plus fours and matching beret which was to become his favourite English attire, the people around began to feel rather proud of their latest asset.

What the Romans had accomplished centuries before in Bath, then abandoned, and later Beau Nash under royal patronage had developed and left to artistic posterity, was now given a shot in the arm by the presence of this author from Vienna.

Zweig, eternally withdrawn into his concern for the fate of his own country and that of all humanity, as well as with his latest literary commitment, nevertheless became aware of this respectful regard, and was increasingly moved by the form it took. Everywhere he went he met with a cordial response, and although he had in many ways deliberately detached himself from the accepted level of social intercourse, sensing that his time was running out and leaving him barely sufficient to complete his work, it was impossible for him to reject the warmth and friendliness extended on all sides.

He had great plans afoot for rewriting the Balzac biography, and although he was to be denied the satisfaction of seeing this completed as he had always envisaged it, the enthusiasm with which he now set to work on the mass of material collected and accumulated over so many years compensated to some degree for the debilitating effect of his mounting depression.

In a postscript to what Zweig referred to as his 'large Balzac', Richard Friedenthal adds his own comments to the work which was placed in his hands by Zweig's relatives after his death in 1942.

In undertaking what must have been an excessively demanding labour, if a labour of love, Friedenthal had to sift through the vast amount of material left by his friend. He comments, 'When I first began to peruse the available material, I doubted whether the book had been left as anything more than a torso. This, however, was not the case. The book had been finished. This is not to say that every chapter was complete or had been given its final shape, but essentially it had been brought to a conclusion.'

Zweig's ambition had been to match, if possible, in tribute form, the literary output and quality that marks Balzac as something of a giant; and although he possessed in his manuscript collection some priceless items from the French author's own hand, and had spent countless hours in preparing texts and files, by themselves sufficient material for a substantial and informed biography, he seemed unable to come to grips with—or perhaps to admit—the fact that the work was ready to leave his hands.

In his postscript to the biography Friedenthal writes 'He had revised the manuscript with the help of his wife, whose coopera-tion was by no means confined to the mechanical labour of copy-ing . . .' Friedenthal's obvious regard for Stefan's second wife during her lifetime, and the warmth with which he now recalls her memory, may be summed up in his published comment: 'Her queries and marginal comments were clear and very much to the point, and frequently they provided a salutary counterpoise to his flights of lyricism. He was tempted at times by his theme to "sing an aria", as he put it. In this final version many changes and deletions had been made by Zweig himself. In other cases the decisions had to be made by me, and I thought often of his quiet wife, Lotte, who had shared his work and his life with the almost passionate unobtrusiveness which was so peculiarly her own. It had seemed a matter of course that she should also join him in death . . .'

Rosemount, with its mellowed stone and windows overlooking the lower valley, in addition to housing the Zweigs, became both museum and storehouse for canned goods. While more and more books, manuscripts and literary equipment were stacked in the room which became Zweig's study, the equivalent in tins of food arrived in the store-rooms beneath the house.

If, as he had always anticipated, German troops actually landed on British soil, Zweig (according to reliable reports from the household help, whose tasks frequently took them down stairs) was either preparing for a lengthy siege, or a last-ditch stand in the field of barter.

Whatever the original reason for such hoarding—and after its installation the emergency stock was completely ignored—its presence indicates the feverish moods that still swung him from hope to despair.

During the winter and early spring of 1940, Stefan and Lotte worked together as a team; she provided the calm or stimulus as it was needed, and valuable professional help on demand. Several members of her family had joined them, amongst them her young niece, Eva, whose memories of Lotte confirm to the picture formed in the minds of all who remember her in London and in Bath.

Perhaps because of her extreme youth—which only occasionally glimpses, and rarely perceives in depth, the unrest of its elders—Eva recalls a lighter side to her aunt's personality, a trait not re-marked by those who remember Lotte's rather sombre expression and somewhat round-shouldered outline.

There is little doubt, however, that this particular period of Zweig's life offered him a measure of consolation; and had not his mental schism widened and crystallized, the material and spiritual benefits of a relatively peaceful existence in such a spot, in addition to the physical nearness of a practically perfect (for Zweig) companion, might have made it possible for him to weather those years which he saw as the end of an existing form of civilization.

'I wrote and I still thought in the German language, but my every thought and wish belonged to the countries which stood in arms for the freedom of the world. Every other loyalty, all that was past and gone, was torn and destroyed, and I knew that after this war everything would have to make a fresh start. For my most cherished aim, to which I had devoted all the power of my con-viction for forty years, the peaceful union of Europe, had been defiled, and what I had feared more than my own death, the war of all against all, now had been unleashed for the second time. And one who had toiled heart and soul all his life for human and spiritual unity found himself, in this hour which like no other demanded inviolable unity, thanks to a precipitate singling out, superfluous and alone as he had never before been in his life.'

In his somewhat brief essay on Zweig, W. I. Lucas comments that the author's sufferings were 'negligible' when compared, for instance, with the brainwashing episode he depicts so vividly in his story *The Royal Game*. But he adds that 'The artist is here speaking for his age in a way that documentary evidence never can.'

What Lucas's analysis seems to leave out is that the precognition which, on Zweig's admission, and on all the evidence from those who knew him, inflicted a degree of suffering comparable in refinement to that of his fictional character Dr B. in *The Royal Game*, enabled him to speak so eloquently for his age.

Though the tide of war was very much against the Allies, Zweig found himself able to enter into a mode of life completely alien, yet even at this late date, somehow refreshing. In place of the solely erudite and the intellectual, he formed relationships with a variety of people in and around Bath.

Fellow refugees from Austria and Germany, aided in some cases by Zweig himself, caught up with him, and although he was pleased to know that yet another human being had escaped the Nazi tyranny, he dreaded to hear from their lips what he already knew as fact in his own mind.

His curious facility for endearing himself, apparently without any effort, to everyone with whom he came into contact, produces today a rash of nostalgic enthusiasm. The long cultivated virtue of being a good listener, brought him close to many of the locals in and around the city, and families still living on Lyncombe Hill recall his quiet but amiable manner as they exchanged pleasantries and the always present and urgent topic of the war and its progress.

While such comments as 'an unusually kind and understanding

man', 'remarkably patient and so interested in everything around', are frequent when the subject of Zweig is discussed today, the underlying tension in him was also marked by the inevitable turn of any conversation when the subject of Nazism came up. 'Do you honestly believe that the Nazis will not come here?' he would ask. And after receiving the usual British assurance that it was impossible, he would shrug and look at these blissfully ignorant stalwarts with pity: 'Nothing can stop them now . . . nothing . . . I know.'

His obvious deep disquiet and equally obvious attempts to disguise it with some effort turning away from the subject of Nazi atrocity, established him now in the eyes of the people living near Rosemount, as the sensitive and compassionate being they had already imagined the author of *Beware of Pity* would be. Admiration and concern for the exile in their midst was a two-way exercise. As the barriers of reserve gradually broke down, Zweig revealed that part of himself which confirms Richard Friedenthal's remembrance of him today.

A particularly satisfying, if somewhat unusual, friendship had sprung up between him and the elderly gardener at Rosemount, and the two would often sit on the garden bench, bound in semi-silent communion. Edward Leopold Miller, was one of the few remaining members of a dying race, a professional gardener in every sense of the word. From the days of his early training at Lyncombe Hall he had progressed to a status where his opinion on all matters horticultural and philosophical was rarely questioned. The courtesy title 'Mr' was never omitted and this alone set him apart from the lower echelons of his gardening colleagues.

He knew every mood of the countryside and reacted accordingly. Though they were social, political and mental opposites, Zweig found great pleasure in listening to the succinct west-country observations, as Mr Miller alternately sucked on his pipe, ruminated and philosophized. If for no other reason than the truly magnificent produce he brought to the house, Zweig saw in his simplicity and dedication to toil some of the answers to a world gone mad with greed.

According to him, Mr Miller's peaches and apples, his flowers
and vegetables were the finest in the world, and the gardens he so
diligently attended were a tribute to God's goodness in man.
In a continual battle against his arch-enemy, the weed, Mr Miller
pulled no punches. He would rise before dawn during the summer
months in an effort to beat the sun to it. And as he moved between
the rows of soldierly vegetables, it would be a brave weed that had
the temerity to poke its head above the even soil of Mr Miller's
gardens. Nurturing the fruits of the earth was a sacred task which
he undertook with efficiency and dignity. God-fearing and rusti-
cally profound, Mr Miller was a rare and provocative character,
even in the rural west country, where such wisdom is not entirely
unknown.

When invitations from the United States and later from South
America arrived at Rosemount, asking Zweig to consider a visit on
the basis of an extended lecture tour, it was to Mr Miller that Zweig
first confided the news. Mr Miller's daughter Ivy still clearly
remembers their conversations.

'But you don't want to leave, Mr Zweig. You're all right here.
You like it, the house and the garden, you've been happy here.
Why must you go?'

'I can't stay, Mr Miller, I must go. Don't you understand? I
don't want to leave, but *they* will be here. They will be here soon,
and I must go. Can't you understand?'

'No, I don't. They'll never get here, and if they dare set foot
on British soil' (Mr Miller saw no reason to quibble with the
contradiction) '. . . if ever they do, they'll wish they hadn't. I
can tell you that, for sure. You take my advice, Mr Zweig, and
stay put. You'll be safe here with us, whatever happens. We're
not afraid.'

The interlude at Rosemount, and indeed the whole episode,
and the depth of affection in which Zweig is still held there, contrasts strikingly with the almost final stage of the negative takeover
in his personality.

Only the desperate desire to complete the Balzac biography,
and the half-determined project of producing an autobiography,

held off his collapse. This last literary effort had nagged at him for some considerable time, more as a necessary task than one which he anticipated with his usual eagerness.

In physical flight his mind saw yet again a straw at which to clutch, a hope that the dreaded Nazis, would not be able to reach out beyond the Atlantic Ocean to consume the remainder of the western world.

When Zweig finally made plans to leave the spot in England he would have wished to call 'home', he left behind all the precious Balzac material he had so painstakingly gathered. Even the great Balzac was temporarily overlooked in the panic flight before the swiftly approaching enemy.

In a letter addressed to Mr Miller from Brazil, he talks eagerly about returning to Bath; and while this news was greeted with sincere joy by everybody there, it was also accepted that poor Mr Zweig's life did not have too much longer to run.

Meanwhile the community at large devoted itself to reading as many of his books as wartime Britain's libraries and depleted bookshops could provide. With *Beware of Pity* high on the list, the figures of Stefan and the shadowy Lotte merged indelibly with the characters of Hofmiller and Edith in the minds of those who perhaps unconsciously now elevated Stefan Zweig, the Austrian Jewish author, to the realm of posthumous genius.

Chapter Twenty-four

It is not possible to place too much credence in any of Zweig's declared intentions during the remaining three years of life left to him. The facts as they are now known, however, portray the depths to which his periods of indecision plunged.

While immersing himself in the preparation of the new Balzac biography, he was already toying with the idea of leaving some sort of autobiography, although its form and the exact tone the work would take presented him with many problems which he was only too pleased to shelve.

As the tempo of the war increased, and the German army, having successfully fulfilled its top priorities of subduing Austria, Poland and Czechoslovakia, turned its attention to the countries of western Europe, Zweig accordingly accelerated his plans for winding up his own outstanding balance of work. Earlier hopes of finding a refuge in Britain had quickly dissipated with the speed of the German advance, and although he knew it was impossible to keep eternally one jump ahead of the Nazis, he had now accepted in his own mind that he would terminate his life.

By June of 1940 Denmark and Norway had both fallen to the Germans, and Zweig's nightmare vision of the Nazi juggernaut riding over Belgium, Holland and France had become fact. With German troops and tanks poised for what he regarded as the final assault on Britain, his gloomy apprehension of many years was confirmed.

Along with thousands of other refugees, Sigmund Freud, aided by a handful of devotees, had also found his way into Britain. Exhausted by physical illness he was nevertheless still struggling, at the age of eighty-three, to hang on to the 'essence of truth' and attempt some rationalization of this latest horror perpetrated by man against man.

Zweig's meetings with the elderly scientist in London served only to increase his admiration for Freud and place the final seal on what he prophesied as the wholesale extermination of the Jewish race.

'I will never forget the sight which once met me in a London travel bureau', Zweig wrote in his autobiography. 'It was filled with refugees, almost all Jews, everyone of them wanting to go—anywhere. Merely to another country, anywhere, into the polar ice or the scorching sands of the Sahara, only away, only on, because their transit visas had expired and they had to go on, on with wife and child to new stars, to a new language world, to people whom they did not know and who did not want to receive them.'

The eternal tragedy of the Jew, of which he had always been conscious and which he saw typified in the figures of his old friend Walter Rathenau and Sigmund Freud, had possibly only lightened during the period of time he had spent with his fellow artists in France and Belgium before the outbreak of the first world war. The added knowledge of years now closed in upon him with terrible pressure.

On Freud's death in September 1939, he mentally turned the last page in his own earthly saga; and, perhaps with some annoyance, Freud's splendid biographer, Ernest Jones, comments on the length of Zweig's speech after the cremation.

Jones's pique may have been due to the fact that in his own grief he overlooked the very human weakness that stamps Zweig's obsessive identification with any member of the Jewish race, and with Freud, his life-long mentor, in particular. At that time, Zweig found it only too logical to relate any isolated personal tragedy to the international disaster of Nazi persecution.

Of the effect Freud's personality and teaching had had on him personally, he wrote in his accustomed dramatic, deeply nostalgic style: 'Long before I grasped the implication of the intellectual revolution which slowly shaped itself from Freud's first fundamental labours, I had yielded to the moral strength and steadfastness of this extraordinary man. Here at last was a man of science, the exemplar of a young man's dreams, prudent of statement until he had positive proof, but unshakeable against the opposition of the world once he was satisfied that his hypothesis had become a valid certainty. Here was a man of the most modest personal demands, but ready to battle for every tenet of his teaching, and faithful unto death to the immanent truth of his theories, which he vindicated.'

One by one the links which provided him with moral and emotional strength were giving way; and in the loss of his friends and advisers he saw a reflection of anticipated world disintegration.

While longing to put an end once and for all to a situation which forced him to be witness to the procession of Jewish catastrophe, he still went ahead with plans for his trip to America.

'I shall be back, Mr Miller, you may rely on that,' he told his gardener friend, just before leaving on what was intended to be a six-month visit to the United States.

It was midsummer. Britain reeled under the double impact of the start of German bombing and Dunkirk and yet the British saw a challenge and a message of hope in the turning of that military débacle into a victory of sorts. And with the safety of England in the hands of a few hastily-trained pilots, Mr Miller was able to reply with confidence, 'We shall all be here, Mr Zweig—and so will England. You come back to us!'

As Britain fought for her very existence over the coasts and countryside, she saw at last the tremendous task she had undertaken in declaring war on the might of the German armed forces under Adolph Hitler.

Zweig left his home in Bath, wanting to return, wanting to work, wanting to die; the effect of such conflicting desires was to keep him continuously and as usual restlessly on the move while he and Lotte were in the United States.

The World of Yesterday, which he called his autobiography, was now near to completion, an historical, emotional and psychological assessment of an era which he claimed had ended for him twice.

Despite the mood of acute nostalgia in which the majority of the book was written, the romantic era to which he refers so persistently seems, on close examination, to be almost non-existent or at least to exist only within the realm of his own idealistic imagination.

The ecstatic references to the early days he enjoyed in France and Belgium described, as he well knew, only a fraction of human existence. And although providing that small elite with a highly satisfactory mode of life, and the public at large with a fruitful and lasting artistic and intellectual renaissance, it could not possibly have provided, as he had always hoped, a social and political structure on which Europe could build her economic and racial policies. Yet Zweig's idealism, or that part of which still survived, was nevertheless to take him back in time in order to complete his work on the autobiography; and then, surprisingly, leave the past for the unexplored future.

The continent of South America had always intrigued him, and he decided to continue his travels to Brazil, instead of returning as originally planned to England. In any case the news from Europe and Britain was increasingly grim. Yugoslavia, Greece and Crete had all fallen to the Germans and Russia, infuriated by Hitler's violation of their non-aggression pact, declared herself on the side of the Allies, and frantically sought to hold the German advance on both the Ukrainian and Dnieper fronts.

Geographically, there seemed no more desirable place in the world than Brazil, with its unsophisticated economy practically guaranteeing immunity from the tragedies of Hitler's new world in the east. Lush, extravagant and politically quiescent, Brazil offered a life that Zweig could live from day to day without listening for the knock on the door. It was, he claimed, free of racial prejudice which encouraged him to write a book which he envisaged as a tribute to this country.

Lotte and he found a new home in what was then known as the summer capital of Petropolis; and there he completed his autobiography and the last of his works of fiction, *The Royal Game*. This last caused him much agony of mind, both in plot construction and in the creation of its characters, culminating in more sessions of appalling doubt in his own capability as a writer.

It is typical of Zweig's difficult passage through life that here again the doubts and the agonies were self-inflicted; in this particular case the work not only stands on its own merits, but has been declared by many critics as possibly the most incisive and powerfully written of all Zweig's collection.

Brazil—Land of the Future, on the other hand, drew both amiable and adverse criticism.

The reader senses at once that this is to be a paean of praise for a country, constitution and way of life that is every man's ideal. Zweig goes into fairly comprehensive detail of the history of the country—its unambitious beginning, plagued by lethargy and intrigue from the then perpetually impecunious Portuguese, who failed to recognize its potential and did nothing about colonizing it until thirty-two years after its original discovery. His enthusiasm fairly leaps out of the page, every word declaring the author's faith in the future of this country, undefiled by the curse of racialism, where tolerance and understanding of the dogmas and isms is the order of the day. Streets, boulevards and squares, laid out by the finest architects, welcome native and traveller alike; and the cordiality and expansiveness of the people as a whole match the luxuriant growth in the virgin forests, rich with untapped mineral wealth.

In all, the book's foremost effect is to make the reader think he has not even begun to live if he has not yet seen Brazil.

It is a point to ponder that, although Zweig was poised on the brink of self-extermination, he chose to write such a song of praise about a country utterly remote from the land of his birth and the continent of Europe to which he had clung for so long.

Although he writes lyrically of this subtropical paradise where war-weary and disenchanted future generations might discover repose, and sees it as the land of the future on economic grounds, it could not replace all that he had lost. Though he succeeds in infecting the reader with the belief that Brazil is a nonpareil among nations, his personal reservations come through, however subtly.

This is in striking contrast to his other writing, where he so envelops the reader within the compass of his own burning belief in a subject that there is no question of standing aside.

Whatever Zweig loses in scholarly approach, he makes up by employing a literary technique aimed at capturing the attention through the emotions, senses and visual imagination. On occasion he is not reluctant to use hyperbole, if it is indicated.

The Balzac biography apart, *Brazil—Land of the Future* and *The Royal Game*, coming from him during the last months of his life in Brazil, possibly represent more than any other the two extremes of his style. The travel documentary, almost everybody's idea of armchair escapism, eulogises on conditions which could not possibly stand up to the microscope of analysis. *The Royal Game*, on the other hand, reveals a Zweig in full command of an emotional and spiritual situation. The economy and power of the words resist any adverse criticism and mark this as one of the author's most durable creations.

In a letter written to Mr. Miller and in a later note addressed to Friderike, Zweig reveals once more the division within himself, contradicting his earlier predictions of a return to his old haunts, and disposing of his belief in the future, whether in polar ice or in the abdundant continent of South America.

Those of his contemporaries and friends who had escaped the Nazis were now dispersed throughout England and America, determined to hack out, if possible, a new existence.

But Stefan and Lotte were already past the point of no return; and although it would seem, on the surface, a useless gesture for

Lotte to give up her life when her expectancy of it could reasonably be stretched beyond what Zweig pessimistically foresaw as the end of civilisation, her willingness to accompany her husband on his final journey seems logical in the light of what has been learned of her personality.

The precious Balzac manuscripts which Zweig had sent for in one of his many resurgencies of mental energy, arrived too late. The final decision had at last been taken, and even with the flowering of a massive nation to counterbalance his vision of the collapse of man's endeavour against tyranny, the fissure within him had widened and could now never heal.

From the somewhat unlikely subtropical and steamy atmosphere of Brazil's fashionable Petropolis, news came out that Stefan Zweig, the author, and his wife, Lotte, had been discovered dead on February 23rd, 1942, and that their deaths were presumed to be due to a drug overdose.

In a final Declaration that Zweig wrote just before he died all the facts were covered in a lucid manner, and presented the proverbial open-and-shut case to the official and enquiring mind.

Chapter Twenty-five

'Towards great persons use respectful boldness.' George Herbert's saintly capacity for preaching in worldly aphorisms sustains and guides the biographer during the difficult task of producing what must be, in fairness to the subject, as balanced and impartial a verdict as possible.

After observing, studying and analysing everything that has allowed itself to be revealed, there need be no apology for extracting the maximum amount of assistance from Herbert's words.

Stefan Zweig succeeded in maintaining almost uniquely amiable relationships with all his contacts and acquaintances in the literary and artistic field during a public life of three decades a facility that might label him as something of a saint or hero.

His self-imposed discipline in all matters involving his work rarely failed; and his ability to keep to schedules and commitments earned him an enviable reputation for dependability. The extraordinary lengths to which he would go to understand all points of view was a particular attraction for such people as his publishers; and the patience he extended to all those claiming undiscovered literary genius was almost legendary. He rarely turned aside from any claim on his time, however inconvenient it might be.

But Zweig, above all, was human, with all the human failings of which he wrote; and with such a tight, self-imposed professional rein, it was inevitable that the patience and understanding was exhausted by the time the pressure was off.

The complexity of his personality is also demonstrated by his desire to live as a recluse, while unable to shed the trappings of a material and marital existence. And until, by a process of elimination and mental refinement, he finally arrived at his conclusion on the principle of compassion in human existence, he embraced and rejected in turn all the tenets of accepted philosophies.

Throughout his life, the activity of his mind gave him very little respite. Its continual concern with the problems of a universal *raison d'etre* left him exhausted; yet his ability to channel this energy creatively resulted in the legacy of his collected work.

Jules Romains, Lycée professor, novelist and one of Zweig's great friends from the early Paris days, refers to Zweig as: 'one of the seven wise men of Europe . . . one of those men whom I have heard oftenest and most regularly say things that were just and wise and human . . .'

If the author's understanding of George Herbert's use of the adjective 'great' is correct, it is submitted that Stefan Zweig's literary work, and therefore the life that made it possible, falls short of such a description on one count. A man of his time, he was nevertheless something of an anachronism.

While today most of his fictional work has great appeal, some of it is still considered 'dated'.

Zweig's membership of an established social class necessarily dictated to some extent the character types he used—master and servant, bourgeois hypocrite and wealthy philanderer—yet the stories he tells are of all time, and the products of his more mature years, notably *The Royal Game* and *The Biblical Legends*, appear so even to the casual reader.

Although, surprisingly, some of his works are not now so easily available, any one of those to be found on the library shelves has this quality of timelessness.

The dissonance in human lives exposed by him through fictional and biographical subjects continued throughout his own life, branding him, despite his aura of social well-being, as a solitary, beyond the reaches of 'normal' boundaries.

Was Zweig, then, at the last, sufficiently objective to recognize the changing image of himself in those periods of constitutional and emotional change that he depicts through his work? And was he able to sustain that objectivity in his autobiography?

Disrespectfully bold as it may seem, the conclusion is unavoidable that this final literary reflection he left with us on his life and times falls short. In using an overdose of nostalgia, he loses some of his identity, although the facts that he chronicles are admittably lamentable. The title *The World of Yesterday*, is perhaps a clue to the book's style; and it seems at first remarkable that, nearing the end of his life, he might even have subsided into a welter of regret. This was mentioned by Friderike as a possible cause for his unwillingness to include in the book any facts about his emotional life or marriage.

Perhaps this surprising inability to clear the mirror and see a reasonably true reflection of himself accounted for the cloudy and at times angry relationship he depicts between man and his destiny.

Once the belief in his capacity as a writer had been established in his own mind, Zweig held fast with unswerving faith to the dogma of compassion as a means of the salvation of the world thereby risking—perhaps without realizing it—hostile criticism. But the production of his autobiography, on several counts an unsatisfactory record of his life reveals a mental disturbance which sought refuge in mourning a pseudo-idyllic past, and horror at mankind's apparent collision course with disaster. His endless preoccupation with man's ultimate destiny was now reaching a point where he saw nothing illogical in presenting the totally opposite states of perfect salvation and utter extinction as the only possible solutions.

The final move to Petropolis, at first glance an unlikely one at such a time, is shown nevertheless to be in character with the rapidly disintegrating mental processes which for so long had swung Zweig's thinking from one extreme to another.

While the fear which had driven him to seek refuge in so many directions had been transmitted to many of his characters he had remained, as author, in control. But his ability to discipline the waves of suffocating depression that always threatened him was now rapidly weakening.

It is agreed that, as W. I. Lucas states, he did not suffer directly from any physical punishment. His lot, compared to that of hundreds of thousands of victims of and refugees from Nazism, was materially good. From an early age he had enjoyed a state of well-being, and in middle life had attracted such a degree of solicitude from both Friderike and later, from Lotte, that it could be stated without exaggeration that he enjoyed (or endured) a pampered and sheltered existence.

Just as England had done, Brazil offered him friendship, comfort and a devoted public following. At all times and on every occasion during his last months of life in that country, he met with a cordial, even ecstatic response. Private libraries were open to him. Automatic entrée into any circle was taken for granted, and on the rare occasions when he emerged from his seclusion to lecture or to appear at a social or diplomatic function he was greeted with affection and acclaim.

Almost every country in the world, and certainly all those which he had visited or lived in, offered Stefan Zweig the homage and loyalty accorded only to great men. But while this outward display of recognition obviously affected and pleased him, he would never allow it to compensate for the fact that his own country had rejected him.

Though this rejection came comparatively late in his life—he was fifty-seven when Austria was occupied by the Germans—his fear of it had been rooted in his mind from his earliest consciousness; and although periodically, as the youthful days in Paris testify, he had managed to relegate this apprehension to the area of the subconscious, its suppression, as events bear witness, served merely to increase the volume of foreboding.

While submitting this as a reason for Zweig's self-extermination, one must examine the two factors which contributed to it: his Jewishness and the collapse of the civilized world as he understood it.

His Jewish heritage, in turn a curse and a blessing, did much to colour his thinking and influence his reactions. As he moved from youth to adolescence, the knowledge of his ancestry and all that it meant in a world where political and military claims were historically often linked to an outbreak of anti-semitism caused him the deepest grief, and was ultimately responsible for his belief that the only answer to violence was the practice of passivity and compassion.

As he turned his literary energies towards what he hoped might be the intellectual foundation of a 'unified' Europe, he enjoyed the dubious reward of observing his own success as an author while those tenets which he described as indispensable to the spiritual and intellectual survival of mankind were smashed to smithereens before his eyes. The public which had recognized the author, his philosophy and his work, saw nothing extraordinary in condoning the violence and racism he condemned; and Zweig's inability to comprehend such tactics moved him a step further along the route of mental conflict. Gradually, he accepted the image of himself as the eternal wanderer, and with this the burden of his own Jewishness increased.

He was so conscious of this precarious status that he tended to react in any situation which even hinted at racism in an exaggeratedly sensitive manner. While others of his race disciplined themselves to use a period of political calm to integrate and stake economic and social claims, however fragile, Zweig deliberately stirred the seeds of dreadful imaginings, in order to forestall the future.

Passionately declaiming the equality of all men in the eyes of God, he saw himself as set apart, heir to a fateful heritage by a mere accident of birth. Yet on his own admission he felt something like relief when the Nazis finally came out into the open and declared their Aryan policy of segregation.

The excessive attention, too, that he paid to his heritage long before it became a political issue, may have indicated a growing half-conscious desire to offer himself as mediator between his own stateless people and a wrathful God.

Obscure though this reasoning may seem, it nevertheless lends substance to the picture of the divided pattern of his thinking.

Under what he felt as an almost unendurable weight Zweig's defences finally broke down; the degree of mental anguish he suffered must seem incomprehensible to those of coarser grain.

But whether this state of awareness was solely a result of his heritage and simply grew with his intellect, or whether the precognition invariably pessimistic which haunted his mortal existence was a legacy of inherent mental disturbance, only God would decide.

The Declaration he wrote immediately before he took his life discloses his terminal passivity. The style is familiar.

Before I depart from this life, of my own free will and with a clear mind, I want urgently to fulfil one last duty: I want to give heartfelt thanks to this wonderful country of Brazil which has been for me and my work so good and hospitable a resting place.

Every day I have learned to love this country better, and nowhere would I more gladly have rebuilt my life all over again, now that the world of my native tongue has perished for me and Europe, my spiritual home, is destroying itself. But one would need special powers to begin completely afresh when one has passed one's sixtieth year. And mine have been exhausted by long years of homeless wandering. It seems to me therefore better to put an end, in good time and without humiliation, to a life in which intellectual work has always been an unmixed joy and personal freedom earth's most precious possession.

I greet all my friends! May they live to see the dawn after the long night is over! I, all too impatient, am going on alone.

Stefan Zweig.
Petropolis.
22.2.1942

It has not been possible to review in detail all of Zweig's works, and it seemed in any case more appropriate to discuss only those most vividly illustrating his own personality and beliefs.

With the exception of his portrait of Magellan, a full length biography published in 1938, which falls into the highly entertaining travel-cum-historical class, the remaining works, while relatively short in length, display his talent for depicting historic and human drama, these are found in a volume entitled *Twelve Historical Miniatures*, first published in 1927. These works disclose Zweig even then as an author always aware of the way in which circumstances may depend crucially on split-second timing. On an entirely different level, but also a product of the earlier years, is the miniature portrait of Georg Friedrich Handels, a slight but unmistakeably perfect account of the great composer's sojourn in London, with near-comical descriptions of *Messiah* rehearsals.

Throughout his life Stefan Zweig believed that this mortal existence is capable of reaching perfection and freedom through knowledge and universal compassion. Having sifted through many layers of fact, calculation and surmise, it is the author's conclusion that Stefan Zweig's life and work and death form a not inconsiderable contribution to that existence.

Of all the shocked tributes that followed upon the news of Zweig's death, the words of Hans Arens seem to a world inured against violence and crime, more than any other to provide a reason, if one is necessary, for a Zweig biography:

'Most of us, in our youth', Arens writes, 'have idolized some favourite author or poet. We have all known that fiery devotion, that craving for human comradeship and for imaginative literature, which is as old as poetry itself. True, such youthful enthusiasms tend to fade when we take up our own particular task, whatever it may be. Yet many of us remain loyal to the hero of our youth. That is how it was with Stefan Zweig and me.'

Bibliography

First Publication in English

YEAR	TITLE	PUBLISHER
1913	*Paul Verlaine*	
1913	*Hymn of Life* (to Verhaeren)	
1914	*Emile Verhaeren* (Critical Biography) (Also titled 'Memories of Verhaeren)	Houghton Mifflin & Co
1921	*Romain Rolland*	Viking
1921	*The Burning Secret*	Allen & Unwin
1924	*Passion and Pain* (Short stories)	Chapman & Hall
1927	*The Invisible Collection*	
1927	*Conflicts* (Collected short stories) (Includes *Twenty Four Hours In A Woman's Life*)	
1928	*Volpone*	Viking
1928	*Adepts in Self-Portraiture* (Casanova, Stendhal and Tolstoy)	
1930	*Joseph Fouché*	Viking
1930	*Three Masters* (Balzac, Dickens and Dostoyevsky)	Viking
1931	*Lamb of the Poor*	
1932	*Amok*	
1932	*Letter from an Unknown Woman*	
1932	*Mental Healers* (Mesmer, Freud and Eddy)	
1933	*Marie Antoinette*	Cassell
1934	*Erasmus*	Cassell

1934	*Kaleidoscope* (Collected short stories) (Includes *Amok*)	Cassell
1936	*The Right to Heresy* (Sub-titled *Castellio Against Calvin*)	Cassell
1937	*The Buried Candelabrum*	Viking
1938	*Magellan*	Viking
1939	*Beware of Pity*	Cassell and Viking
1939	*The Living Thoughts of Tolstoy* (ed.) *Master Builders: A Typology of The Spirit*	
1940	*The Tide of Fortune* (Twelve Historical Miniatures)	Cassell
1941	*Brazil, Land of the Future*	Viking and Cassell
1942	*Amerigo* (A Comedy of Errors)	
1942	*The World of Yesterday* (Autobiography)	Cassell
1944	*The Royal Game*	Cassell
1946	*Balzac* (Biography) (Begun by Zweig in 1939 as a full-scale work (as opposed to the earlier shorter biography) and later edited by Dr Richard Friedenthal)	Viking
1951	*Kaleidoscope Two* (includes *Buch Mendl* and *Leporella*	Cassel (Hallam Edition)
1952	*Legends* (including *The Buried Candelabrum*, *Rachel Arraigns God* and *Virata, or the* *Eyes of the Undying Brother*)	Cassel (Hallam Edition)

A note on the series 'Master Builders of the World': Zweig originally conceived the idea of bringing out a book to be called *Master-Builders of the World*, four volumes, each containing three biographical portraits. The titles were: *Three Masters, Adepts in Self-Portraiture, Struggle With the Demon* and *Mental Healers*. Each volume was published separately in German (see German Bibliography). In 1935 *Master-Builders of the World* appeared as one volume, containing *Three Masters, Struggle With the Demon* and *Adepts in Self-Portraiture* (all in German). *Mental Healers* was not included.

Three Masters and *Adepts in Self-Portraiture* were published in English, but *Struggle with the Demon* has not been translated as far as can be ascertained. Therefore, *Master-Builders of the World* has not appeared in its entirety in English.

First Publication in German

1901	*Silver Strings*
1902	*Paul Verlaine*
1904	*The Love of Erika Ewald*
1906	*Die Fruhen Kranze*
1907	*Tersites*
1910	*Emile Verhaeren*
1911	*Erstes Erlebnis*
1913	*The Sculptor*
1917	*Polypheme*
	(written in 1917; ? actual date of publication)
1920	*Three Masters*
1920	*Marceline Desbordes-Valmore*
1920	*Fear*
1921	*Romain Rolland*
1922	*Amok*
1923	*Collected Poems*
	(Zweig deliberately witheld the inclusion of 'Silver Strings' from this edition)
1925	*The Struggles with the Demon*
	Critical Essays on Holderlin, Nietzsche and Kleist
1926	*Volpone*
1927	*The Invisible Collection*
1927	*Der Fluchtling*
1927	*Vervirrung der Gefuhle*
1927	*Eulogy on Rilke*
	(Originally delivered in Munich State Theatre)
1927	*The Tide of Fortune*
1928	*Adepts in Self-Portraiture*
1929	*Little Chronicles*
	(Originally published in *The Star Hours*)
1929	*Joseph Fouché*
1931	*Mental Healers*
1932	*Marie Antoinette*

1934   *Erasmus*
1935   *Mary Stuart*
1935–6 *Masters of the World*
1936   *The Right to Heresy*
1936   *Gesammelte Erzahlungen*
        (Includes *The Kette* and *Kaleidoscope*)
1937   *Georg Friedrich Handels*
1938   *Magellan*

N.B.—An early Essay on Albert Schweitzer was published, year uncertain. Also a one-act play *Flight to God* based on a Tolstoy drama was
performed by (quote from Friderike) '. . . five theatres and broadcast
by the German Radio'.

Index by Lilian Rubin, M.A.

Note: Titles in italics are by Zweig unless otherwise indicated.